Contesting the Market

Contesting the Market

Pay Equity and the Politics of Economic Restructuring

Deborah M. Figart and Peggy Kahn

Wayne State University Press • Detroit

01 00 99 98 97   5 4 3 2 1

Library of Congress Cataloging-in-Publication Data

Figart, Deborah M.
    Contesting the market : pay equity and the politics of economic
restructuring / Deborah M. Figart and Peggy Kahn.
        p.   cm.
    Includes bibliographical references and index.
    ISBN 0-8143-2664-1 (pbk. : alk. paper)
    1. Pay equity—Michigan.   2. Women in the civil service—Salaries,
etc.—Michigan.   3. Job evaluation—Michigan.   4. Sex discrimination
in employment—Michigan.   5. Civil service positions—Michigan—
Classification.   I. Kahn, Petty, 1953–   .   II. Title.
HD6061.2.U62M536   1997
331.331.2′153′09774—dc21   96-29583

For Ellen, and in memory of Adeline Malek Figart
For Bob and Jonathan

Contents

Tables

Figures

Acknowledgments

This book would not have been possible without the diligent and generous assistance we received from current and former Michigan Civil Service officials, union officers and staff, and labor and women's movement activists, who provided primary documentation, made themselves available for interviews, and discussed issues related to pay equity in Michigan.

Martha Bibbs, former director of the Department of Civil Service, opened many doors for us. We are extraordinarily grateful to Joseph Slivensky, director of the Planning and Development Bureau in the Michigan Department of Civil Service, and to Hilda Patricia (Pat) Curran, who until her reassignment was director of the Office of Women and Work in the Michigan Department of Labor (as well as a member of the Michigan Women's Commission and an activist in Women in State Government and the Michigan Pay Equity Network). Carol Mowitz, Richard Crittenden, and Linda Coe from the Department of Civil Service and Thomas Hall and Paulette Granberry from the Office of the State Employer rendered assistance and answered many questions. We are also indebted to Mary Pollock, the affirmative action/EEO coordinator in the Department of Civil Service and also a Women in State Government activist.

Jon Ogar, director of communications at the Michigan AFL-CIO, Sheila Strunk from UAW Local 6000, and Tim Hughes from the Michigan AFL-CIO were particularly helpful in locating materials related to collective bargaining over wage adjustments and labor's perspective on many issues. The late Olga Madar, a Coalition of Labor Union Women and Pay Equity Network activist at the time we interviewed her, shared her extensive experience with us. Elizabeth Giese from the Michigan National Organization for Women and Michigan Women's Hall of Fame helped us in several ways. However, we alone are responsible for the judgments and conclusions we express in the book.

Most of the written documentation we used is not held in public archives and was made available to us by the organizations and individuals who cooperated with the research. Full records of the *UAW v. State of Michigan* civil action (No. 85CV75483DT) are, however, available at the U.S. District Court in Detroit. The State of Michigan Library and Archives in Lansing holds a number of published reports, state newspapers, and other historical documents relating to state government. The Michigan Democratic Party records we consulted are available at the Bentley Historical Library at the University of Michigan.

It is difficult to express the myriad of ways in which Ellen Mutari contributed to our work. She engaged in endless hours of discussing theoretical and conceptual issues, as well as assisting in editing various drafts. Ronnie Steinberg, Melissa Barker, and Lynne Revo-Cohen also helped us refine our arguments, particularly on classification issues. June Lapidus and Melissa Barker provided guidance as we developed the statistical analysis. For research assistance, we appreciated the efforts of Darcel Smith, Trish Steding, Evanthia Leissou, and Colleen Scott. Colleagues who have read and commented on the entire manuscript or portions of it include Marilyn Power, Marie Richmond-Abbott, Ken Harrison, Peter Gluck, and several outstanding anonymous reviewers. Over the years, we have been inspired and supported by a number of feminist researchers and activists whose work has contributed to our perspective.

Portions of this research were presented at conferences of the Institute for Women's Policy Research, the North Central Sociological Association, and the Western Economic Association. Support for our work was provided by an Eastern Michigan University Faculty Research Fellowship and two University of Michigan-Flint Faculty Research Grants. We appreciate the support and assistance of the staff at Wayne State University Press, especially its director, Arthur Evans, and managing editor, Kathryn Wildfong; Mary Gillis was a thorough and skilled copy editor.

We would not have been able to complete our research without the unlimited support of Ellen Mutari, Bob Bix, and Jonathan Bix. Catherine Jiang, Trish Steding, and Michelle Witzke provided loving care of Jonathan, who has grown as this project has done over five years.

Abbreviations

AAUW	American Association of University Women
AFL	American Federation of Labor
AFL-CIO	American Federation of Labor-Congress of Industrial Organizations
AFSCME	American Federation of State, County, and Municipal Employees
ASE	American Society of Employers
BNA	Bureau of National Affairs
CATF	Citizen's Advisory Task Force on Civil Service Reform
CETA	Comprehensive Employment and Training Act
CLUW	Coalition of Labor Union Women
CRC	Civil Rights Commission
CSC	Civil Service Commission
CWTF	Comparable Worth Task Force
DCS	Department of Civil Service
DLC	Democratic Leadership Council
ECP	Equitable Classification Plan
EEO	Equal Employment Opportunity
EEOC	Equal Employment Opportunity Commission
ERA	Equal Rights Amendment
ERB	Employee Relations Board
ERP	Employee Relations Policy
FEPA	Fair Employment Practices Act
FSC	Federal Supplemental Compensation
FY	Fiscal Year
GAO	General Accounting Office
IP	Impasse Panel
LPER	Legislative Program Effectiveness Unit
MBES	Michigan Benchmark Evaluation System
MCO	Michigan Corrections Officers
MEA	Michigan Education Association
MESC	Michigan Employment Security Commission
MMA	Michigan Manufacturers Association
MNA	Michigan Nurses Association
MPES	Michigan Professional Employees Society
MSEA	Michigan State Employees Association
MSPTA	Michigan State Police and Troopers Association
NCPE	National Committee on Pay Equity

NOW	National Organization for Women
OLS	Ordinary Least Squares
OSE	Office of the State Employer
OWW	Office of Women and Work
PAQ	Position Analysis Questionnaire
PCEL	Position Comparison Equivalency Level
PCS	Position Comparison System
PEN	Pay Equity Network
PERA	Public Employment Relations Act
RRS	Representative Revenue System
SEIU	Service Employees International Union
UAW	United Automobile Workers (United Automobile, Aerospace, and Agricultural Implement Workers of America)
UTEA	United Technical Employees Association
WSG	Women in State Government

1

Introduction

Working women, and the movements that represent them, have contested their secondary status in the labor market through a variety of strategies. The pay equity movement, in particular, confronts forms of discrimination not addressed by previous policies such as equal pay for equal work or affirmative action. In the United States, legislation addressing individual access to jobs and requiring equal employment opportunity by race and gender has been in force since passage of Title VII of the Civil Rights Act of 1964. The Equal Pay Act of 1963 mandates equal pay for men and women working in the same job for the same employer. Yet, despite more than thirty years of federal legislation, most women continue to work alongside other women in jobs which average lower pay and fewer promotion opportunities than men's jobs.

Pay equity advocates argue that through occupational segregation certain jobs have become identified as women's work, and these jobs pay less primarily because women do the work. Low wages in these female-dominated occupations are related to women's work being labeled "unskilled" and the assumption that women workers do not have the same need as men for a "family wage" or "living wage" (Davies 1982; Reverby 1987; Steinberg 1990; Kessler-Harris 1990). In addition, women have remained for the most part outside the unions that increased the labor market power of male workers (Hartmann 1976; Walby 1986). This pattern of wage discrimination continues to be manifested by a negative correlation between wages and the percentage of female workers in an occupational category (Treiman and Hartmann 1981; England 1992; Sorensen 1994).[1] In other words, the higher the percentage of females in a job, the lower the average wage.

To remedy wage discrimination, feminists and labor activists have introduced the idea that female-dominated jobs should be paid the same as male-dominated jobs within the same organization when they are of comparable value to the employer. Jobs can be compared and evaluated based on the skill, effort, responsibility, and working conditions they entail. Equal pay for work of comparable value, or comparable worth, represents a departure from other approaches to improving women's economic status because it seeks to address discrimination against entire job categories rather than individual workers.

In fact, several terms have been given to this type of policy and are generally used interchangeably. The expression "comparable worth" is often used to connote the reevaluation of the worth of women's work through a technical process of linking pay to points in an organization's job evaluation system (see Reskin and Roos 1987; Evans and Nelson 1989a). "Pay equity" is the term preferred by scholars and activists who emphasize the continuity between new strategies for rectifying gender-based wage disparities and the equal pay for equal work principle in the Equal Pay Act. We use "pay equity" as a broader concept, encompassing a wide range of approaches to the reevaluation of predominantly female jobs. Thus, pay equity refers to traditional comparable worth wage reform closely allied to pay-for-points exercises as well as wage adjustments based upon less formal evidence of the undervaluation of women's work. We also use pay equity to refer to other ways of addressing low pay for women's work, including low-pay campaigns, which target wage increases to low-wage jobs regardless of their gender composition but have significant effects on predominantly female jobs, and career mobility programs, which restructure job ladders to recognize skills and improve pay in female-dominated positions. While previous research frequently has been critical of compromises and strategies that deviate from "true" comparable worth, our analysis values a wide range of pay equity reforms.

The pay equity movement, broadly understood, contests not only the devaluation of women's work, but also the belief in benevolent market forces found in traditional economic doctrine. Pay equity advocates emphasize that concepts of skill are historically constructed, socially contingent, and strongly gendered (Horrell, Rubery, and Burchell 1989; Steinberg 1990; Wajcman 1991). Orthodox economic models which view market wages as solely reflecting productivity are contradicted by the role institutions and internal structures play in wage-setting. These institutions have ideas of gender-appropriate work and pay embedded in them, pay equity proponents argue, and the market is an aggregate of these institutions (Bridges and Nelson 1989; Steinberg and Haignere 1991; England 1992). While comparable worth advocates are sometimes criticized for accepting job hierarchies and embracing job evaluation as potentially objective and value-free, in fact the movement recognizes and tries to reveal the power and social dimensions of the wage-setting process (Feldberg 1984; Brenner 1987; Peterson 1990; Blum 1991; McCann 1994).

The emergence of the pay equity movement in the United States during the early 1980s was driven by a number of economic, social, and political developments. While women continued to be segregated in low-paid jobs, they won increasing access to economic and political organizations (Steinberg 1988; Evans and Nelson 1989b; Blum 1991). Other equal opportunities programs created a powerful impetus for women to claim this new right to fair pay, while a few highly visible court cases amplified this possibility (McCann 1994). Alliances among public sector unions, feminist bureaucrats and politicians, and Democrats made it possible to put pay equity for state workers on the political agenda in a number of cases (see Evans and Nelson 1993). In addition, large public organizations traditionally relied upon elaborate personnel systems which used job evaluation and adhered to formal ideas of equal treatment. State bureaucracies were therefore relatively receptive to comparable worth arguments and techniques (Johansen 1984; Johnston 1994). In the 1980s, while the presidential administration of Ronald Reagan blocked pay equity developments in national law and policy, over twenty states and several localities adopted some sort of pay equity reform for their employees (NCPE 1989).[2]

However, the expansion of the pay equity movement in the United States in the mid-1980s occurred at a contradictory moment. At the same time that social and political developments generated the movement, business was expanding its use of relatively inexpensive women's labor to succeed in a changed economic environment; further, the state and its workers were increasingly seen as a drain on the market economy. Pay equity opponents also gained strength from the new politics of deregulation and the dismantling of the welfare state. Business organizations, which resisted pay equity even in state employment, found receptive ears among the conservative politicians whose numbers had increased in federal, state, and local governments. Both have claimed that pay equity reform represents destructive interference with the market mechanism and that it introduces wage rigidities and inefficiencies (see Williams and Kessler 1984; Killingsworth 1985; Paul 1989; Rhoads 1993). The invocation of market determination of wages resurfaces again and again not only in the Michigan pay equity endeavor but also in national opposition to pay equity (see, for example, McCormick 1981; Berger 1984; Bergren 1984; O'Neill 1984; Rabkin 1984; Smith and Ward 1989; Hill and Killingsworth 1989; O'Neill 1990; Rhoads 1993).[3] This is because the process of reclassification and wage-setting for female-dominated occupations in the public sector has implications for gendered and class-based wage hierarchies in the private sector.

It is this changing context within the public sector and the political economy that pay equity developments in Michigan illuminate. Tensions existed between the integration of women into the labor force and economic restructuring, between strong labor and women's politics and renewed conservatism, and between the need for public services and cutbacks in the public sector in the face of taxpayer revolt. The state workers who issue driver's licenses, nurse patients in state hospitals, counsel the unemployed, inspect bridges and railroads, protect wildlife and maintain parks, and guard prisons have been buffeted by these tensions. The fight for pay equity in Michigan therefore involves a set of conditions that will be increasingly faced by the movement nationwide.

CONFRONTING WAGE DISCRIMINATION THROUGH PAY EQUITY

During the past few decades, working women have seen some progress in their employment status. The U.S. labor force is almost evenly divided between women and men. Women comprise 46 percent of today's workforce. The percentage of women in traditionally male occupations has increased and a range of jobs formerly dominated by men have become integrated, though professional, managerial, and technical jobs are relatively more open to white women. African-American women, historically concentrated in domestic service work, have shifted towards clerical and other predominantly white female occupations.[4] Nevertheless, according to U.S. Department of Labor statistics, 6 out of 10 working women are still employed in occupations that are at least 70 percent female while 8 out of 10 men are employed in occupations that are at least 70 percent male.

Occupational segregation continues to affect men's and women's relative earnings despite changes in legislation and society. In the past few decades, the difference between men's and women's earnings has narrowed but not closed. As illustrated in figure 1, the median weekly earnings for women who worked full-time measured 62.0 percent of men's in 1975. Twenty years later, the ratio was 75.5 percent, a slight setback from the peak of 76.8 percent in 1993. That is, the gender-based wage gap declined only 13.5 percentage points, from 38 to 24.5 percent, from 1975 to 1995. Numerous studies have estimated that from one-fourth to more than one-third of this wage gap may be due to occupational segregation and the devaluation of women's work.

Pay equity policies targeted to eliminate discrimination against female-dominated jobs can be established at the federal, state, local, or firm level. However, the process of determining whether wages are equitable occurs within individual organizations or workplaces. In conventional comparable worth implementation, a study helps determine whether there is gender or racial bias in an organization's classification system. In other

Figure 1

U.S. Gender-Based Wage Ratio and Gap
for Full-Time Workers

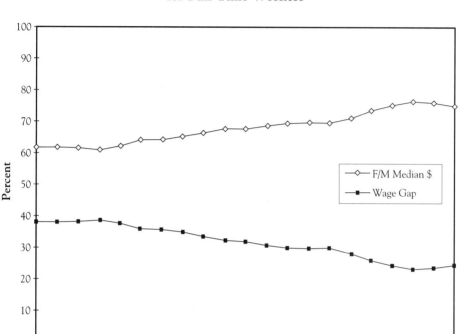

Source: U.S. Department of Labor, Bureau of Labor Statistics, Employment and Earnings, annual averages, various years.

words, is there a significant relationship between the gender or race of a job category within an organization and its rate of pay? Joan Acker (1989: 3) succinctly describes the procedure: "Comparable worth projects determine the amount of undervaluation by comparing the complexity and responsibility of female- and male-dominated jobs, then institute pay increases to eliminate the identified discrimination."

Job evaluation, traditionally a management tool, can be used to ascertain whether jobs of comparable value are paid equitably and to estimate the size of the inequity. It is a formal procedure for hierarchically ordering a set of jobs according to their worth within or value to an organization. Thus, job evaluation can be used to break the link between a job's rate of pay and the predominant gender (or race) of its incumbents. The most common method of job evaluation in larger firms and in the public sector is the point factor method.[5] In *a priori* point factor job evaluation, an organization selects job attributes (compensable factors) which it believes are valuable. The most common categories of compensable factors are skill, effort, responsibility, and working conditions, although the individual factors selected may vary among job evaluation systems. Job descriptions, questionnaires, and/or interviews are used to rate all positions or key positions on each factor and total point scores are tallied for each position or job class.[6]

However, many job evaluation procedures and techniques may incorporate gender bias even as they are used as part of a project to remedy the devaluation of women's work. In writing job descriptions, women or their supervisors may understate their tasks. In identifying how job content reflects the compensable factors of skill, effort, responsibility, and working conditions, demands traditionally associated with women's jobs may remain invisible. For example, job evaluation plans traditionally value the physical effort in lifting heavy objects much more than the mental effort of entering data. Skills such as the ability to deal with resistant clients or an impatient public are often overlooked.

The next step is comparing jobs with similar point scores to ascertain whether they are paid similarly under existing wage policies. Job classes are categorized as male, female, and neutral (gender-integrated). Using simple regression, one technique estimates the relationship between points and pay for men's and women's jobs separately. This methodology plots two salary lines—one for men's jobs and one for women's jobs. A hypothetical example is portrayed in figure 2. The wages of individual job categories, or job classes, will generally cluster around each line. In most comparable worth job evaluations, the female salary line is lower and flatter than the male line, indicating wage discrimination. The average distance between the two lines represents an estimate of the degree of wage depreciation for female-dominated jobs.

If such inequity exists, a consistent and nonbiased method of translating job evaluation point scores into salary ranges must be determined. This usually entails selecting a nondiscriminatory salary line relating points to pay. The wages of undervalued jobs are raised to the level of wages along this accepted standard. Most pay equity advocates argue that the male salary line should be used as the standard, as this represents the wages which would be earned in the absence of discrimination. However, few jurisdictions utilize the male line as the standard. Other possibilities for the chosen salary line include the nonfemale line, consisting of male plus neutral (integrated) job classes or an average line of all jobs, which includes correction for possible gender bias.[7] As in the case of Michigan government workers, a fourth option can be used by employers seeking to minimize pay adjustments. The salaries of male, female, plus neutral job

Figure 2

Points-to-Pay by Gender of Job

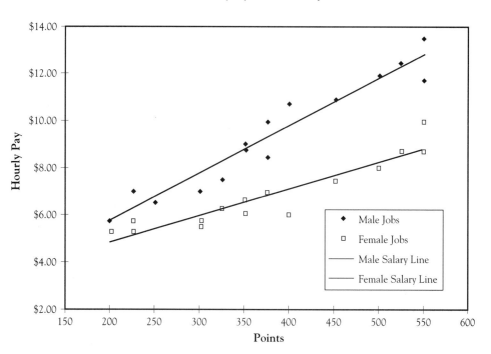

classes can be averaged and this (uncorrected) average line can be used to show how salaries should correspond with evaluated points. In keeping with the legal requirements of the Equal Pay Act, the general practice is never to reduce pay to achieve equity.

In actual implementation, employers rarely close the entire discrepancy between similarly evaluated male- and female-dominated positions. Rather than calculating wage increases based on the depreciation for *each* individual job class, many employers raise all female-dominated classes based on the amount of the average disparity. In the public sector, for example, a fixed sum for a pay equity adjustment fund is generally allocated either by the legislature or as a result of a collective bargaining agreement. Compromises are often made in determining how to allot the pay adjustments.

EVALUATIONS OF PAY EQUITY

The early literature on pay equity focused on the technical issues involved in defining and remedying wage discrimination. Researchers documented the male-female wage gap and analyzed what proportion was attributable to gender rather than education, experience, and other measurable factors (see, for example, Corcoran and Duncan 1979; Treiman and Hartmann 1981; England 1982, 1984; Aldrich and Buchele 1986; Sorensen 1991; England 1992; Sorensen 1994). Researchers also surveyed existing job evaluation systems and discussed the doctrine of comparable worth in relation to existing sex discrimination law (Treiman and Hartmann 1981; Remick 1984; Heen 1984; Beatty and Beatty 1984). The feminist critique of the neoclassical economic model of wage determination that emerged from these studies had two central premises. First, relative wages are determined by structured organizational hierarchies, not merely individual employee characteristics. Second, prevailing market wage rates perpetuate preexisting wage hierarchies based on the gender composition of occupations.

As comparable worth reform began to be implemented in the public sector, researchers turned to the task of analyzing the movement's successes and failures. The new studies evaluate comparable worth or pay equity reform as a political process involving a variety of actors exerting varying degrees of control over wage determination. Often distinguishing two phases of reform—putting pay equity on the policy agenda and implementing reform—these accounts are particularly concerned to show the politics not only of overtly political decisions but also of implementation "techniques."

Because implementation techniques are central to reform and reveal the deeply gendered nature of assessments of work yet are relatively obscured by technical language, many of the important pay equity studies focus their attention on the politics of the implementation process. These studies suggest that while politicians and bureaucrats could rhetorically endorse women's claims to equal pay for work of equal value, the cost and cultural impact of reform could be contained through implementation decisions. In their important formulation anchored in a study of Minnesota, Evans and Nelson (1989b) argue that the centrality of complex implementation created a paradox of comparable worth: it was a democratic movement with a social vision, dependent upon and disempowered by a highly specialized management technology. Acker (1989) saw comparable worth implementation as a process of reproducing gender and class hierarchies and wage structures within organizations. Describing closely the activities of the Oregon Task Force on State Compensation and Classification Equity on which she sat, Acker analyzed several implementation struggles. Both Acker's (1989) and Steinberg's (1991, 1992) descriptions of how job evaluation reproduces gender and class hierarchies create a solid foundation for understanding how job evaluation tools themselves are gendered and contribute to the gendering of organizations—the structuring of advantage and disadvantage, exploitation and control, action and emotion, meaning and identity through and in terms of distinctions between male and female (Acker 1991: 17).

Those writers who have examined agenda-setting attribute explicit political decisions to adopt some sort of comparable worth reform to the national pay equity movement combined with state-specific coalitions of unionists, feminist bureaucrats, and Democratic politicians (see Evans and Nelson 1989b, 1993). Two studies by Blum (1991) and McCann (1994) take a social movement approach to evaluating pay equity developments. While agreeing on the limitation of policy outcomes, these authors are especially interested in how social movements and the experience of women workers generate pay equity and its impact on their activity and their consciousness.

THE POLITICAL ECONOMY OF PAY EQUITY

Our study assesses the lengthy and yet unfinished development of pay equity policies for state of Michigan workers within the larger context of the political economy and the institutional context of civil service industrial relations. It is in the tradition of the literature on the political processes of pay equity reform within state and local government, though it places more emphasis on the historically changing political and economic forces that permitted and constrained reform. We see our study as a political economy of pay equity, one that takes seriously the political articulation of the interests of capital and labor, the interests of male and female workers, and the appropriate roles of the market and the state in political life outside the state administration as well as within it.

While the state is a gendered organization, it is a particular type of organization, the employment practices of which are related to the broader politics of the economy, of political parties, and of political debate about the state and the market. To understand the recent history of pay equity in Michigan and elsewhere, we must discern the dynamics not only of organizational class but also of political-economic interests and power.[8] The actions and inaction of feminist organizations, labor unions, political parties, elected officials, and state employers in relation to pay equity reform occur in a broader political and economic context. Placing pay equity reform in this context, we can see more clearly that pay equity arrived on the political agenda at a historical moment that combined generative forces and political blockages. Pay equity was contained not only by administrative and technical maneuvers but also by larger forces.

In addition, we emphasize the institutional constraints faced by public sector (civil service) unions in winning pay equity. It is obvious that pay equity is potentially a union issue in that it addresses pay and classification in particular workplaces. Other studies have examined unions as part of the alliance to win pay equity reform decisions. Evans and Nelson (1989b), Blum (1991), and others have documented tensions over putting the pay equity issue on union agendas and how implementation ought to be pursued. What has been less clear in previous studies is how state institutional structures and broader politics shape union strategies for pay equity and what that range of strategies is.

This political economy approach helps us understand the history of pay equity reform and its future in different ways. Other writers have appropriately regretted the limits of compromised reforms in the states, interpreting them as the reproduction of gendered power relations within organizations (Acker 1989) or policy containment (Steinberg 1991; Steinberg and Haignere 1991). However, it is also important to see these disappointments in the context of the changing political and economic situation that made winning pay equity more difficult. Further, while the limits of union activity regarding pay equity are partly due to the gender dynamics of unions, they are also constructed by the institutional structures in which unions operate and the multiple pressures on public sector unions and the union movement as a whole.[9] Understanding the complex context of pay equity gives added import to social movement analysis and its focus on the consciousness of union and feminist activists. In a period in which policy reform was increasingly difficult to win, one of the movement's greatest contributions may have been its impact on consciousness— its calling into question in the minds of working women the purported fairness of the market.

Our study emphasizes that progress on pay equity depends critically on the strength of the broader labor and women's movements. Progress also requires political discourses, including a critical feminism, which insist upon more than a "free market" as the measure of a good and just social order. In a restructuring and decentralizing economy in which the state has lost its ability to command legitimacy and resources, future efforts need to be more decentralized and informal, reaching beyond the civil service into other parts of the public sector and the private sector.

THE PLAN OF THE BOOK

Pay equity reform in Michigan began relatively early in comparison with other states. As the chronology in table 1 indicates, pay equity advocates within state government commissioned an initial comparable worth study in 1979. However, pay equity did not reach the political agenda of those with the power to enact reform—in the case of Michigan the Civil

Table 1

Chronology of Pay Equity
Development in the Michigan Civil Service

1937   Legislature authorizes a merit system for state classified workforce.

1938   Position Comparison System implemented as classification plan.

1939   Legislature passes "Ripper Act" severely restricting the merit system.

1940   Voters authorize a merit system and Civil Service Commission as an
        amendment to the Michigan Constitution.

1965   Michigan Department of Civil Rights established.

1968   Michigan Women's Commission established.

1971   Republican Governor William Milliken orders a special
        Employment Practices Review to investigate gender employment
        practices in the merit system.

1975   Civil Service begins to implement the Michigan Benchmark
        Evaluation System; system phased in through 1981.

1976   Civil Service Commission grants collective bargaining over noneco-
        nomic issues to employee organizations.

1979–   Office of Women and Work created in Michigan Department of
1981   Labor; completes preliminary study of comparable worth; examines
        discrimination in the Benchmark system; issues Request for
        Proposals to assess whether single job evaluation is possible; Arthur
        Young and Company chosen to conduct study.

1979   Women in State Government, an independent group of civil
        servants advocating for women, founded.

1980   Civil Service Commission extends collective bargaining to wage and
        other compensation issues.

1981   U.S. Supreme Court issues landmark decision in *County of
        Washington, Oregon v. Gunther*.

1981   Karon Black and MSEA file a class action suit alleging sex discrimination in the civil service.

1981   Office of Women and Work transmits Arthur Young study to Civil Service Commission.

1981   Office of Women and Work helps organize Michigan Comparable Worth Task Force, a grassroots coalition of women's and labor organizations, academics, and government agencies; dissolves in 1982.

1982   Internal Department of Civil Service staff report to the Civil Service Commission on occupational sex segregation in the civil service.

1983   Civil Service Commission asks Department of Civil Service to develop "cross–walk" classification model to convert 11 segregated groups into single job evaluation system. Department instead recommends more affirmative action to desegregate occupations. Civil Service Commission establishes a Comparable Worth Task Force.

1983   District Court finds in favor of plaintiff in *AFSCME v. State of Washington*; reversed on appeal in 1985.

1985   Comparable Worth Task Force issues its report to the Civil Service Commission. Recommends reclassification; multiple groupings; pay increases for female–dominated occupations.

1985   Michigan Pay Equity Network founded at a Coalition of Labor Union Women conference in response to shortcomings of Comparable Worth Task Force report.

1985   Representation of administrative support bargaining unit changes from MSEA to UAW; UAW files pay equity lawsuit, *UAW v. State of Michigan*, in U.S. District Court.

1985–   Incumbents in female–dominated job classes receive limited pay
1986   equity wage adjustments.

1986   Pay Equity Network tries unsuccessfully to persuade Democratic governor James Blanchard to set aside a pay equity fund in the state budget.

1987   Pay Equity Network drafts new regulatory legislation similar to Manitoba and Ontario, Canada, to prohibit discrimination in job evaluation systems. UAW lawsuit fails; upheld on appeal in 1989.

1988   Pay Equity Network abandons regulatory act effort; works on com-
        plaint–triggered legislation to amend existing state Civil Rights Act
        to define as a violation failure to provide equal compensation
        for work of equal value; bills in successive legislative sessions never
        pass committee.

1990   Equitable Classification Plan for Group One (nonprofessional)
        employees completed and implemented.

1993   Equitable Classification Plan for Group Two employees completed
        and implemented.

Service Commission—until the mid-1980s. Pay adjustments followed in
the mid-late 1980s, but reclassification of nonsupervisory civil service positions was not completed until the early 1990s. This long-running reform
provides an especially broad window through which to understand changes
in the economy and politics, their mediation by the state's institutional
structure, and their impact on pay equity.

The next chapter of this book, chapter 2, discusses the political
and economic context of Michigan pay equity reform from the early 1980s
through the mid-1990s. It begins by examining major developments in the
national and Michigan economies. Ranking among the top ten states in
both overall gross state product and manufacturing output, the Michigan
economy exemplifies both the cyclical processes of recession and recovery
and the longer-term process of economic restructuring, which have disproportionately affected the northeast and midwest industrial heartland. The
chapter then explores in some detail the state politics which developed
during the two administrations of Democratic governor James Blanchard
(1983–1990) and the first administration of Republican governor John Engler (1991–1994). We argue that it was not economic dislocation but the
response of political actors to economic developments that created a poor
climate for reform during those years. Democratic and Republican politicians espoused an antistate politics and targeted state workers, as did politicians in other states. Grassroots women's groups and organized labor,
though nominally supportive of pay equity, were preoccupied with maintaining reproductive choice and jobs lost through deindustrialization and
state cutbacks.

Chapter 3 summarizes the battle to put pay equity on the agenda
of the Civil Service Commission, the institution with exclusive constitutional jurisdiction over approximately sixty-three thousand state employees, of whom 51 percent are women. The chapter explores the critical
policy decisions taken by the commission and adopted within the civil
service. In the absence of a strong grassroots movement, we identify the

importance of the Office of Women and Work in the Michigan Department of Labor and Women in State Government, a voluntary association, in persuading the Civil Service Commission to consider pay equity. The commission delegated decisions about whether and how the civil service should undertake pay equity to an appointed Comparable Worth Task Force. The task force's recommendations did not represent a commitment to a strong pay equity reform.

Chapter 4 is the first of two successive chapters which examine implementation of pay equity within the framework set by the task force. It explores the attempts of the civil service unions to negotiate special pay equity wage increases. Nearly three out of four state employees are represented by unions. We emphasize the efforts of the two large unions representing many incumbents in female-dominated jobs: the United Auto Workers (UAW) and the American Federation of State, County, and Municipal Employees (AFSCME). The implementation of the Equitable Classification Plan, the new nondiscriminatory job evaluation and classification plan mandated by the Comparable Worth Task Force, is discussed in chapter 5. The new classification plan, developed by the Department of Civil Service rather than an outside consultant, is evaluated in detail. The exercise, largely controlled by professional staff in the Department of Civil Service, was not particularly visible to women workers, their male coworkers, or supervisors, partly because the points assigned by the plan never became the basis for pay. Our statistical analysis of the civil service wage structure indicates that job classes are not remunerated in accordance with the relative valuation captured in the new reclassification plan and that substantial gender-based wage disparities persist.

Although the civil service was clearly the key arena for pay equity reform within Michigan, chapter 6 focuses on efforts to reach beyond state employment. Frustrated with the slow pace and limited results within the civil service, a small Pay Equity Network led by feminist labor activists attempted to broaden and deepen the pay equity reform. Ultimately unsuccessful, the Pay Equity Network launched a discussion of legislative possibilities and strategies and repeatedly articulated the issue. As within the civil service, these efforts ran up against larger political and economic forces in the state. Nevertheless, they represent the construction of a broader pay equity strategy.

The final chapter, chapter 7, revisits the Michigan case, restating and elaborating our interpretation of the limits of pay equity reform as currently constituted. We discuss the need for a more informal and decentralized movement that goes beyond state employment. Thus, we reflect on what a political-economic approach to pay equity and the specific Michigan experience tell us about the future of the pay equity movement.

CONCLUSION

Michigan's pay equity reform provides a lens through which to examine not only the organizational dynamics that may reproduce women's subordination but also the changing political economy of state employment, the sector which has provided the focus of much actual pay equity activity and scholarly analysis of reform. The reform originated in the optimism of the early 1980s but has had a long and as yet incomplete implementation period. Experiences of working women struggling for pay equity nationwide mirror the problems faced by Michigan government workers in the context of the political economy.

In 1984, Glennis Ter Wisscha, a bank employee from Wilmar, Minnesota, gave hopeful testimony at congressional pay equity hearings: "Millions of American women will never have college degrees nor professional jobs. For them work means the daily grind in offices, factories, hospitals, and schools. But they deserve the pride that comes from doing a job well and being paid fairly. They deserve their pride in themselves. Today with these hearings, you are beginning to recognize these claims of pride" (Wisscha 1984). Ten years later, Marilyn Jancey, a cafeteria worker from Everett, Massachusetts, testified to new obstacles preventing women's claims:

> Since no one in the city really knew what we did—their impression of us was that we made some sandwiches every once in a while and chatted with fellow co-workers for the rest of the time—they did not realize that we were in charge of the maintenance of all equipment, cleaning, menu organizing, handling of money, carrying heavy cases of food, and preparation of original recipes for 6,000 to 7,000 students. It was also not uncommon for us to suffer from cuts, back injuries, burns and other injuries as cafeteria workers. . . . Even though the school knew what we did, they didn't value our work nor did they pay us accordingly. . . . In September of 1991, we went to court. . . . the remaining women were laid off when the City of Everett decided to privatize the cafeteria workers and suppliers. The same company that has been a food supplier was now contracted to also provide cafeteria workers. (Jancey 1994)

The voices of these two working women directly challenge the low value placed upon predominantly female work. They both call attention to the failure of employers and society as a whole to see and value the demands associated with women's jobs. Separated by a decade, their experiences and perspectives are also shaped by a changing political economy. The first speaker is optimistic that national pay equity policy might address the underpayment of women's work; the second speaker, whose job has been privatized in the midst of a discrimination claim, illustrates the limitations of a movement which has been largely confined to state and municipal workers. We argue that it is only by expanding pay equity strategies beyond narrow, state-centered, comparable worth techniques that the movement can adapt to the emerging political economy.

2

The Context of Pay Equity Reform: The Political Economy of Michigan in the 1980s and 1990s

The pay equity reform movement gained momentum nationally and in the state of Michigan in the late 1970s and early 1980s. Its rise was related to social changes such as the increasing (though gender-segregated) labor force participation of women and women's growing financial responsibility for families. Political developments—such as the rise of a women's movement with a multifaceted agenda, the increased membership of women in workplace-based organizations, and the development of an array of equal opportunities programs that at once raised women's expectations yet left many in low-paying jobs—also fuelled the movement. The pay equity reform movement, once initiated, was developed through national organizations, including both unions and specific pay equity networks, and bolstered by a few early court cases with high visibility. Pay equity made its greatest progress in state and local government.

Yet the early 1980s represented a singularly unpromising, or at least contradictory, economic and political period for pay equity. A set of paradoxical conditions was present both nationally and in the state of Michigan. First, increased global competition induced deindustrialization in the Midwest and Northeast, while tight money policies of the Federal Reserve precipitated a more general recession. The decline of the primarily male manufacturing economy and shift toward a more feminized labor force in the 1970s and 1980s was precisely one development from which pay equity gathered some of its strength. But at the same time, capital and many politicians were intensifying the attack on high wages in the private and public sectors as undermining competitiveness and productivity. While women were increasingly drawn into the workforce in this period, they were often employed precisely as a strategy to reduce labor costs.

Secondly, as a result of increasing public sector unionization, the election of feminist politicians, and the creation of advocacy offices for women within state bureaucracies, a movement advocating pay equity reform developed in the public sector. However, the 1980s was a period during which "big government" and the taxation required to support it were delegitimized. The quest to reduce the number and cost of state workers overrode the image of the state as a model employer.

Third, the pay equity movement was "between feminism and labor" (Blum 1991). That is, it was dependent upon the strength of both labor and feminist organizations. It was both contingent upon and conducive to combining labor movement and feminist forms of consciousness. In the 1980s, despite the relative success of service unions in the public sector, however, unionism was under attack, and the political organizations of the union movement as a whole were focused on defending the conditions of its predominantly male core constituency. The women's movement was similarly preoccupied, fighting abridgements of reproductive choice.

This chapter initiates the exploration of the long-running Michigan experience of pay equity reform by discussing the problematic political-economic context of the 1980s and the early 1990s in Michigan. It begins by examining major developments in the national and Michigan political economy—the longer-term processes of deindustrialization and restructuring on the one hand and the cyclical processes of recession and recovery on the other. It then explores in detail the state politics which developed during the two administrations of Democratic governor James Blanchard (1983–1990) and the first administration of Republican governor John Engler (1991–1994) during this period of economic change. Both governors led state government during a period in which politicians had abandoned the perspective that the state is a positive mechanism for stabilizing the economy and securing social justice; the state had been redefined as interfering with the private market and individual freedom. This discussion puts the bureaucracy-centered pay equity reform in the state in broader context and sets out some important political dynamics related to the containment of reform in Michigan. At a broader level, this analytic approach illustrates the relationship between pay equity as an internal state-bureaucratic reform and a much broader politics, a politics of the economy, of political parties, and of public discourse.

THE MICHIGAN ECONOMY IN THE EARLY 1980S

Following World War II, a key segment of manufacturing workers in Michigan and other industrial states experienced the "glory days" of high demand for domestic manufactured goods, high and stable levels of employment, and high wages. But in the 1970s, in place of the boom years of the immediate postwar decades, a period of sluggish growth and inflation coincided with the appearance of intensified competition from Japan and Western Europe. "Deindustrialization," widespread, systematic disinvestment in basic productive capacity, was accompanied by high rates of unemployment among industrial workers as their jobs disappeared. Eventually, a new international division of labor emerged, with export-oriented manufacturing in newly industrialized countries promoted by international development agencies. The service sector expanded in the United States and other advanced industrialized countries.

Economists have argued that, in the 1970s and 1980s, the overall composition of employment shifted towards "bad" service-sector jobs, with less job security, lower wages, fewer benefits, and few prospects for advancement (Kuhn and Bluestone 1987; Sokoloff 1987; Harrison and Bluestone 1988; Albelda and Tilly 1994; Badgett and Williams 1994). By 1984, service sector employment constituted 74 percent of all employment nationally, compared to 58 percent in 1948 (Kuhn and Bluestone 1987). In all sectors, employers sought labor cost reductions and increased labor flexibility. Three types of "contingent" work, work not based upon full-time permanent jobs with benefits, grew in the 1970s and 1980s: part-time work, temporary work, and contract work (Beechey and Perkins 1987; Blank 1990; Callaghan and Hartmann 1991; duRivage 1992; Engberg 1993).

When recession and restructuring began in the mid-1970s and early 1980s, Michigan, like much of the Midwestern "rustbelt," was distinguished from the rest of the nation by the importance of manufacturing to its economy. Before the recession of the early 1980s, manufacturing provided more than one third of all wage income in the Midwest, compared to less than a quarter in the country as a whole. In addition, Michigan depended largely on durable goods manufacture, particularly the automobile industry, and a large share of workers were employed in the auto industry (Rom 1988: 18–54).

The booming Michigan economy of the postwar years had been founded upon the extraordinary economic success of the "Big Four" auto manufacturers—General Motors, Ford, Chrysler, and American Motors—which profited from the physical destruction of European and Japanese industry and from domestic oligopoly. The U.S. auto industry produced 8 million or three quarters of the 10.6 million cars and trucks produced worldwide in 1950 (Bluestone and Bluestone 1992: 62). After the war, Wayne County, Michigan (comprised of Detroit and its surrounding communities), produced about 50 percent of all cars manufactured in the United States, according to Aronowitz (1984). The auto industry's loss of more than half its world market share between 1950 and the late 1980s and of its share of the U.S. domestic market (as imports increased from about 4 to 30 percent), therefore, had a critical impact upon the Michigan economy (Bluestone and Bluestone 1992: 62–63).

The response of auto manufacturers was largely to attack labor costs, not only because labor costs were a high proportion of total costs for manufacturers but also to enable investment in new technology to match the production efficiency, product quality, and product variety of foreign competitors (Moody 1988; Bluestone and Bluestone 1992; Zurvalec 1995). Auto production drifted away from southeast Michigan, first to the southern United States, then overseas (Aronowitz 1984: 261; Moody 1988: 100–101). General Motors, Ford, and Chrysler (which had acquired the American Motors Corporation), all introduced technology to reduce labor costs in the long run. Plants were closed in an effort to concentrate production at the most efficient and profitable sites. Then, beginning in 1979, the auto companies began demanding concessions from unionized workers, first on wages and benefits and then on work rules and working conditions, as the tradition of pattern bargaining in the auto industry began to break down (Bluestone and Harrison 1982; Cappelli and McKersie 1985; Harrison and Bluestone 1988; Moody 1988: 169–174).

The contraction of auto and durable goods manufacture in Michigan had a considerable impact upon employment. In January 1980 the state's jobless rate of 10.3 percent was far ahead of the 6.2 percent national average (Department of Commerce 1991: 5) and gave Michigan "the dubious, unwanted honor of having the highest unemployment rate of any of the nation's industrial states," as the *Michigan AFL-CIO News* reported in February 1980. Between 1980 and 1983 annual average unemployment ranged from 12.3 to 15.5 percent (Department of Commerce 1991: 5). The rise in unemployment was due largely to layoffs in the auto industry, which, in turn, led to layoffs in parts and suppliers plants and other businesses dependent upon the income of autoworkers.

Women workers in Michigan were concentrated outside the blue-collar occupations of the durable goods manufacturing sector and so their employment followed a somewhat different course. As in the national economy as a whole, Michigan women continued to join the labor force through the mid-1980s as the service sector expanded on the basis of low-wage, part-time and often female labor, and as the manufacturing sector itself became feminized (Hagen and Jenson 1988: 10–11; Amott 1993). Women were employed overwhelmingly in administrative support, services, and managerial and professional jobs such as teaching and nursing, and were a disproportionate number of part-time workers. Women's unemployment rate in 1982 was 13 percent, as compared to 17.3 percent for all workers in Michigan. Despite more favorable official unemployment rates in the 1980s, Michigan women had lower median incomes than men, and African-American and Hispanic women had lower incomes than white women. Michigan women who headed households with children were disproportionately impoverished (Sarri et al. 1987: 82).

Michigan's severe, cyclical recession ended in the mid-1980s, but the long-term restructuring of the state economy continued. The late 1980s and early 1990s represented an improvement in the overall economy as measured by several indicators of overall economic performance. But aggregated measures disguise the increased earnings inequality that characterized the 1980s and the considerable downward mobility both within and across generations that characterized many blue-collar and other families (Danziger and Gottschalk 1993; Newman 1988, 1994).

Between 1984 and 1987 unemployment rates ranging from 7 to 9 percent in the state remained above the national average but considerably lower than in the early 1980s (Department of Commerce 1991: 3–5). The number of Michigan jobs grew 17.1 percent, while the national average growth was 18.5 percent. The level of employment recovered to more than 4 million in 1986, up 400,000 since 1982. All the net job growth in Michigan was in non-manufacturing jobs, however, with the largest growth in retail and wholesale trade; business, health, and other services; finance, insurance, and real estate—sectors with lower average wages and less unionization than manufacturing (Department of Commerce 1991: 3–5). Michigan income per person grew 8.2 percent from 1979 to 1990, after adjusting for inflation. However, this was lower than the national real income growth of 13 percent (Department of Commerce 1991: 12). In the early 1990s, a buoyant national economy revived the demand for cars, creating increased overtime and strikes against speed-up in the plants. By 1993 the rate of unemployment was 7 percent, and in 1994 it fell to 5.9 percent (MESC 1995).

Economic trends in the postwar period also affected labor unions. Unions as organizations had been relatively strong in the period after the war, with approximately 30 percent of all wage-earning workers and 60 percent of production workers unionized nationally (Aronowitz 1984: 259). During this uniquely prosperous period, organized labor's increased wages and benefits were compatible with job security and did not substantially decrease profits (Freeman and Medoff 1984; Bluestone and Bluestone 1992). Unions' industrial base had already eroded slowly in the 1960s and 1970s, but the success of public sector organizing had maintained a substantial proportion of union membership in the workforce as a whole (Aronowitz 1984: 259–60). By the early 1980s, however, employers and conservative policymakers blamed unions for the American economy's lack of competitiveness. Corporate strategies and national policy, including the dramatic example of the dismissal of the striking air traffic controllers and Reagan's appointment of antilabor staff to the National Labor Relations Board, aimed to weaken unions, already debilitated by unemployment and deindustrialization. Overall, national union density in 1986 was 17.5 percent, while manufacturing workers were 24.8 percent organized (Moody 1988: 4). By the 1990s, less than 15 percent of the entire labor force was made up of union members. Michigan's unionization rate, 37.3 percent in 1980 (second in the country to New York State at 38.8 percent), fell to 25 percent in 1991. Private sector union membership fell to 19 percent, while the public sector remained 55 percent organized (MESC 1992: 4).

During the nationwide recession of the early 1980s, therefore, the Michigan economy underwent a particularly severe dislocation. Automobile and other manufacturing workers, relatively heavily unionized and well represented in party and legislative political action, were suffering immense losses in employment and considerable deterioration in terms and conditions of work, a sharp contrast to the security they had experienced in earlier decades (Bluestone and Harrison 1982; Harrison and Bluestone 1988; Moody 1988). The multiplier effect of these job losses affected other workers, who struggled to support themselves in lower-paid service sector jobs. The percentage of unionized workers fell as the composition of private sector employment shifted, and unions, facing a generally hostile climate, failed to organize the service sector aggressively. In the service sector in particular, women's employment increased, but outside of the professions women worked at relatively low-wage jobs, often without the benefits associated with male employment in the auto plants. During the 1980s, beset by the crisis in industrial manufacturing affecting its membership core, the organized labor movement in Michigan had little concern with these low-wage feminized jobs or with women's wages relative to men's. The cyclical swings and structural changes in the Michigan economy shaped the political priorities of business, labor, and political parties in the state in the 1980s.

THE BLANCHARD YEARS, 1983–1990: ECONOMIC CRISIS AND FISCAL PRESSURES

Democrat James Blanchard was governor of Michigan from 1983 until 1990, predominantly a period of economic dislocation. While governor, Blanchard, nominated and supported by organized labor, was preoccupied by a dual economic crisis: economic restructuring and recession on the one hand and budget scarcity and antitax pressures on the other. Blanchard was interested in working with private business, especially in the durable goods manufacturing sector, to maintain jobs and production in Michigan. Blanchard was a "moderate Democrat" oriented towards a traditional male labor constituency rather than towards redistributive economics or gender and race equality. Although Blanchard adhered to the notion of creating incentives for business to invest, he declined to attack labor's wages and benefits. Organized business, however, tried to reduce labor costs by assailing such state-level programs as unemployment insurance and workers' compensation. When, early in his first term, Blanchard attempted to manage an unbalanced state budget by raising the state income tax without cutting services, a dramatic tax revolt flared in the southeastern part of the state. Tax-cutting had become a key political word across the United States in the 1980s, as taxation came to represent an overweening and inefficient state, misusing money that rightly belonged to individuals and making "free enterprise" uncompetitive. In response to the tax revolt, Blanchard and the state Democratic Party moved to the right, both responding to and defining a more conservative political and economic climate.

THE DEMOCRATIC PARTY, THE UNIONS, AND BLANCHARD'S ELECTION

The Democratic leadership and organized labor had worked together to recruit James Blanchard, whom they saw as a winning candidate, to run for the governorship in 1982. The Michigan AFL-CIO, UAW, and Michigan Education Association (MEA) all took the unusual step of endorsing Blanchard in the primary ("Status Quo on the Line in Primary," *Detroit News*, August 1, 1982: 1 and 9, "Blanchard Blazed a Positive Trail," November 3, 1982: 12A; Buffa 1984: 263–71). The primary was seen as a test of the power of labor in general and of the UAW specifically, and the Michigan AFL-CIO, dominated by the UAW, campaigned energetically ("Status Quo on the Line in Primary," *Detroit News*, August 1, 1982: 1; Buffa 1984: 263–71). Blanchard was seen as sympathetic to labor, traditionally a powerful force in the Michigan Democratic Party organization (Buffa 1984), at a time when labor was desperate for political solutions to its mounting economic and organizational problems. When he was endorsed by labor for the governorship, Blanchard was a young congressman from Oakland County, a northern suburb of Detroit, who was closely associated with organized labor yet generally seen as pragmatic and moderate rather than liberal. While in Congress, he had played an important role in devising a controversial plan which combined federal guarantees for loans to the Chrysler Corporation with demands for concessions from labor (Buffa 1984; Press and Verburg 1985: 221–22; Moody 1988).

In the 1982 elections themselves, labor campaigned vigorously for Blanchard and other Democrats ("Blanchard, Griffiths Push Jobs Plan," *Michigan AFL-CIO News*, November 1982: 5; see also Press and Verburg 1985: 221–23; "Blanchard Acts While Headlee Talks," *Michigan AFL-CIO News*, October 1982: 1). The Michigan AFL-CIO mounted a campaign

> aimed at reaching every rank and file union member and members of union families with the message that the only way to reverse the present deep recession is to elect labor endorsed candidates pledged to opposing Reaganomics at every level of government. In Michigan the races are clear cut between labor-endorsed Democrats who are committed to creating and preserving jobs and the Republican opponents who are staunch supporters of the same Reagan policies which have brought record unemployment to the state and nation. (*Michigan AFL-CIO News*, October 1982: 1)

In the November 1982 elections, not only was the labor-endorsed gubernatorial candidate, James Blanchard, elected 51 to 45 percent, but the Democratic Party won majorities in both the Michigan house and senate. It was the first time since 1938 that Democrats held both the governor's office and the legislature.

State Politics and the Restructuring Economy

For the eight years of his governorship, Blanchard worked to support private business initiatives and diversify the state's economy. Established during his formative first term, his strategy was to encourage high-wage manufacturing jobs, as well as service sector jobs associated with tourism. Libby Maynard, former chair of the Michigan Democratic Party and a cabinet member in the Blanchard administration, characterized Blanchard's focus on job development as follows: "We were in tough economic times, and so most of the emphasis [of the administration] was on job development. Michigan began losing its manufacturing base so we were looking at skilled high-tech jobs for the 21st century and service sector jobs linked to tourism. For 30 years previously neither labor, management, nor the governor had looked at the economic issues" (Maynard 1993).

One economic objective of the Blanchard administration was to attract manufacturing jobs. His office worked with other departments to attract specific manufacturing and research establishments to Michigan with incentive packages. Some of these, such as the new Mazda plant at Flat Rock, were unionized sites in the Detroit area. His Commission on Jobs and Economic Development, chaired by Lee Iacocca of the Chrysler Corporation and Doug Fraser, former president of the UAW, stressed job creation and retention in a diverse set of manufacturing industries—food processing, forest products, and auto supply.

The 1984 report of a Task Force for a Long-Term Economic Strategy for Michigan became the basis for one broad thrust of economic policy. Blanchard had commissioned the study shortly after his election. Economists from Michigan's three major public universities—the University of Michigan, Michigan State University, and Wayne State University—were influential on the task force. Anticorporatist in tone but rejecting "tax relief" and lowered wages as solutions to Michigan's economic problems, the report argued that Michigan "must become a world center for the export of the new industrial technologies and manufacturing machinery that will form the basis of the factory of the future" ("State Urged to Focus on High Tech," *Detroit News,* November 19, 1984). In a set of strategies aimed more at small business, Blanchard created the Michigan Strategic Fund to make loans and grants to small business, the Michigan Business Ombudsman to provide information about legal and regulatory issues to business, and a tourism marketing board.

While Blanchard did not attack the unions' organizational base or the benefits they had won for their members, state Republicans kept up a decade-long effort to "improve the business climate" by decreasing costs to business of employing labor and producing goods. The Michigan Manufacturers Association (MMA), the largest proportion of whose members are in automotive supply and auto manufacturing but also include large food processors and chemical corporations, summarized their priorities as "improving Michigan's competitive position relative to other states and nations . . . the goal is effective, full employment for Michigan citizens and profitability for the business community who provide jobs." Reduction of labor costs was key in large, high-wage manufacturing concerns, which saw their wage costs as "not as high as in Europe, but not as low as South Carolina, either" (Zurvalec 1995). The MMA centrally identified the need for further modification of the workers' compensation system and unemployment insurance law, as well as reduction of costs associated with product liability, regulatory policies, and occupational health and safety legislation (MMA 1986). The Chamber of Commerce, a more diverse and inclusive group of business interests, including many small businesses, shared these concerns but also had as high priorities the reduction of taxes on small business and maintenance of a low minimum wage (Chamber of Commerce [Michigan] n.d., Proposed Legislative Priorities; Moving Michigan Forward). Both the Michigan Manufacturers Association and the

Chamber of Commerce wished to minimize overall business taxation and state regulation of business.

Defense of jobs and benefits for its core, mainly male, manufacturing constituency remained organized labor's key objective in the 1980s. At both state and federal levels, organized labor fought for plant-closing legislation. The proposed legislation required pre-notification of closures to employees and communities. It also incorporated both automatic emergency measures to alleviate distress and longer-term programs to save jobs and retrain workers. Organized business opposed this "industrial hostage" legislation.

With many of their members on layoff and then unemployed, maintenance and improvement of unemployment benefits were high priorities for the unions. In December 1982, as a direct result of the recession, the state's unemployment fund was insolvent, and a four-year emergency plan froze benefits and tightened eligibility, while requiring employers to pay higher taxes. When the emergency program expired, labor fought against business and Republican proposals to institute a waiting week (an initial week of unemployment for which benefits would not be paid), limit benefit levels, and restrict eligibility. Simultaneously, Michigan labor worked to try to improve benefits available through the Federal Supplemental Compensation (FSC) program, which extended benefits in states with higher rates of unemployment. While labor fended off most of the proposed Republican modifications during the 1980s, unemployment taxes for businesses and benefits for unemployed workers were dramatically cut in 1995, early in the second term of Republican John Engler ("House Votes to Cut Benefits for Jobless," *Ann Arbor News*, March 24, 1995: C5).

Workers' compensation, like unemployment compensation, was seen by the business community and many Republicans as an unfair tax on business that deterred economic development. The *AFL-CIO News* took exception to this depiction, defending workers' compensation as a necessary cost of doing business, and argued that Michigan did not have unusually high unemployment benefit costs. Labor tried with uneven success to defend the relatively progressive changes to workers' compensation that had been enacted in 1980 and 1981.

Both state and national mimimum wages became preoccupations for organized labor in Michigan. The steep decline in the real value of the minimum wage not only hurt minimum wage workers but also lowered the floor above which unions negotiated wages for their members. By the end of the 1980s the federal minimum wage brought a family of three to 70.5 percent of the (artifically low) federal poverty level, down from 104.6 percent of the poverty level in the 1960s. Labor simultaneously supported an increase in the federal minimum to $4.25 or 81.5 percent of the poverty rate for a family of three, as well as an increase in the state minimum to

$4.55 in 1991 and $5.00 by 1993 ("Garrison: Boost Minimum Wage," *Michigan AFL-CIO News*, February 1990: 1; Danziger and Gottschalk 1993). While labor was fighting to raise wages, business unsuccessfully sought to overturn Michigan's prevailing wage law, a law which required that wage rates on all state-funded construction projects be not less than those generally prevailing in the locality, that is, the union rate (MMA 1986).

FISCAL CRISIS AND ANTITAX PRESSURES

Nearly as soon as he was elected, Blanchard found the state deep in fiscal crisis, and the first-term struggles over the state's fiscal status critically shaped his entire period in office. Michigan's $900 million deficit was the result of a combination of factors. Federal aid to the state was cut as part of Reagan's new federalism and new budgetary priorities. New federalism reduced funding to the states, while reorganizing categorical grants into block grants. It also placed more regulatory and administrative responsibilities on the states, which continued to administer well-established programs to which there was a strong sense of entitlement (Eisenger and Gormley 1988; Kaplan and O'Brien 1991). Rising unemployment rates reduced tax revenues, while making new demands on them.

On the recommendation of a Fiscal Crisis Council comprised of business, labor, education, and government leaders, Blanchard introduced a recovery program which he described as "stern medicine for a very ill patient." The program included a 38 percent increase in the state income tax, from a flat rate of 4.6 to 6.35 percent. The council also recommended targeted budget cuts.

The increase in the state income tax provided the rallying cry for a dramatic antitax revolt in the state. The antitax revolt involved several different organized campaigns. The centerpiece was an attempt to recall two Democratic senators, Phil Mastin of Pontiac and David Serotkin of Mount Clemens, who had voted for the tax increase and who were perceived as particularly vulnerable to Republican challenges. The two Democratic senators lost recall elections in November 1983 and were replaced by antitax Republicans. About a dozen other legislators were targeted, but unsuccessfully ("Tax Cut Bid Fails to Cool Recall Fever," *Detroit News*, January 23, 1984: 3A). A referendum on a Voter's Choice Amendment, which would have required voter approval for all future tax increases, failed. An effort to recall Blanchard also went down to defeat, but the tax revolt in general created widespread public sentiment that Blanchard was a "one-term governor" ("Tax Revolt Alive and Kicking," *Detroit News*, January 15, 1984: 19; "Voters Reject Proposal C," *Detroit News*, November 7, 1984: 1; Cole 1989).

The tax-related recalls were partly a specific Republican strategy to change the political balance in the state senate. But they were also one manifestation of the more general tax revolt and antigovernment sentiment of the late 1970s and early 1980s. In Michigan, as elsewhere in the country, activists opposed tax increases even though they had been enacted purely in order to remedy the budget deficit, not to increase services to citizens (Kuttner 1988). The revolt was bolstered by the association of taxation with government activity, which was seen almost wholly negatively. The tax revolts were a dramatic indication of the shift from public commitment to the use of government for broad social improvement to public condemnation of tax burdens. They represented a popularization of the Reagan era's supply-side economics, the idea that tax cuts would stimulate work, savings, and investment, which would in turn increase jobs and productivity, lower inflation, and balance the budget (Sawhill 1986: 97, 100). The Reaganite ideology resonated with many middle-income families as they experienced an increased tax burden, as inflation pushed them into higher tax brackets, and as more of the national tax burden shifted onto personal income and property. In his study of Democratic defectors in the 1984 presidential election residing in Detroit's predominantly white working-class suburbs, Stanley Greenberg also found the sentiment that government spending went to "undeserving" African-Americans (Greenberg 1985: 13–18), an idea that could also have contributed to the tax revolt.

The Michigan tax revolt explicitly articulated the idea that state taxation was responsible for Michigan's economic decline. "Michigan . . . is letting its economic strength dwindle away. Companies are leaving or failing to expand in our high-tax state," John Lauve, the coordinator of the campaign to recall Blanchard, wrote in a letter to the *Detroit News* on January 6, 1984. He saw Michigan's levels of taxation as "tax abuses that drive industry from Michigan." The campaign also focused on the idea that public sector workers were overpaid. "Michigan workers made concessions to keep their jobs. Lansing is unwilling to do the same," the letter from Lauve continued. While it was clear from both the report of the Fiscal Crisis Council and census data that Michigan had a lower public-employee-to-population ratio than all but five other states, the tax rebels continued to attack pay and particularly the absence of employee contributions to retirement benefits (John Lauve, letter to the editor, *Detroit News*, January 6, 1984; "The Budget Gamble," *Detroit News*, January 8, 1984; "Who's in Charge Here?" *Detroit News*, April 19, 1984).

With the election of two Republicans in place of the Democrats Mastin and Serotkin, the partisan split in the state senate became twenty Republicans to eighteen Democrats. In general, it became more difficult to maintain "liberal" policies, as not only the partisan balance changed but also the political climate. After the 1983 recall elections, Blanchard, mirroring the trajectory of many Democrats at national and state levels, began increasingly to speak the language of budget-cutting, tax relief, cuts in social spending, and decreasing the size of government (Aronowitz 1984: 258).

In a clear attempt to limit political damage to the Democratic Party and because of progress in resolving the budgetary shortfall, the rate of the state income tax was decreased in 1984, sooner than originally planned, and then lowered again in 1987. For 1984–85 Blanchard proposed a more or less "zero growth" budget, more disciplined, leaner and tighter than he might have otherwise. Following the Michigan tax revolts and the crushing defeat of Walter Mondale in the 1984 presidential election, Blanchard in 1985 associated himself with the Democratic Leadership Council (DLC), the central theme of which was "avoidance of any association with organized labor, minorities, feminists, or other 'special interest' groups" (Moody 1988: 144).

In his 1982 campaign Blanchard had promised to reduce "waste" in state government and decrease the size of the state workforce. During his first two years he continued to warn department heads that he intended to decrease the number of state employees (*Michigan Report*, August 19, 1983: 1). In his 1984 State of the State Address, Blanchard spoke publicly about cutting the number of public employees as a means of making state government more efficient:

> What this means for the State of Michigan is that we will work harder, we will work smarter, we will work better to deliver the same services at higher quality for less money. . . . one yardstick for measuring this commitment is the level of state government employment. Over the past 12 months we have reduced the number of state employees by 1,200. Over the next 12 months we will bring the number down by another 1,200. Those reductions will not only mean greater efficiency . . . but also . . . that more funds will be available for our priorities for the future.

In fact, during his first administration the number of state employees decreased by about 7,000 (Blanchard 1984; *Detroit News*, February 10, 1984, letter to the editor by Robert Naftaly; DCS, Management Services Division, 1992: 3). A subsequent increase in state employment was due solely to the massive expansion of the prison workforce.

Blanchard and Women's Issues

While Blanchard supported reproductive choice, the main demand of the organized women's movement in Michigan, he showed little interest in other women's issues, including the economic status of women. In the 1982 gubernatorial election Blanchard had won considerable women's support due to the actions of his opponent, Richard Headlee, a conservative Republican who belitted women's issues and organizations and opposed the Equal Rights Amendment. Blanchard also won support by selecting as his running mate Martha Griffiths, a leading congressional supporter of women's issues (George 1982; Harrison 1988; Press and Verburg 1985; Cooke 1993). In an interview in 1993, Libby Maynard, a member of the Blanchard cabinet who subsequently became chair of the state party and ran unsuccessfully for lieutenant governor with Blanchard in the 1994 gubernatorial race, said Blanchard was perceived as "fair-minded" on the issue of women and favoring women's reproductive choice (Maynard 1993).

In his report on Democratic defection in southeast Michigan in the 1984 presidential election, Greenberg had found that "the position of women, particularly working women, represents the largest area of opportunity for the Democrats," with blue-collar voters expressing "extraordinary sensitivity" on women's workplace issues (Greenberg 1985: 31–32). But neither Blanchard nor other leading Michigan Democrats showed interest in this agenda. Blanchard felt that he could secure the votes of women by taking a pro-choice position. Blanchard's neglect of working women's issues was tied to his marginalization of the social justice agenda. Similarly, Blanchard paid little attention to the problems of Detroit urban residents, largely African-Americans, towards whom traditional white Democrats, rather than showing sensitivity, harbored resentment. Republican party politics of the 1980s had set the tone nationally, identifying equal opportunity politics as reducing individual rights, abridging business freedom, and defending "special interests" (Shafran 1982; Moody 1988).

The predominant issue for women's organizations during Blanchard's administrations was not the need for women's increased wages or economic resources, but women's reproductive choice. The focus of the National Organization for Women and other organizations was dictated by the strength and intensity of the Michigan Right to Life movement, which almost annually introduced legislation restricting women's access to abortion. Right to Life focused its efforts on prohibiting state payment for abortions for poor women. The reproductive choice issue, according to former NOW president Marian McCracken, also helped the organization rebuild its membership and resources after the national defeat of the Equal Rights Amendment (McCracken 1993). Blanchard made clear his support for choice. He vetoed a bill prohibiting Medicaid funding for abortion on November 28, 1983, and a March 1984 effort to override the veto failed. However, in November 1988, as a result of a state-wide ballot initiative and referendum, Medicaid-funded abortion was prohibited in Michigan.

The Blanchard years in Michigan were not, therefore, auspicious for the implementation of pay equity. Governor Blanchard was largely pre-occupied by issues of economic recovery, and worked hard with manufacturers to attract investment and jobs to the state. He paid little attention to women's issues, except on the crucial problem of reproductive choice, where he closely monitored developments, made public statements, and exercised an important veto. Blanchard attached little importance to the economic status of women within the civil service, or in the economy generally. Pay equity made some progress during the Blanchard years, mainly as the result of women in state government and despite the disinterest of the governor. It was during the Blanchard years that the Civil Service Commission finally appointed a task force to study comparable worth and make recommendations. Between 1985 and 1989, state workers received small wage adjustments on the basis of comparable worth criteria.

THE ENGLER ADMINISTRATION 1991–94:
"THE TAXPAYER'S AGENDA"

John Engler, a conservative Republican who had been majority leader in the Republican-dominated senate, won a narrow electoral majority in the gubernatorial election of 1990 (and was reelected in 1994). Blanchard's defeat was due to a combination of his abandonment of urban voters, particularly in the city of Detroit, and the appeal of his opponent's antitax agenda to white working-class voters in the Detroit suburbs, many of whom had already defected to the Republican Party in the three previous presidential elections of 1980, 1984, and 1988 (Kaza 1991; "Post Election Analysis," *Detroit News*, November 8, 1990; Greenberg 1985). Engler also benefitted from a massive effort mounted by anti-abortion forces in the state, even though Engler himself did not emphasize abortion as an issue in the campaign (Kaza 1991; "Emotion-Charged Abortion Issue," *Detroit News*, September 25, 1990).

As senate majority leader, Engler had led the state Republican efforts to roll back the 1983 income tax increase and taxes in general in the 1980s. From the beginning of his administration he asserted the importance of tax cuts to increasing business prosperity and individual freedom. In his first State of the State message, he declared:

> Through the 1980s our national economy experienced a
> record-breaking peacetime expansion. It should have

been a time for all states to set themselves on a firm, low-tax, pro-growth foundation. . . . Ours did not. Year after year, even though our population has not grown at all, government spending in Michigan has grown relentlessly. And, in spite of greater and greater amounts of taxes paid by the working citizens of our state, government has persistently failed to live within its means. . . . As we chart a new course for Michigan we must first recognize that the hand of government reaches all too far into the pockets of the people. . . . [Taxes] have imposed an enormous cost on the state in the form of lost jobs, lost businesses, and lost population. . . . We must cut taxes now.

Engler's tax initiatives initially focused on property tax reductions. At his swearing-in in January 1991 he promised also a new commitment to "free enterprise," declaring "Our industrial might was not forged in the planning divisions of state agencies . . . sadly, because of government, it has been impaired" ("Do Good, My Friend, Do Good," *Detroit News,* January 2, 1991).

While Blanchard's concern about a balanced budget was coupled with reluctance to cut services, Engler's more militant budget-cutting stance was joined to an ideological commitment to decrease the size and functions of the state. In a set of policies that combined fiscal conservatism with social conservatism, Engler began his welfare reform initiatives with the abolition of Michigan's General Assistance program, the state supplementary program for those not qualifying for other income maintenance programs. This measure presaged later social welfare reforms that aligned him with the conservative wing of the national Republican party. Engler faced a recall campaign, but it was less well-organized than the effort that had been made to remove Democratic legislators during the Blanchard administration. Directed against Engler rather than individual legislators, neither the Democratic Party nor the AFL-CIO supported the drive undertaken mainly by welfare recipients and their advocates.

In fact, Engler's first administration combined broad ideological antistate pronouncements with successive reforms designed to reduce the size of the state and increase its efficiency. The abolition of the General Assistance program and cuts in state funding for the arts during his first year withdrew the state from certain functions without any certainty that the private sector would take them up. Engler also took measures to "streamline government," invoking the efficiency argument but reorganizing and reducing finance for departments based partly upon political priorities. His proposed 1991–92 budget, for example, cut spending for eleven of nineteen departments, while increasing funding for education. The largest cuts were in the Department of Commerce, which conservatives saw as dispensing "corporate welfare" through programs such as the Michigan Strategic Fund and the departments of Labor, Civil Rights, and Agriculture. In a widely discussed move condemned by consumer groups, Engler abolished the Department of Licensing and Regulation, which included the Insurance Bureau, and transferred its functions to the Commerce Department.

Engler also attempted a systematic "privatization" initiative in the state. A movement animated in the mid-1980s by conservatives hostile to the idea of public services but also including efficiency-minded managers, the privatization movement had by the 1990s advanced quite far in intermediate physical and commercial services in states and localities and increasingly involved human services (Starr 1987; National Commission for Employment Policy 1987; Gormley 1991; Henig 1989–90; Donohue 1989; AFSCME n.d., *Fact versus Fiction*). In July 1992 Engler issued an executive order creating the Michigan Public-Private Commission to review a draft report prepared by the Department of Management and Budget. The commission, chaired by James Barrett, president of the Michigan Chamber of Commerce, broadly accepted the desirability of diminishing state activity and subjecting remaining state services to more commercial discipline. The commission tied the necessity of reducing state activity to economic imperatives and argued that the public sector represented an inefficient monopoly. The commission argued: "Taxes and demands for economic resources by government must be minimized so as to allow Michigan to retain the employers it has while encouraging other job providers to locate here. . . . In large part because government itself operates without competition, many demands experienced by individuals and firms in the private economy are not experienced by those in public sector employment. . . . The result is often low productivity and poor accountability" (Michigan Public-Private Partnership Commission 1992: 26). The commission's final report, *Privatize, Eliminate, Retain, or Modify* (1992), recommended that all state programs and activities be reviewed for possible privatization or, alternatively, complete elimination, retention without modification, or modification. It established a set of criteria, offered an analytical methodology, and listed pilot programs for review. As of June 1995, moves toward privatizing some activities had occurred in most departments, but the largest privatization was the controversial sale of the Accident Fund, the state's workers' compensation fund, to Blue Cross/Blue Shield of Michigan.

While defense of state workers had never been a priority of Blanchard's, reduction in the state workforce became a very high priority for Engler. Both UAW Local 6000, the largest union in the civil service, and the Democratic Party had polling data from 1990 showing that "public sector workers are out of favor." Sheila Strunk, the former legislative chair of Local 6000, said in an interview in 1992, "Engler has both jumped on and helped to create this sentiment."

In his first nine months, state civil service employment declined 5 percent, with 71 percent of the decline attributable to layoffs. In 1992, the number of state civil servants fell (from 67,000 two years previously) to about 61,000; the total civil service workforce continued to approximate that number through the mid-1990s (DCS, Management Services Division, 1995). In July 1991, state employees, over the objections of their unions, were laid off for four days without pay, in order to help balance the budget. This "unpaid furlough" resembled measures being taken by governors in other states, such as New York and California ("The Chastening of Public Employees," Governing, January 1993: 26–30). Wages and benefits were frozen in fiscal year 1992–93, and the freeze was accompanied by a strong statement deploring the growth of annual payroll costs at 8 percent a year. Annual wage settlements fell in subsequent Engler years. They often amounted to annual increases of 1–2 percent; in some years, workers won only, or as part of a larger settlement, lump-sum awards not rolled into base pay. The attack on public sector labor costs paralleled the discussion about high labor costs in the private economy, but the size of the state's payroll was condemned in light of its financing by taxpayers. Privatization was one device to weaken the civil service unions and lower labor costs in state government (National Commission for Employment Policy 1987; Donohue 1989: 140).

Like Blanchard, Engler took a strong position on abortion questions, but while Blanchard had prominently supported reproductive choice, Engler opposed it. Engler supported the liberalization of market forces and deregulation of business, rather than development of policy to improve women's economic status. In February 1991, one month after being sworn in, Engler abolished the Office of Women and Work (OWW) by exercising his line-item veto (Keeley 1994). The OWW had a long history of supporting women in the civil service and pressing the comparable worth issue within the state, but it also supported women in the private sector. The Michigan Women's Commission, which had always had a broader focus than women's employment, and which was previously in the Department of Management and Budget, was reassigned with a reduced budget to the Department of Civil Rights, the smallest and perhaps least powerful department in the state. Engler eliminated the Displaced Homemakers Program and reduced the program for Women-Owned Business.

The Engler years, therefore, represented an inauspicious political setting for the continued development of pay equity reform. While Governor Blanchard's discourse about reducing the state and its workers reflected the increasing antigovernment sentiment of the period, he simultaneously affirmed the importance of state services; he was driven partly by the state's fiscal problems. Engler, however, espoused a clear and purposeful antistate and antitax policy and valorized the efficiency and freedom associated with the market. As part of this political program, he strongly insisted upon the reduction of numbers and costs of state workers, as he argued that the state should withdraw from numerous functions. The administration had no political commitment to improving the economic status of women inside or outside state government; the political discourse of the Engler years called no attention to issues of economic equity for women. Pay equity made virtually no progress under the Engler administration, as the Republican governor was strongly committed to reducing labor costs in the state and in the private economy and resolutely opposed to modifying the sway of "the market" in any way.

Michigan Economics and Politics as Context for Pay Equity Reform

A restructuring economy, economic recession, a fiscal crisis in the state, and an antitax politics characterized the Michigan political economy of the early and middle 1980s. This was the period during which pay equity emerged on the state's political agenda. Both in the workplace and in representational politics, the relatively strong Michigan labor movement was weakened and preoccupied with job loss in unionized manufacturing industries and with deteriorating terms and conditions for organized labor's core male constituency. The women's movement, while conscious of the fact that women were not faring well in the recession as workers and as family members, rallied around defense of reproductive choice, as social conservatives tried repeatedly to pass laws abridging such rights. The Democratic governor of the state, partly in response to tax revolts, associated himself with the need to reduce taxes and cut the size of the state workforce. In the early 1990s, while the economy recovered from another cyclical downturn, antistate politics linked to fundamental economic restructuring intensified. Pay equity, therefore, not only slipped off or down the agenda of the larger political forces in the state, it also ran headlong into the priorities of business, legislators, and governors: the improvement of the private sector business climate and the diminution of state government and its costs.

It was this conjuncture of the demand for pay equity with both the economic crisis in the state and an antistate politics that created serious obstacles to comparable worth reform. In a telling comment that spoke to this timing, Libby Maynard argued that "There was a budget crunch for Blanchard's whole eight years, and if he had not faced this, I think he would have supported pay equity, just because he had a sense of fairness. But he had different priorities, given the situation. In the mid-1970s, we would have gotten it" (Maynard 1993). The "given situation" was not only economic dislocation, but the new, more conservative politics of the 1980s, which took the state as something to be reduced rather than as ameliorative of broader social and economic problems or as an employer that might serve as a positive model.

Despite this difficult "given situation," state-level pay equity advocates, located mainly in state government itself, succeeded in putting pay equity on the agenda for civil service workers, as the following chapter shows. Pay equity was first undertaken as a reform within the Michigan Civil Service. However, private business associated public sector wage adjustments with potentially higher taxes; further, it feared a dangerous precedent that would challenge market-based wages and might have a demonstration effect on private labor markets. Later, as reformers tried to amend broad civil rights legislation to include comparable worth, the business community's opposition grew. The political parties themselves, the two governors, the legislature, the labor movement, and the women's movement placed little pressure on the Civil Service Commission, the body charged with regulating state employment. Nor did political organizations and social movements press the legislature, which may pass state employment law, to implement serious pay equity reform. The economy and politics of the 1980s and 1990s remained a critical force containing those policy reforms.

3

(Not) Above Politics: The Civil Service Determines Reform

Prior research suggests that pay equity reform is more likely to be initiated in a state that has public sector collective bargaining, Democratic control of the state government, and an energetic Commission on the Status of Women (Evans and Nelson 1989b, 1991). While these factors predisposed Michigan toward some sort of pay equity reform, getting pay equity on the policy agenda was difficult because of the problematic political economy of the 1980s, which focused unions and many Democrats on revitalizing the private manufacturing sector and created widespread antagonism toward the state and its workers. It was also difficult because the state constitution assigned exclusive control over state employment to an appointed, "independent" Civil Service Commission, a powerful but somewhat obscure state body. Officially "above politics," the commission operated cautiously and with an eye toward what it perceived as a broad political consensus. The formal power to engage both in political decision-making about pay equity and oversee its implementation rested with the Civil Service Commission.

In Michigan, pay equity reform was pressed onto the agenda of the Civil Service Commission primarily by the small Office of Women and Work (OWW) in the Department of Labor and by a well-organized and energetic voluntary group, Women in State Government (WSG). Both drew upon the momentum, ideas, and strategies of the national pay equity movement. In the early stages, neither unions nor the broader women's movement was centrally involved in advancing the issue. Preoccupied with other problems, both labor and feminist organizations were also unaccustomed to civil service rules and procedures.

After persistent representations and argument by the Office of Women and Work, the Civil Service Commission established a Comparable Worth Task Force to study and make recommendations about whether and how to implement pay equity for state workers. The report of the Comparable Worth Task Force failed to endorse the comparable worth principle that pay for both male- and female-dominated classes be consistently related to evaluated job points. But it did acknowledge pay inequities in the Michigan civil service and outlined corrective measures involving pay awards and classification redesign.

This chapter is divided into two main parts. The first section examines the position of the Civil Service Commission in the state of Michigan and how activists finally managed to place pay equity reform on the commission's agenda. The second part explores how the Civil Service Commission appointed a task force to make recommendations and how the task force set the framework for pay equity reform in the state.

GETTING PAY EQUITY ON THE CIVIL SERVICE COMMISSION AGENDA

THE CENTRALITY AND DISPOSITION OF THE CIVIL SERVICE COMMISSION

The Civil Service Commission has been central to pay equity reform in Michigan because regulation of state employment is reserved to and ultimately determined by the commission. The commission itself determines how much weight to attach to the representations of other political bodies, such as the governor, the legislature, and various departments of state government. Unlike the federal government and other state jurisdictions, which have departments of personnel and separate bodies to protect the merit system, the state of Michigan centralizes its personnel functions in a Civil Service Commission, the independence of which is constitutionally specified and whose power over state employment is exclusive.

Because the Michigan legislature may not pass state personnel laws setting priorities or practices in public employment, Michigan lawmakers could not legislate pay equity for public employees. In other states, many of which have adopted some form of pay equity reform, the legislature and executive retain more authority over state classified employment (Remick 1986; Winebrenner 1986; Steinberg 1988; Acker 1989; Evans and Nelson 1989b). According to the National Committee on Pay Equity (1989), fourteen states have relied upon legislation to some degree in instituting pay equity.

Article XI, Section 5 of the Michigan Constitution authorizes the

Civil Service Commission to regulate all conditions of employment in the classified civil service. The classified service is defined comprehensively.[1] The constitution authorizes the CSC to classify positions, assign rates of pay for all job classes, administer examinations, make rules and regulations covering all personnel transactions, and approve/disapprove disbursements for personal services. The commission is responsible for providing for periodic and ongoing reviews of all positions in the classified civil service (CSC 1989: 47–52). Whereas the constitution allows the Michigan legislature to enact laws concerning dispute resolution for public employees, it prohibits the legislature from enacting laws which regulate the resolution of disputes in the civil service.

Overall, the state constitution assigns the commission a combination of legislative, executive, and quasi-judicial functions. When it makes general rules about employment, for example, a general rule prohibiting discrimination or setting guidelines for political activity of civil servants, the commission is exercising powers traditionally regarded as legislative. When it implements these general rules, it is acting administratively. When the commission resolves disputes between labor and management, its powers are judicial. According to the constitution, the legislature must appropriate not less than 1 percent of the state payroll as an operating budget for the commission and department each fiscal year. The commission does not, therefore, enter the same budget battles as other departments and agencies. While the commission has sometimes presented itself as a third-party neutral, merely ensuring efficiency and fairness in state employment and refereeing disputes between management and labor, its independence from executive and legislative authority and its power seem to render it a fourth branch of government.

These powers are formally discharged by four uncompensated civil service commissioners, appointed by the governor for eight-year terms. No more than two commissioners may be of the same political party, and their terms are staggered such that no two will expire in the same year. The day-to-day business of the commission is carried out by the Department of Civil Service (DCS) headed by a state personnel director, who is a civil servant. Because the commission is comprised of part-time appointees, the department substantially guides its decision-making.

The commission has ceded some power to the Office of the State Employer (OSE), the creation of which it approved in 1980 when it granted state employees collective bargaining rights. The commission has recognized the authority of the OSE to conduct, coordinate, and administer negotiations with civil service employees in areas of collective bargaining, contract administration, unfair labor practices, improvement of work performance, and administrative efficiency. However, the commission retained authority over an area critical to pay equity reform, that of classification of the civil service workforce. Although the commission does not direct the Office of the State Employer, which answers both to the governor and Department of Management and Budget, it must approve contracts OSE negotiates.

In view of these constitutional and institutional arrangements, the commission would have to act as decision-maker about pay equity, performing essentially a legislative function, and it would also oversee and coordinate implementation. It might, in fact, have established a new Merit Principle (a general rule governing employment and compensation within the civil service) affirming comparable worth as a basis for pay, thereby creating the equivalent to a legislative mandate.

Not surprisingly, however, the Civil Service Commission itself did not initiate pay equity reform. Through the 1970s, neither the commission nor the Department of Civil Service had any substantial presence of women in authoritative positions. In the 1970s, only three women served on the commission, none with a relationship to the organized women's movement. A special Employment Practices Review, ordered in 1971 by Republican governor Milliken and conducted jointly by the Department of Civil Rights and the Department of Civil Service, found that the Department of Civil Service, like other departments, was comprised of a (white) male bureaucratic elite with a female support staff (Department of Civil Rights and Department of Civil Service 1971). Still, in 1980, white men, many lifelong civil servants in their fifties, continued to dominate the Department of Civil Service.[2]

In fact, the department presided over a state-wide gendered employment structure, much like that of other organizations at the time. In state employment as a whole in 1980, women comprised only 9 percent of officials and administrators, but 94 percent of office and clerical workers statewide. In 1980 women's median salary was $15,686, while the male median was $19,993. As salaries increased, the percentage of men in the salary range increased, while women dominated the lower salary ranges (DCS, Management Services Division 1980: 111).

The state acted upon gendered stereotypes in employee selection and did little to recruit, reassign, or train women for jobs that were not predominantly female.[3] Successive classification structures segregated workers by gender, and job evaluation devalued women's skills (see chapter 4). Career tracks were generally masculine, with the idea of a career civil servant premised on a full-time male worker with an uninterrupted work record. Women's job ladders were short, and promotion prospects limited. The Civil Service Commission resisted the Michigan Civil Rights Department's ruling that the pregnancy discrimination practiced in state employment through the 1970s was prohibited sex discrimination (Pollock 1992; Cooper 1993; WSG, *WIRE*, March 1984: 1).[4] The problem of sexual harassment only began to be addressed in the mid-1970s (WSG, *WIRE*, April 1983: 3), and in the mid-1980s women struggled to put child-care provision on the employment policy agenda (see WSG, *WIRE*, September 15, 1983; WSG, *WIRE*, November 1983: 1, 3; December 1983: 1; April 1984: 5; May 1984: 1–3, 9 ff.; September 1985: 1–2).

The institutionally central Civil Service Commission, therefore, did not initiate pay equity reform. Rather, it responded belatedly and minimally to external and internal pressure from feminists: from the national pay equity movement, from the Office of Women and Work, and from Women in State Government.

THE NATIONAL PAY EQUITY MOVEMENT

The national pay equity movement both directly and indirectly put considerable pressure on the Michigan Civil Service Commission to act. The movement's arguments for comparable worth and the large legal cases against state employers created a degree of receptivity among state managers. For women employed by the state of Michigan, the national movement created a general awareness of the comparable worth issue, suggested strategies and tactics to advance comparable worth agendas, and provided political and moral support for organized activity.

The national movement which developed in the early 1980s was the result of a number of different economic, social, and political changes. By 1980, the percentage of women participating in the labor force was 52 percent and growing, and women comprised 43 percent of the total labor force. Women were increasingly responsible for supporting families (Bergmann 1986: 20–21, 227–38). Yet women remained segregated in a few low-paying jobs and occupations, often with little autonomy, invisible or undervalued skills, and poor working conditions (Reskin and Hartman 1986; Reskin and Roos 1990). The Equal Pay Act of 1963 was not a full remedy for women's low pay, as it required that men and women be paid equally only for substantially equal jobs in the same establishments. Affirmative action had resulted in limited progress for the majority of women (Kessler-Harris 1994; Blum 1991).

As the public sector began to extend collective bargaining rights in the late 1960s and 1970s, women increasingly joined unions and professional associations. They therefore became more aware of structural gender discrimination and gained access to institutions that might improve their terms and conditions of employment. The growing presence of women in government as administrators and elected politicians and the growth of politically organized women's groups also created an awareness of women's economic status and a resource for remedying various problems of women at work.

A legal strategy supporting comparable worth—the idea that paying men and women differently for work of comparable worth or value to the employer is sex discrimination—developed among lawyers working in the Equal Employment Opportunity Commission (EEOC) and the U.S. Department of Labor during the 1960s and 1970s. In 1977 the EEOC chair, Eleanor Holmes Norton, commissioned the National Academy of Sciences and National Research Council to study the issues involved in a comparable worth concept of job compensation. Organized labor, professional associations, and women's groups also took up the idea. Between 1973 and 1976 the first comparable worth studies in state jurisdictions and the first major legal cases were filed. Pay equity advocates, wishing to coordinate their efforts, created the National Committee on Pay Equity in 1979 (McCann 1994: 48–58, 123).

The Supreme Court handed down a landmark decision in 1981 in *County of Washington v. Gunther* (452 U.S. 161 1982), the impact of which was to open the door to cases of sex discrimination in pay where different jobs were involved. In 1983 Judge Jack Tanner of the U.S. District Court ruled in *AFSCME v. State of Washington* (578 F. Supp. 846 D. Wash 1983) that the state had discriminated against women by systematically paying female-dominated job classes lower wages than comparably rated male-dominated classes. Judge Tanner accepted aggregate statistical disparities, discriminatory hiring decisions, and departures from an employer's own job evaluation study as sufficient to make a *prima facie* case of discriminatory treatment of women in predominantly female job classes; he authorized a remedy that could include ordering affirmative action and awarding hundreds of millions of dollars in back pay (Heen 1984; Willborn 1989).

Though the Washington decision was reversed on appeal, the Washington and Gunther cases attracted considerable attention and provided tremendous momentum for comparable worth as a policy in state and local government. McCann (1994) has shown how these early cases jump-started the pay equity movement. In 1985, just two years after the Tanner ruling, the National Committee on Pay Equity reported that all but five states had taken some action, from the establishment of task forces or commissions to appropriation of funds for reform, on pay equity. Thirty-nine states had or were engaged in research and data collection; thirty-four had established task forces or commissions; ten had established pay equity policies; twenty-two had embarked on job evaluation studies; and six had engaged in some form of implementation. Thirteen states were the object of Title VII pay equity lawsuits (NCPE 1985).

In fact, the momentum had shifted to state and local government not only because of the positive developments in women's organizing, but also because the climate for reform at the federal level had deteriorated. The largely favorable National Academy of Sciences/National Research

Council Report commissioned by the EEOC, *Women, Work and Wages: Equal Pay for Jobs of Equal Value* (Treiman and Hartman) was issued in 1981. But by then the EEOC and U.S. Civil Rights Commission, led by conservative Reagan appointees, were opposed to comparable worth. The Reagan administration's stance reflected an underlying politics that abandoned ideas of using the state to correct market and "private" discrimination. In 1985, after many years of inaction on comparable worth complaints, the EEOC announced that it would act only on gender-based wage discrimination where there was evidence of intent to discriminate (Withers and Winston 1989). Not only the Reagan administration but also business and political groups forced the debate onto the ground of the cost of comparable worth and difficulties of implementation.

MICHIGAN'S OFFICE OF WOMEN AND WORK AND WOMEN IN STATE GOVERNMENT

As the pay equity movement developed nationally in the late 1970s, women working in state government in Michigan became interested in the concept of comparable worth as a way of identifying and remedying problems for women in the state's civil service classification and pay structure (Curran 1991, February 19). The Office of Women and Work (OWW) within the Department of Labor, Women in State Government (WSG), a voluntary association of state employees, and the Michigan Women's Commission, a gubernatorially appointed body, all took an interest in pay equity.

The overall charge of the Office of Women and Work, established within the Michigan Department of Labor in 1979, was "to improve the position of women in the work force and in Michigan's economy." Its responsibilities were both intra- and extra-bureaucratic. The Office of Women and Work was to monitor and guide the Department of Labor's issuance of rules, regulations, and standards; proposals of legislation; conduct of statistical surveys; and publication of reports and periodicals. It was to coordinate its work with that of the executive branch, a large employer of women. It was to organize and support women in the labor force throughout the state by, for example, offering (in conjunction with the Michigan Department of Civil Rights) referral services and guidance in cases of gender discrimination (Department of Labor 1984). Hilda Patricia (Pat) Curran was appointed director of the Office of Women and Work; the office had two other full-time workers. Its annual budget was approximately $150,000.

Drawing upon its overall charge, the Office of Women and Work embarked upon a series of efforts on behalf of pay equity. The OWW approached comparable worth as a concept addressing the relationship between gender composition, but not the race composition, of jobs and pay; these efforts preceded by several years key national discussions about comparable worth as a remedy for race-based wage discrimination (Scales-Trent 1984; Malveaux 1985; NCPE 1987, 1989). Between 1980 and 1981 the Office of Women and Work was responsible for the production of three reports critical of gender bias in the existing civil service classification and pay systems: an August 1980 general critique of the Michigan Benchmark Evaluation System, entitled "What's Wrong with MBES? A Critique of the Michigan Benchmark Evaluation System"; an August 1981 paper on the impact of gender-dominant jobs on salaries, "Impact of State of Michigan Compensation Policy on Salaries for Sex-Type Jobs"; and a study commissioned from Arthur Young and Company, A Comparable Worth Study of the State of Michigan Job Classifications (Arthur Young and Company 1981). The findings of the reports, the most important of which was the Arthur Young study, converged around the theme that Michigan's job evaluation system and pay practices embodied gender discrimination.

The Office of Women and Work sparked the state's pay equity reform by enlisting Arthur Young and Company of Detroit, a reputable consultant, to do two things. First, the OWW wanted to identify the extent to which the state's existing job and wage classification systems undervalued certain skills and responsibilities. Secondly, it wanted to identify a more appropriate job evaluation system that might form the basis for a new classification and wage structure free of gender discrimination. The study was funded by the Comprehensive Employment and Training Act (CETA) and a special gubernatorial fund. While Arthur Young and Company served as consultant, a Technical Advisory Committee, in which the civil service participated, helped guide the project.

For the study, approximately 675 state employees in 209 job classifications described their jobs to both female and male trained job analysts. Each job was then evaluated by two job evaluation plans, both different from the existing classification system, the Michigan Benchmark Evaluation System (MBES). The first was the Position Analysis Questionnaire (PAQ), a structured job analysis questionnaire that consisted of 187 job components. The second plan was an analytic point-factor job evaluation plan, that is, a plan that assigns points to jobs based upon degrees of complexity of several key job factors, or job demands. The Office of Women and Work was involved in negotiating the point factor plan, as were staff from the American Federation of State, County, and Municipal Employees (AFSCME), the Equal Employment Opportunity Commission (EEOC), and the Department of Civil Service. The consultants were pressed to think carefully about what would constitute an appropriate list of factors and factor weights in public employment, though some bias against women's jobs may have remained (Curran 1991, February 19).

The Arthur Young study demonstrated that it was possible to use a single job evaluation system for all jobs within the state classified service. It also showed that the existing Benchmark System contained gender inequities. Analyses showed that pay rates were actually higher than would be predicted from job evaluation for male-dominated jobs and lower than would be predicted for female-dominated jobs. The pay differential was $100–$300 a month between women and men in similarly evaluated jobs (Arthur Young and Company 1981).

Although the study was completed in 1980, the Office of Women and Work decided not to transmit the result immediately to the Civil Service Commission. They reasoned that the deep recession into which Michigan had plunged would produce an unsympathetic, even dismissive response to the Young report. Meanwhile, in 1981, using evidence from the Arthur Young study, Karon Black and the Michigan State Employees Association (MSEA), on behalf of all female employees in the classified service, lodged a civil complaint of sex discrimination with the Michigan Civil Rights Commission and Equal Employment Opportunity Commission. The MSEA demanded that the Civil Service Commission and Department of Civil Service act immediately to correct discrimination in classification and pay between male and female employees. The complaint was not acted upon.[5]

In June 1981, a few months before the filing of the legal complaint, the Office of Women and Work helped organize a "grassroots comparable worth task force," independent of state government. Its aims were to support the attempt to achieve pay equity for state employees and to build broader support for pay equity among legislators, labor unionists, and other women. Chaired by Pat Curran, the group included women in classified civil service positions, on state legislative staffs, in university labor education programs, and on union staffs. By October, the task force had set for themselves two main objectives: to increase general understanding of comparable worth among themselves and other working women and to explore legislative and legal means of achieving comparable worth in the public and private sectors. As a group the task force did not support specific workplace efforts to win comparable worth adjustments or engage in rank-and-file union education and organizing on the issue (Comparable Worth Task Force [grassroots] 1982).

The group supported a successful amendment to the Payment of Wages and Fringe Benefits Act of 1978 which made it unlawful for an employer to discharge, threaten, or otherwise discriminate against employees for revealing their wages. They saw this measure as a prerequisite to comparable worth progress in the private sector. In August 1982, as the time and energy of members was strained and the civil service seemed to be moving forward on the issue, the group dissolved.

In December 1981, the Office of Women and Work decided that they had to transmit the Arthur Young report to ensure the currency of their data and to apprise the commission of data related to the MSEA/Karon Black legal complaint. The Department of Labor formally transmitted the report to the Civil Service Commission, Office of the State Employer, and civil service unions. The Office of Women and Work attached four key recommendations to the report: (1) the civil service should revise and update pay-setting; (2) the civil service should eliminate its overdependence on market rates of pay; (3) the civil service should recognize the pay gap based on gender and address it; and (4) the civil service should use a single job evaluation system (Michigan Women's Commission 1982).

The Department of Civil Service acknowledged the report in a memo to the Civil Service Commission: "There were no surprises in the results . . . we have been aware that women in the state classified service are paid 74 % of the rates paid to men. . . . [A]dopting a comparable worth policy in the Michigan state classified service would require a very basic change in the Commission's pay setting policy. That policy is based on collective bargaining and has long been based on comparison with rates paid in the general labor market" (Ross 1981). In August 1982, confirming the fears of the Office of Women and Work and demonstrating the sensitivity of civil servants to economic developments and the political climate, a civil service staff report to the Civil Service Commission concluded that the economic climate was not conducive to immediate action on pay equity. The report also noted that there was a lack of clarity on issues regarding comparable worth and that a remedy had to be accomplished through the pay-setting process (Bibbs 1982). The department's inaction condoned market rates of pay and the gender (and class) hierarchies implicit in their construction.

Women in State Government, an independent, registered, nonprofit organization with membership from a variety of occupational classifications, bargaining units, and levels in the executive and legislative branches of government, helped the Office of Women and Work press the issue on the Civil Service Commission. The organization, led by higher-level staff women in government, was committed to "promot[ing] the career development of all women employed by the State of Michigan by providing resources and education to facilitate job performance, by securing greater recognition of women's accomplishments and contributions in state government, and by improving communication among women state employees" (WSG 1984: 1).

With a membership of about three hundred, WSG was established in May 1979. The group saw itself as a collective advocate for women's interests, interacting with the Civil Service Commission, the legislature, the governor, the Office of the State Employer, unions, and other organizations to win equity for the state's women workers. It regularly issued a newsletter, a rich source of information on the national pay equity movement and other issues of concern to women workers in the state. As part of the effort to force the state to engage seriously the comparable worth issue, Women in State Government presented a detailed proposal to achieve pay equity to the civil service, in Coordinated Compensation Panel hearings before the Employment Relations Board in October 1982.[6] Women in State Government would continue to press for pay equity. They appeared before the Employment Relations Board of the Civil Service Commission and before the Comparable Worth Task Force that the commission eventually appointed. They also gave evidence before the Federal District Court in the case of *UAW v. State of Michigan*, the Title VII lawsuit that grew out of the Karon Black/MSEA complaint.

Evans and Nelson (1989b) suggest that in Minnesota the Council on the Economic Status of Women, a legislatively established body, was crucial to efforts to place pay equity reform on the state political agenda, and that women's commissions have been indispensable advocates in other states. In some respects, the Office of Women and Work functioned like Minnesota's Council on the Economic Status of Women.

Yet in Michigan, the Women's Commission, a gubernatorially appointed body, took no pay equity initiatives. Established in 1968, its fifteen members and chair were appointed by the governor, and governors appointed women who were loyal party workers or who represented a range of established women's organizations, such as the National Organization for Women (NOW) and the American Association of University Women (AAUW). State political leaders encouraged appointees to think of themselves not as representatives of their organizations but as individuals. In the late 1970s and early 1980s the commission had only two staff.

Though its charge was broad, the commission tried not to take on issues being addressed by other government bodies. It was more interested in broad statewide concerns than issues affecting "a limited number of women or women in a particular location, occupation, or situation" (Cooke 1993). The commission did, for a time, have a State Employees Task Force, which compiled a list of barriers that prohibited women's advancement in state employment and made a list of recommendations to the civil service (WSG, *WIRE*, April 1983: 2). But beyond supporting and publicizing the work of the Office of Women and Work and Women in State Government, it had no substantial involvement in pay equity. Margaret Cooke, a Women's Commission member from 1975 to 1979 and executive director from 1979 to 1984, said, "On pay equity, we let the Office of Women and Work and Pat Curran provide the leadership, but we did what she asked" (1993).

THE CIVIL SERVICE COMMISSION RESPONDS

INITIAL RESPONSES

Until 1982, the Office of Women and Work and Women in State Government, with some support from the Michigan State Employees Association (MSEA), campaigned for comparable worth reform alone. But in his State of the State message in 1982, Governor Milliken, a moderate Republican in office since 1969, instructed the Department of Civil Service, the Office of the State Employer, and the Office of Women and Work to assess jointly the economic, social, and labor relations implications of basing wage policies on the principle of equal pay for jobs which were actually of equal or comparable worth and to devise a plan for effectively dealing with these cases. An Interdepartmental Committee on Comparable Worth met, declined to allow Women in State Government to participate, and did little.

It was only after a breakfast meeting between Pat Curran, director of the Office of Women and Work, and the Civil Service Commission chair in January 1983 that the commission took responsibility for seriously examining the issue and its policy implications. "It might have been buried if Curran had not presented it directly to the Commissioners, and without Commission as well as staff support, the issue wouldn't have progressed at all," recalled Mary Pollock (1992), an equal opportunity officer for the Department of Civil Service who was active on the issue at the time.

Following the direct representations of the Office of Women and Work in early 1983, the Civil Service Commission asked Department of Civil Service staff to conduct two studies that would provide background for but not address directly the pay issues raised in the Arthur Young report. Only one study was completed. That study found gender segregation in 80 percent of civil service job classifications. The department recommended more affirmative action to desegregate occupations in the civil service. They offered the creation of departmental trainee classes as one solution. These classes were proposed to facilitate career movement for employees without bachelor's degrees from primarily clerical classes to professional classes typically not requiring specialized educational credentials. The department also recommended that the commission should seek the cooperation of many entities—the executive branch, legislature, unions, and public and private groups in working through the issue of comparable worth. "It is imperative that the Commission seek involvement of these groups before deciding on a course of action," the report stated (Hueni 1983).

Finally, in June 1983, in response to the changing political environment for comparable worth nationally, the transmission of the Arthur Young comparable worth study to the commission, the continued activity of Women in State Government, and the pressure of the Karon Black/ MSEA legal complaint and national legal activity, the commission set up the Comparable Worth Task Force. The commission feared a loss of jurisdiction if it did not take any action on its own. Defenders of the independent Civil Service Commission worried that an activist pay equity movement might form a coalition with other groups in the state that already wanted to amend the constitution to abolish the commission as a "fourth branch of government" (Pollock 1992; Massaron 1992).

The task force was charged to make authoritative recommendations to the commission for removing pay inequity. The task force, one of the commissioners said, would "not discuss the issue of whether wage disparities based on sex should be eliminated, but will make recommendations how" (CSC minutes, June 27, 1983). Echoing claims of comparable worth proponents themselves, Civil Service Commissioner Michael Dively explained, comparable worth "is a major issue of the 1980's, and the Commission is in a national leadership role in addressing it" (CSC minutes, June 27, 1983).

THE ESTABLISHMENT OF THE COMPARABLE WORTH TASK FORCE

The Civil Service Commission chose to address comparable worth by setting up for several reasons what civil service commissioners and members described as a "blue-ribbon" Comparable Worth Task Force (CWTF). First, the Civil Service Commission and Department of Civil Service wanted to build and ascertain consensus. Pat Curran, crediting the Civil Service with wanting to act but to do so on a consensual basis, observed, "The Civil Service seemed to want more people in their boat if the sharks went after them" (Curran 1991, February 28). The commission also wanted their task force to examine civil service employment data, critically review the Arthur Young study, regain control over definition of the issue from the low-status, advocacy-oriented Office of Women and Work, and explore the complicated policy alternatives facing the state. The charge of the task force was to "thoroughly review the disparities between average male and female wages and recommend actions to eliminate wage discrimination based on sex to the extent it may exist in the state classified service" (CWTF 1985: 1).

The Comparable Worth Task Force was a committee of eleven private- and public-sector executives, state women's commission members, elected representatives, and labor unionists. Task force chair, Edward Cushman, a former automobile executive and vice-president emeritus at Wayne State University, was appointed by the CSC. Along with then state personnel director John Hueni, Cushman was largely responsible for assembling the task force. Cushman was one of Michigan's leading advocates of a constitutionally independent Civil Service Commission, who had been a prominent participant in the 1961 state constitutional convention. Both Republicans and Democrats had appointed him to various state government study committees. Former vice-president and director of American Motors Corporation and a former executive director of the Michigan Employment Security Commission, he had been an official of the Michigan Chamber of Commerce, the Employers Association of Detroit, and the Automobile Manufacturers Association, as well as a member of the National Business Council for the Equal Rights Amendment. He probably wished to preserve the Civil Service Commission's independence and authority, maintain existing labor markets in the private sector, and insure equal treatment, within existing economic and political structures, for women in state employment (Madar 1992; Massaron 1992; Brown 1993; WSG, *WIRE*, September 1983: 2).

The task force as it was finally constituted consisted of:

> Edward Cushman, chair, executive vice-president emeritus, Wayne State University
> Mary Jane Kay, vice-president of the Detroit Edison Company
> Martha Griffiths, lieutenant governor
> Mary Brown, state representative, Democrat-Kalamazoo
> William Sederburg, state senator, Republican-East Lansing
> Larry Glazer, legal adviser to Governor James Blanchard
> Malcolm Denise, retired vice-president for labor relations, Ford Motor Company
> Edward Thomas, president, Detroit Receiving Hospital and University Health Center
> Mildred Jeffrey, member, Wayne State University Board of Governors
> Yolanda Alvarado, former member, Michigan Women's Commission
> Barbara Roberts Mason, member, state board of education and Michigan Education Association

Feminist representation. Five of the eleven members of the committee were women, yet only three, Martha Griffiths, Mildred Jeffrey, and Mary Brown, had much experience with feminist politics or any acquaintance with comparable worth issues. While Martha Griffiths attended several task force meetings, participants had difficulty recalling her contributions. She asked that her name be removed from the final task force report. The Michigan Women's Commission had one representative on the committee, but she had little experience of feminist politics and no knowledge of comparable worth. While Women in State Government submitted a list of government, academic, and corporate nominees, only one of the women suggested by Women in State Government, state representative Mary Brown, was appointed to the task force (WSG, *WIRE*, 1983: 4).

Labor representation. Two traditionally powerful labor organizations which did not represent state employees at the time the task force was formed, the International UAW and the Michigan AFL-CIO, were both invited to appoint representatives. The commission's philosophy, according to Mary Brown, was that the task force should be without "vested interests," in other words, that those directly affected by the reform should not be represented on the task force. (However, the Department of Civil Service acted as staff to the committee and exercised a good deal of influence.) The UAW appointed international representative Charlene Knight, who had close ties to women in the UAW, and the AFL-CIO appointed Paul Massaron. Charlene Knight left the task force due to poor health, and Paul Massaron resigned because he became a UAW International representative at a time that the UAW was campaigning to represent state workers. Neither was replaced. Mildred Jeffrey had a long history in the union movement. She had served as first director of the UAW Women's Bureau (later the Women's Department), after having worked as a union organizer in the textile and garment industries, and she continued to support working women within the UAW and through broader coalitions (see Gabin 1990). She was not appointed as a labor representative but as a member of the Wayne State University Board of Governors; by the mid-1980s her official ties with organized labor had been attenuated. Nevertheless, she penned a vigorous dissent on the task force's recommendations regarding job evaluation. Barbara Mason Roberts represented the Michigan Education Association. The representatives sat on the task force as individuals, and were asked not to disclose proceedings (Massaron 1992; Madar 1992).

In other states, task forces were formed for purposes both of implementation and policymaking. Those committees also marginalized pay equity advocates. In Oregon, the official task force overseeing the evaluation study had a majority of representatives from women's and union groups, but the consultants nevertheless minimized the impact of reform proponents (Acker 1989: 10; Evans and Nelson 1989b: 78–79; McCann 1994: 200–1).

THE DELIBERATIONS OF THE TASK FORCE

The state's legal position and vulnerability. The Comparable Worth Task Force was clearly preoccupied by legal developments in the area of pay equity, as had been the commission and department themselves in establishing the task force. In some respects its deliberations may be seen as an effort to take into account uncertain legal requirements. While Karon Black had filed a civil complaint involving comparable worth claims in 1981 against the state for gender discrimination under Title VII, the UAW's major case against the state was not filed until November 27, 1985, several months after the task force issued its report. The task force charge itself had used the legally derived language of gender discrimination, and at its first meeting the chair suggested that the task force arrange for "an expert in the area of the evolving interpretation of the law" to address the next meeting (CWTF minutes, October 7, 1983: 2).

At the subsequent meeting, Theodore St. Antoine, professor of law, University of Michigan Law School, described how the Gunther decision had opened the door to claims alleging violations of Title VII of the Civil Rights Act of 1964 with regard to differences in pay even though jobs were not equal, or substantially identical. He emphasized that the lower courts could now entertain claims challenging pay differentials between different jobs but he noted that market conditions was an acceptable defense in comparable worth cases. However, he alerted the task force to the fact that case law was still evolving, and that the courts were applying disparate impact, as well as disparate treatment, theory. That is, the courts were finding discrimination where there was a facially neutral practice that had disproportionately negative effects upon protected groups, as well as in cases where employers could be shown to have discriminated intentionally.

But the task force's final report noted that acting upon comparable worth analysis was not mandated by federal law (CWTF 1985: 14–16; 25–36, and passim). An argument used in both Gunther and *AFSCME v. Washington* to show intentional discrimination was that the employment jurisdiction had evidence from their own studies of gender discrimination but that they neglected to remedy the documented discrimination. The Legal Subcommittee of the Comparable Worth Task Force contended: "Is the Arthur Young study the State's 'own' . . . ? We think not. The Department of Labor has no power or jurisdiction in the area of setting pay rates for State classified employees. The Young study was done without request or authorization from the CSC. Vis-a-vis CSC, the Department of Labor stands in the position of an advocate, and the Young study is no more binding on the State as an employer than it would be had it been contracted for by an employee organization" (CWTF 1985, appendix to CWTF report: 2).

The role of the market in wage-setting. While there was a consensus within the group that the state should act to mimimize its legal liability, the main debate within the group was over the role and effects of the market in wage-setting (Brown 1993). The task force had a strong representation of free-market proponents, those who argued that the main factor in wage-setting should be the market rather than internal relationships of classes to one another. In fact, there is some evidence that the anti-comparable worth representatives on the task force aggressively challenged their charge to recommend action to eliminate wage discrimination (WSG, *WIRE*, January 1984: 2). On the task force, employer representatives were the strongest advocates for market forces (Brown 1993). They were aware that the Michigan civil service was a dominant employer in the labor market for clerical work in certain localities, and they believed the wage practices of the state could have an impact upon private sector employers (Massaron 1992; Brown 1993).

In fact, the one public hearing that the task force called before the completion of their draft report was a hearing about economic ramifications of pay rate adjustments. "We're not looking for rhetoric on the equality or equal rights of men and women," the task force chair announced. "We want to know what people with a direct interest in total labor market rates, both public and private, think might happen to the economy or labor relations in the event of rather significant changes brought about through resolution of questions being examined in this study" (WSG, *WIRE*, January 1984: 2).

The Michigan Manufacturers Association argued that civil service reform could directly affect the private sector's employment and pay. Its spokesman, Henry Earle, warned:

> When the rhetoric is stripped away, Comparable Worth constitutes a tinkering with one of the basic laws of our economy. That is the law of supply and demand. If wage rates are artificially created without regard to supply and demand, there would be a serious disruption of our economy which, among other results, could mean an end of collective bargaining. . . . If artifically high wage rates are created in the name of Comparable Worth, other inequities in pay among employees of the same sex, as well as among employees of the different sexes will be asserted as the basis for still further artificially inflated wage rates. The end result would be, if not chaos, a totally government-controlled economy, which is antithetical to our political and economic history. (Earle n.d. [1985])

During this period the Michigan and national chambers of commerce were vigorously denouncing the concept of comparable worth, and the Michigan chamber would later argue that the report did not go far enough in rejecting the concept because the task force had contained political supporters of comparable worth (Grattan 1985). The Employers Association of Detroit argued against the concept of comparable worth even in state employment and would later applaud the task force for not endorsing the implementation of a comparable worth job evaluation study, insofar as "such studies are inherently subjective and, hence, worsen pay disparities" (Carter 1985).[7] The literature and testimony of all three associations argued that comparable worth would create burdens on taxpayers. The Women in State Government newsletter observed, "Employer representatives . . . forecast major economic dislocations if female-dominated jobs are paid equivalently to male-dominated jobs" (WSG, WIRE, January 1984: 2).

Civil service staff in the task force meetings emphasized the importance of the labor market in setting pay rates. However, they pointed out that with the beginnings of collective bargaining over pay, salary surveys ascertaining wages in the labor market were playing a more limited role (CWTF minutes, November 18, 1983: 2; December 12, 1983: 2).

Single job evaluation? In addition to debate over the general import of the legal position and the role of the market, there was considerable disagreement within the task force over the desirability of single job evaluation for state of Michigan workers. Early in its deliberations, the Subcommittee on Reasons for the Wage Gap, suggested that the state institute a single job evaluation system and contract a consultant to develop as bias-free a system as possible. They suggested that at the same time the state develop a single notification system to inform applicants of the availability of jobs or that each department develop a notification plan to be reviewed and approved by the civil service. Task force chair Cushman quashed the recommendation by arguing that job evaluation was the provenance of the Job Evaluation Subcommittee (CWTF minutes, August 6, 1984: 2). That subcommittee, chaired by Mary Jane Kay and including Malcolm Denise, Lawrence Glazer, and Paul Massaron, recommended only modifications to the existing system to reduce occupational groupings and limit their gender segregation (CWTF minutes, August 6, 1984: 2–3). It rejected a single job evaluation system.

Massaron, still a member of the task force and its Job Evaluation Subcommittee, dissented, as, in the final report, did Mildred Jeffrey. A single job evaluation was strongly supported by the Office of Women and Work and major female-dominated employee unions, such as UAW Local 6000, AFSCME Council 25, and MSEA, as well as the UAW International (Collette 1985; Komer 1985; MSEA 1985; Strunk 1992).

THE REPORT OF THE TASK FORCE

Following two years of work extending from June 1983 to June 1985, the task force issued its report, comprised of findings, recommendations, and supporting documentation. The report was a complex and contradictory document. It acknowledged that state classified service was characterized by pay inequities, and gender-based wage disparities, which ought to be reduced. However, the task force report did not endorse the concept of comparable worth, that is, a pay policy based upon equal pay for work of equal value. While not endorsing comparable worth, it did make some concessions to its principles: that the value of work should be determined by gender-neutral job evaluation and that pay should take into account the value of work, as well as being influenced by collective bargaining and the market. The report apportioned some responsibility for pay disparities to the civil service itself, while also arguing that such inequities are created externally, by "society," through gender stereotyping and steering, through market mechanisms and through collective bargaining. Despite the fact that the Michigan Civil Service was 20 percent African-American, the task force was not charged with reviewing disparities in pay based upon race, and it did not itself raise this issue in the course of its deliberations. Here, we summarize the main recommendations of the task force report. We discuss some of the recommendations in more detail in chapters 4 and 5, where we examine pay equity implementation.

Failure to endorse comparable worth. The report failed to endorse a comparable worth principle that pay for both male- and female-dominated classes be consistently related to evaluated job points. Nowhere does the report recommend a change in the Civil Service Merit Principles, which would formally commit the commission to comparability as a key determinant of wages. Women in State Government had argued that Merit Principle 3 should be altered to include language similar to that found in new personnel statutes in other states. They suggested wording such as: "It is the policy of this state to establish an equitable compensation relationship between female-dominated and male-dominated classes of employees in the classified service. Compensation relationships are equitable within the meaning of this policy when the primary consideration in negotiating, establishing, recommending and approving total compensation is comparability of the value of the work in relation to other positions in the classified service." Nadine Korth from Women in State Government underlined this in her affidavit in *UAW v. State of Michigan* (1985).

The principle as written stated that equitable compensation should be provided for work of equal value. But, according to the Department of Civil Service, reference to equal value was to jobs within the same class and to classes within the same skill level (within occupational groups) attracting the same pay unless there was a compelling reason they should not. The rule also stated that "appropriate consideration of the relevant compensation provided by other employers" was an acceptable factor in pay determination (CSC 1989: 4).

However, the task force report made no such recommendation and so declined to undertake what in Michigan would have constituted an equivalent to comparable worth legislation. The failure to establish comparable worth in pay setting was tied to the task force's view that they were not compelled to do so by law.

Desegregating jobs. Yet the report accepted the concept of pay inequity, that is, the existence of gender-based pay disparities which must be reduced. It identified the main source of these disparities as various forms of gender segregation: "The major cause of wage disparities between male and female employees of the State classified system is their unequal distribution among the eleven service groups and by skill level" (CWTF 1985: 7). It argued that "at the core of pay equity [are] the concepts of equal employment opportunity and affirmative action" (CWTF 1985: 22). The report recommended a number of measures to increase the eligibility of and recruitment of women into predominantly male entry-level jobs and a number of measures to improve women's advancement, especially into supervisory, managerial, and executive positions. While accepting the responsibility of the civil service for perpetuating gender segregation, the report also argued that it was a result of gender stereotyping and steering, perpetuated in, among other places, the Michigan public schools.

The report therefore recommended affirmative action, that is the movement of women into different jobs, often at higher levels of the hierarchy, as a means of remedying gender-based pay disparities, rather than comparable worth, a method of revaluing women's existing jobs. Nationally and in Michigan the demand for comparable worth, however, rested on the limited accomplishments of affirmative action for women and upon women's assertions that they liked the jobs they did and thought them undervalued (Blum 1991; WSG, *WIRE,* April 1985: 4–6).

On release of the draft report of the task force, Women in State Government protested that fourteen years of affirmative action, directed first by the civil service, then by the Michigan Equal Employment and Business Opportunity Council, had not integrated most gender-segregated occupations. Nadine Korth, president of Women in State Government, declared,

> Affirmative action or job desegregation is not pay equity. We don't want nurses to become state troopers to be paid fairly. We want nurses to continue to do the job they choose to do and were trained to do while being paid a fair wage for the skill, effort, and responsibility required by their jobs. . . . [T]he bulk of employed women are still in the relatively low-paid pink-collar ghettos of clerical work, direct care work in state mental hospitals, unem-

ployment claims workers and welfare workers. Their jobs
need to be recognized for the value they have to the
state, without regard for the gender of the person hold-
ing the job. (WSG, *WIRE*, May 1985: 2)

It is not surprising that the Comparable Worth Task Force report fell back
on affirmative action as a remedy. Affirmative action encourages women
to change their place in the gendered hierarchy of authority and worth in
organizations rather than challenging the gendering of the hierarchy or
the principle of hierarchy. It does not involve major changes in pay-setting, which challenge market rates, and organized business in Michigan
has generally supported it.

Reformed job evaluation. However, the report also suggested remedies that could be broadly defined as pay equity measures closely related
to comparable worth methods. These instructed the Department of Civil
Service to establish a less gender-biased job evaluation system and directed
the commission and Office of the State Employer to make some pay adjustments based upon skill levels. The task force endorsed nondiscriminatory
job evaluation based upon factors of skill, effort, and responsibility. It argued that such evaluation should be applied to all classifications. The task
force recommended that within four years the Bureau of Classification of
the Department of Civil Service reduce the eleven gender-segregated service groups that existed under the Benchmark System to five non–gender-
dominated groups. They argued that this reduction would provide consistent classification and greater access to career advancement (CWTF 1985:
20–21). Feminist and labor activists saw the task force's recommendation
of five separate groups differentiated on the basis of education/skill level as
a major defeat.

Pay adjustments. As well as recommending affirmative action and
non-discriminatory job reevaluation as medium-term goals, the task force
made some general recommendations about pay setting in state employment. The report suggested, in no particular order of priority, that collective bargaining, prevailing labor market comparisons, and coordinated pay
setting remain important and legitimate determinants of pay for state
workers. The report also specifically stated that any collective bargaining
or coordinated pay setting should address the issue of pay equity (CWTF
1985: 22). These two recommendations are quite vague in that they neither specify the relative importance of various factors in pay setting nor
propose mechanisms to operationalize various factors, such as "market"
and "pay equity." The recommendations can also be seen as contradictory,
as gendered market rates are often in conflict with relative wage rates established through gender-neutral job evaluation.

In the short term, the task force recommended special pay adjustments for female-dominated classes. The task force defined female-dominated jobs as those 70 percent or more female, thereby excluding from pay adjustments incumbents of classes between 60 and 69 percent female. Yet there is evidence that proportions of women well below 70 percent lower an occupation's pay. Studies have shown that each additional percentage point female in an occupation is associated with significantly lower median annual earnings (see, for example, Reskin and Hartman 1986: 10; McDermott 1991: 25).

The report recommended that the Office of the State Employer develop a salary line composed of the average wages of all classes; the female-dominated classes which were below the average line should receive special adjustments of a substantial percentage of the gap between their current wage and the average for all classes. Collective bargaining was recommended as the mechanism for determining the proration and extent of these adjustments, beginning in fiscal year 1985–86 and coordinated over four years. Yet, pay equity adjustments, like all wage increases, should be subject to budgetary constraints (CWTF 1985: 21).

An average salary line based upon all classes contains within it discrimination against female jobs. The average line, therefore, would be artificially depressed by including both male and female job classes. A more equitable standard, as the civil service unions argued, would have been the average salary line of the male-dominated classes, a line which would be free of discrimination (AFSCME n.d.; MSEA, n.d.). Sorensen (1994) points out that there are four types of pay lines (average, male, corrected average, and non-female) and that the majority of states using job evaluation for pay equity reform have used average or corrected average lines. Sorensen notes that the state of Minnesota used a male line, several states used a corrected line, and some, such as Wisconsin, used the non-female line (*Report of Wisconsin's Task Force on Comparable Worth* 1985).

In addition, however, the recommendation to construct a pay line in the absence of a gender-neutral single job evaluation system, which would not be developed for some years, was problematic. How could the state construct a single pay line showing pay for points when "points" were awarded in eleven occupational service groups on different bases? How could point scores be relied upon when scoring systems previously and currently in place in state employment were understood to have incorporated gender bias? In the end the state resorted to use of PCELs, a set of twenty-one levels derived from the old Position Comparison System, an outdated single classification system used between 1938 and 1975 in civil service employment.

Furthermore, though the report recommended pay adjustments, there was a strong emphasis upon leaving it to the unions to negotiate these increases rather than upon administratively requiring them. The collective bargaining process as a route to pay equity involved two elements of uncertainty: whether the unions would raise such demands and whether the employer would concede them. The commission's abstention from pay determination might be seen positively as noninterference with union autonomy and bargaining rights, but in context it appears that the task force simply was not strongly committed to pay equity.

Women in State Government was concerned about both union and management commitment to pay equity. On the problem of unions carrying the weight of the pay reform, WSG president Nadine Korth commented:

> [T]he classified service has only had collective bargaining since 1980; therefore, the problem of discriminatory wage rates clearly was not caused by the state classified employee unions, but rather was caused by management actions. The State of Michigan cannot now abrogate its responsibility and expect unions with diverse memberships to solve this problem. It has been said that providing equal rights for women statute-by-statute instead of by an Equal Rights Amendment is comparable to freeing the slaves plantation by plantation. Similarly, achieving comparable worth bargaining unit-by-bargaining unit would be not only like freeing the slaves plantation-by-plantation but also expecting them to negotiate with other [slaves] and with the plantation owners. (WSG 1984: 9)

Several concrete recommendations might have indicated more commitment to pay equity on the part of the state. The report might have recommended establishment of a pay equity fund, based upon previous staff estimates of the cost of implementing comparable worth. It might have recommended that pay equity become a management objective in bargaining. The state had previously put into a place a process of evaluating collective bargaining agreements for their impact on equal opportunity and affirmative action goals, and the state might have set up a program that made approval of agreements contingent on progress towards pay equity (WSG, *WIRE*, n.m. 1983: 3). No such recommendations appeared. Of course, the task force also did not argue that once the new classification system was complete, it should be a primary factor in setting pay.

CONCLUSIONS

Inside the gendered bureaucracy of the state of Michigan, the Office of Women and Work, Women in State Government, and the civil service unions forced the issue of pay equity onto the agenda of the Civil Service Commission, a body constitutionally central to reform, which would oversee both political decision-making about and implementation of pay equity. Pay equity activism in the state itself was, in turn, dependent upon the broader national pay equity movement. Through 1985 Michigan represents a case of limited "legal leveraging" (McCann 1994). There is no doubt that the Gunther case in particular as well as other lower court decisions in general forced the attention of the civil service towards issues of classification and pay discrimination. The court cases had an impact upon the commission both indirectly—they built the resolve and activity of the Office of Women and Work and other advocates—and directly— they shaped the awareness and receptivity of the Comparable Worth Task Force and the state's own legal experts. But state officials were also aware that the law might allow it to escape liability through both a market defense and a denial that it had an authoritative job evaluation study showing discrimination. The specific complaint against the state lodged by Karon Black and the MSEA languished in the Department of Civil Rights, and this inaction was noted by the task force (CWTF minutes, May 21, 1984: 2).

The commission, after much resistance, set up a task force. The conflict between opponents and advocates of comparable worth was largely played out within the task force, whose members were asked not to disclose the content of discussion. The task force process was not open to business, labor, or feminist mobilization the way a traditional legislative process would have been, and the task force and commission reiterated to themselves and others their legal independence in the matter of pay equity. The task force presented itself as independent from general economic and political interests as well as civil service management and labor. Its view of its own independence is analogous to the professed independence of the commission itself. In fact, the task force was dominated by a chair drawn from the ranks of business executives and included other representatives of higher managerial ranks, who succeeded in limiting change. Concerned to present a "reasonable" set of policy recommendations which the commission could adopt, the task force was bound not to offend the business interests which had protested so loudly against the concept of comparable worth (Grattan 1985; Parish 1985; Carter 1985; Earle n.d. [1985]; Shattuck 1985).

Despite union and feminist criticisms, the Civil Service Commission adopted the recommendations of the Comparable Worth Task Force and directed the Department of Civil Service, the administrative arm of the commission, and the Office of the State Employer, an agency attached to the governor's office, to begin implementation. The Civil Service Commission had thus engaged in an important rule-making function analogous to legislating for public employees, but in a more privatized setting than the legislature. The commission did not set a requirement that comparability form the basis of pay, but established a more partial and fragmented policy that some pay inequities be removed.

Several specific recommendations—the acceptance of the appropriateness of (gendered) market wages; the use of a pay line comprised of male and female classes and based upon a tainted, outdated job classification system; the definition of predominantly female jobs as those that were at least 70 percent female; the separation of pay from long-term reclassification; the acceptance of budgetary constraints as reasons not to adjust the pay of female-dominated classes more quickly and fully; and the recommendation of multiple job evaluation plans—produced "palatable" policy on comparable worth (Steinberg 1989; McCann 1994) and sabotaged any "true comparable worth" outcome (Acker 1989). Many of these apparently technical decisions reflected concerns about the costs of adjustment in a context of fiscal stringency and a changing political economy, as well as an absence of committed urgency about resolving women's inequitable pay. The commission made clear that it did not take direct responsibility for adjusting pay in the short run or in the longer term as the new classification system was developed. In this way the commission presented itself as both acting to remove discrimination and acting in a fiscally responsible and business-friendly fashion.

Finally, in Michigan, a coordinating body, the commission, and its task force deliberately instituted a non-coordinated reform. The task force framework granted considerable independence to different agencies and aspects of the reform. The Office of the State Employer was free to use considerable discretion in negotiating wage adjustments, and in fact would become more resistant to pay equity increases over time as antistate politics and antagonism toward state workers intensified. The OSE was not required to respond to the Department of Civil Service's reclassification. The Department of Civil Service also had considerable freedom in designing job evaluation and instituting reclassification, as we show in chapter 5. The different time scales of the different parts of the recommended reforms, as well as the fact that different recommendations would be overseen by different agencies, thus created an improvised and incomplete reform.

4.

Conflict at the Bargaining Table: Limited Pay Equity Raises

Pay equity implementation in Michigan occurred within the framework determined by the Comparable Worth Task Force (CWTF). Although unions representing incumbents in female-dominated occupations attempted to raise the issue of pay equity at the bargaining table in the early 1980s, they had no success until the UAW officially filed a pay inequity lawsuit against the state and until the task force completed its report, both of which occurred in 1985.[1] The task force indicated pay equity wage increases were to be immediate, prior to the implementation of the Equitable Classification Plan (ECP). Therefore, following the report of the task force, Michigan civil service unions such as the UAW, AFSCME, and SEIU (Service Employees International Union) negotiated specific pay equity increases for female-dominated occupational classes in fiscal years 1985–86 and 1986–87.

The first phase of the Equitable Classification Plan (Group One) covered nonprofessional employees, who comprise the majority of civil service union membership. After the Group One reclassification was completed in 1990, the UAW tried unsuccessfully to use the new classification points as the basis for additional comparable worth adjustments. Pay equity claims in the 1990s have been denied, partly due to a changed political climate in state government following the gubernatorial election of Republican John Engler. The classification plan, therefore, never became the explicit basis for pay.

On one side in the collective bargaining process was management, represented by the Office of the State Employer (OSE). The office was

headed by a director, a gubernatorial appointee. The other staff were professional negotiators and career civil servants directly answerable to the
governor. The governor's political priorities were a factor determining
what management would agree to in negotiations. Negotiations were thus
constrained by the politics of the state government and, in particular, of
the governor's office. The perception of union negotiators has been that,
"Since the governor appoints the director of the OSE, we get nothing in
bargaining that the governor hasn't already agreed to" (Strunk 1992). In
negotiations with labor in the mid-1980s, the period of pay equity negotiations, the state budget and the market were invoked in a way that reflected
gubernatorial priorities. During both Governor Blanchard's and Governor
Engler's terms, reducing state budgets and restricting compensation increases for state employees were priorities.

On the other side of the bargaining table, civil service unions had
to respond to their members. If not, negotiated tentative agreements would
not be ratified, or worse, workers might vote to decertify the union—a
real possibility in view of the history of civil service unions in Michigan.
However, the collective bargaining process established for civil service employees was not "true collective bargaining" between two independent parties as it exists in most settings, but a modified version (see appendix A for
a model and description of collective bargaining for civil service employees). Not only are civil service employees prohibited from striking as a last
resort, but unresolved issues are sent to a board appointed by the Civil
Service Commission that has the power to impose a settlement upon the
unions. Proposed settlements or negotiated agreements are subject to approval by the commission. The legislature and governor also have formal
power to reject or reduce negotiated pay agreements. Some unionists have
described this procedure as "collective begging." In fact, the former president of AFSCME Council 25, James Glass, commented in the *Michigan
AFSCME News:* "Even today, bargaining in the Civil Service is a strange
animal. The agreement, once ratified by the Union and the employer, is
still subject to approval—and selective, unilateral veto!—by the Civil Service Commission" (1984 August/September: 1).

The strategies and results of negotiations over pay equity, given the
political, economic, and institutional constraints faced by both labor and
management, are the subject of this chapter. Although the Michigan
Comparable Worth Task Force set the framework for pay equity collective
bargaining, wage increases had to be negotiated by individual civil service
unions. There were some demonstration effects during bargaining, where
raises in one unit were extended to others, and often to the nonunion
staff in confidential occupations. However, the specific outcomes of the
negotiations varied over time, depending on political and economic con-

straints, and across unions, depending on the occupational and gender composition of the bargaining unit.

A brief summary of the history and structure of civil service industrial relations sets the context for negotiations by individual unions. Discussion of pay equity negotiations and outcomes are divided into three analytical and chronological sections: (1) initial pay equity adjustments based on gender composition of the job; (2) unions' shift to broader pay equity strategies while management awaited the new classification system; and (3) stalemated attempts to link new ECP points to pay in the Engler era. Although previous researchers, most notably Acker (1989), have viewed similar transitions from "true comparable worth" to broader pay equity strategies as a dilution of feminist consciousness in favor of class-based politics, we argue that these nontraditional approaches are a more realistic response to the political economy of the 1990s. In conclusion, we evaluate the impact of the limited special wage increases on the gender-based wage gap in the Michigan Civil Service.

CIVIL SERVICE INDUSTRIAL RELATIONS IN MICHIGAN

MANAGERIAL IDEOLOGY AND STRATEGIES

The state of Michigan has been part of a nationwide trend to cut the cost of government, as we noted in chapter 2. Governors and their managers have employed fiscal considerations and market forces to justify their attempts to hold the line on wages, including pay equity adjustments. They have also placed increased emphasis on subcontracting work to the private sector (Staudohar 1983; Mitchell 1988). In Michigan, budget- and personnel-cutting initiatives intensified with the election of Republican governor John Engler in 1990. These political priorities were manifested in pay equity negotiations by the state's avowed use of the market as arbiter of pay rates and the importance of "fiscally responsible" employment and pay practices. However, the meaning of market rates and their relation to other factors affecting wage rates has never been clearly defined. Thus, the invocation of market rates and fiscal responsibility by state negotiators has always been selective.[2]

The selective use of market rates has tended to disadvantage female-dominated job classes. While pay increases for some classes have been justified on the basis of market rates and the state's need to attract qualified workers, female-dominated classes, which are perpetually short of qualified applicants, did not receive pay adjustments based upon supply and demand factors. Examples cited by Women in State Government in their newsletters include several data-processing classes and nurse consultants. In contrast, the market argument was used extensively by the state in defending against a claim of discrimination in *UAW v. Michigan* in the mid-1980s, as well as in pay equity wage negotiations in the 1990s. Reliance on market wages has been employers' most common litigation defense in pay equity suits, according to McCann (1994: 31–34, 40–41; see also Patten 1988).

The civil service pay policy is reproduced, verbatim, in the *Report of the Comparable Worth Task Force* (CWTF 1985: Attachment B). The first point of the pay policy describes the state's role in establishing compensation levels that are competitive with other major employers, enabling the state to recruit and retain employees. The second principle, which discusses "the financial ability of the state to provide necessary services" can be interpreted to mean that there is an interest in low-cost state services and in maintaining the health of the state economy. These principles in combination imply that the state should hold wages near market rates of pay. The merit principles of the civil service, printed in the commission's *Rules*, also emphasize "appropriate consideration of the relevant compensation provided by other employers" (CSC 1989: 4). Since the market incorporates both historic gender and class differentials, adherence to the pay policy serves to reproduce these wage hierarchies. The reference to market rates of pay and the reproduction of the full pay policy in the task force report legitimated the rejection of comparable worth policy in favor of a more incomplete and improvised pay equity policy.

The Office of the State Employer's initial strategy in pay equity wage negotiations appears to have been to follow the letter of *The Report of the Comparable Worth Task Force*. The report recommended collective bargaining as the mechanism for determining the proration and extent of pay adjustments, beginning in Fiscal Year 1985–86 and coordinated over four years. Management would begin to negotiate pay adjustments before completion of the new classification system, although the task force anticipated four years would allow time for the new system to be in place. The task force also defined the specific methodology for determining eligibility for wage increases. In short, adjustments were to be given to female-dominated classes (defined as 70 percent female). The state should develop a salary line composed of the average wages of all classes (female, male, and neutral). Female-dominated classes below the average line should receive special adjustments of "a substantial percentage" of the gap between their current wage and the average for all classes. Finally, the task force cautioned that pay equity adjustments, just as all wage increases, should be subject to budgetary constraints (CWTF 1985: 21).

HISTORY OF PUBLIC SECTOR COLLECTIVE BARGAINING

To appreciate labor's priorities and constraints in negotiating pay equity, it is important to understand the history and distinctive nature of public sector collective bargaining in the state of Michigan. Michigan reflects overall national trends in public sector unionism in the U.S. (see, e.g., Bell 1985; Burton and Thomason 1988; Horowitz 1994). While Michigan historically had significant private sector union membership, before 1965 Michigan public sector workers had no legal right to representation. But in Michigan, as elsewhere, there was a rapid expansion of the public sector, public sector employment, and laws permitting public sector unionization in the 1960s.[3] Michigan was one of eleven states to pass legislation authorizing collective bargaining by public employees between 1965 and 1966, and one of thirty to have such legislation by 1969. Michigan's statute, the Public Employment Relations Act (PERA), passed in 1965, but this legislation excluded civil servants. The act provided other public employees the right to organize, join, or assist unions; engage in lawful concerted activities; present grievances; and bargain collectively with their employers over wages, hours, and other terms and conditions of employment (White and Crabb 1988).[4]

Civil service unionization in Michigan was slower in coming.[5] The civil service did eventually grant collective bargaining rights in stages as the legislature, civil service employee associations, and public advisory groups or task forces applied intensifying pressure. First, voluntary employee associations were granted formal recognition and the right to "meet and confer" under the Civil Service Commission's first employee relations policy (ERP) in 1964.[6] Twelve years later (in 1976), civil servants were granted limited collective bargaining rights over noneconomic issues (i.e., excluding compensation) by the commission.[7] The constitutional independence of the Michigan civil service and its control over state employment were considered an obstacle to the extension of full bargaining rights over economic issues to all units (see STAFER 1975: 3).

Not satisfied with limited bargaining rights, employee associations such as AFSCME launched several campaigns, with the support of sympathetic legislators, to establish collective bargaining through a constitutional amendment (see LPER 1976). State police troopers and sergeants went directly to the voters, initiating a successful statewide petition drive to gather signatures to place a constitutional amendment on the ballot granting them collective bargaining rights. The ballot initiative generated by the troopers passed on election day in November 1978.[8] In the meantime, a legal opinion by Michigan attorney general Frank Kelley in 1978 confirmed that it was within the commission's constitutional powers to extend collective bargaining to compensation as long as it reserved its right to modify or approve agreements. Michael Cain, a past director of AFSCME Council 25, expressed his frustration in 1979: "In order to understand why state classified employees remain[ed] the only segment of employees in this state without collective bargaining rights and hence saddled with an ineffective employee relations policy, one must realize that Michigan is the only state in the nation that has a constitution giving the civil service commission plenary authority over all matters in state classified service" (Cain 1979: 1).

When faced with the possibility of another constitutional amendment granting bargaining rights to the majority of civil service employees, the civil service sought to retain regulatory control. The commission appointed a Citizens Advisory Task Force on Civil Service Reform, which recommended that the commission extend collective bargaining rights to civil servants (CATF 1979).[9] The Civil Service Commission granted "full" collective bargaining over wages, benefits, and working conditions without constitutional amendment in 1980, although the right to strike is prohibited. Today, nearly 70 percent of women and men in the Michigan civil service are represented under agency shop agreements.[10]

The Structure and Membership of Civil Service Unions

Since the 1980s the bargaining units in the civil service have been organized loosely by occupation, often across state departments. The ten bargaining units and their union representatives, with 1990 employment levels, are listed in table 2. Each union typically represents employees in occupations which serve a particular purpose in state government: for security (guards) in state institutions, the Michigan Corrections Officers (MCO); for the state police, the Michigan State Police Troopers Association (MSPTA); for human services support workers, the Service Employees International Union (SEIU); and for scientists and engineers, the Michigan Professional Employees Society. However, UAW Local 6000 and the Michigan State Employees Association (MSEA) each represent employees in two employment units.

The division of employees into bargaining units on the basis of occupation and job expertise, rather than by location in state departments, follows the traditional craft model of trade unionism. Occupational uniformity homogenizes members' interests and strengthens differential occupational identities. On the other hand, organizing across departments physically separates members and maintains divisions based upon skill hierarchies within individual departments. This occupational division clearly distinguishes certain units as being female-dominated and therefore invested in pay equity policy.

In fact, among the largest bargaining units listed in table 2 are those with a concentration of female-dominated occupations: the administrative support and human services units represented by the UAW and the institutional unit represented by AFSCME. UAW Local 6000's two units include nonprofessional clerical workers and professionals such as nurses

Table 2

State of Michigan Civil Service Exclusive Bargaining Agents

Employment Unit	Employees in 1990	Union Representative
Administrative Support	11,601	United Auto Workers (UAW Local 6000)
Human Services	10,991	United Auto Workers (UAW Local 6000)
Human Services Support	1,259	Service Employees International Union (SEIU Local 31–M)
Institutional	6,081	AFSCME, Council 25
Labor and Trades	3,834	Michigan State Employees Association (MSEA)
Safety and Regulatory	1,668	Michigan State Employees Association (MSEA)
Scientific and Engineering	1,878	Michigan Professional Employees Society (MPES) (SEIU Local 517)
Security	7,167	Michigan Corrections Officers (MCO) (SEIU Local 526)
State Police	1,916	Michigan State Police Troopers Association (MSPTA)
Technical	1,627	United Technical Employees Association (UTEA)
Total Exclusively Represented Employees	**48,022**	

Source: Department of Civil Service [Michigan], *Annual Work Force Report*, Fiscal Year 1989–90.

Note: All bargaining agents have at least one job class in Group One. Total non–exclusively represented employees number 19,194.

and librarians. AFSCME represents a variety of workers in the state's hospitals and other institutions, such as practical nurses, launderers, cooks, and youth specialists. A smaller unit where the majority of the members work in female-dominated job classes such as unemployment claims workers is SEIU's human services support unit.

The United Auto Workers, the preeminent union in Michigan's manufacturing sector, is a relative newcomer to civil service collective bargaining. In Michigan, as nationwide, initial representation elections in state employment in the 1970s were typically fights between an independent employee "association" such as MSEA and a public employee "union" such as AFSCME (see Stern 1988: 81).[11] In Michigan, of the 54 percent of civil servants represented after limited collective bargaining was established in 1976, 62 percent belonged to MSEA, 20 percent to AFSCME, and the remaining 18 percent to others (*Michigan Report* 1977: no. 35). The UAW did not represent any civil service units.

Clerical workers in the Michigan civil service voted in a representation election in June 1981. At the time, the bargaining unit had 13,500 members; it was the largest of the seven which had already held representative elections. MSEA and AFSCME were again on the ballot (*Michigan Report* 1981: no. 94), and MSEA won, having also secured a victory over AFSCME in a runoff election to represent the human services workers. In 1981, MSEA represented four of ten bargaining units: two male-dominated and two female-dominated.

The two largest bargaining units represented by MSEA (administrative support and human services) were involved in jurisdictional battles in the mid-1980s. Karon Black, the lead name on the Benchmark classification (gender discrimination) lawsuit against the state and former director of MSEA's clerical unit, announced on September 16, 1982, that she was taking steps to switch the unit's affiliation from MSEA to its state rival, AFSCME. One of her major reasons for wishing to do so was that the MSEA Executive Board tried to overturn a contract ratified by 11,500 clerical unit members. She was cited by a Michigan daily political news service as accusing MSEA of "broken promises regarding autonomy and contract negotiations." Further, in her opinion, MSEA was trying to systematically stifle dissent within the bargaining unit (*Michigan Report* 1982: no. 179). AFSCME, she added, had a reputation for decentralized and democratic bargaining. In an interview in 1994, Mary Trombley, a nurse consultant and member of the human services unit, recalled that MSEA was dominated by male workers who were not clericals and attended more to its male than female bargaining units. In AFSCME, nationally, clerical members were second in membership only to members in the health care field (Stern 1988: 84–86). AFSCME's attempt to decertify MSEA's clerical unit was ultimately unsuccessful.

But a subsequent decertification drive undertaken by the UAW resulted in a runoff election with the MSEA. Clerical activist Karon Black favored the UAW despite her previous allegiance to AFSCME, and said her newest decision was a difficult one.[12] Several local activists felt that MSEA, formed in the pre-collective bargaining era, was not a "real union" that could effectively bargain. A large number of the state's clerical workers were also familiar with the UAW, as their spouses, partners, and other family members worked at the nearby Lansing Buick-Oldsmobile-Cadillac plant, a sprawling complex several blocks from state government offices. Many civil servants saw the UAW as a union with considerable national resources and support services. As an unaffiliated state-level association, MSEA had limited resources, according to Mary Trombley, who served as a union steward under both MSEA and the UAW (Trombley 1994).

The UAW also has a history of feminist labor activism. Nevertheless, critics asserted that the UAW failed to understand civil service employment, formed as it was on an "industrial model" which emphasizes an adversarial shop floor culture and the right to strike. In contrast, state workers were thought to identify with the employer's mission of public service and view their work altruistically—"a different kind of workforce" (Curran 1991, March 28). Further, because of the segmented structure of automobile industry employment, the UAW historically focused on employment discrimination and affirmative action (to encourage women's entry into nontraditional jobs) rather than pay equity (Milkman 1987: 158–59; Gabin 1990: 190–93).

In the representation election of November 1985, the UAW won the female-dominated administrative support and human services units while the male-dominated units (labor and trades, safety and regulatory) were retained by MSEA. One reason for the split in affiliation may have been frictions between the primarily male and female units over pay equity (and the complaint against the Benchmark classification system). UAW Local 6000 became the largest state employee union. In fact, the largest UAW local in the state of Michigan is not affiliated with automobiles; it is now UAW Local 6000, the twenty-two thousand strong local of state workers. Although not new to white-collar unionism in the private sector, the UAW quickly became a major player in public sector unionism in the state, often negotiating standards used for pattern bargaining within the civil service.[13] (The two MSEA units later affiliated directly with the AFSCME International—but not Michigan's Council 25—as a separate new local in 1986).

UNIONS' INTERESTS AT THE BARGAINING TABLE

Because of their membership in administrative support and human services occupations and in state institutions, the UAW and AFSCME were at the forefront of negotiating pay equity wage adjustments, with SEIU and other units containing female-dominated classes generally relying on their bargaining precedents. The largely female bargaining units were the administrative support, human services, and human services support units, and the institutional unit (with employees in health and other service occupations at state institutions). The UAW represents a number of the largest female-dominated job classes, such as secretary, typist clerk, and assistant payments worker in the administrative support unit. While the UAW's human services unit contains some professional employees, members of SEIU's human services support unit are overwhelmingly nonprofessional. AFSCME's institutional unit contains job classes with a majority of female incumbents, such as practical nurse, dental aide, and resident care aide.

Nationally, AFSCME, along with the Coalition of Labor Union Women (CLUW) and the International Union of Electrical Workers, used its influence to be both a pioneer and a leader in the struggle for pay equity in public employment by means of collective bargaining, litigation, and lobbying (AFSCME n.d., *AFSCME's Record*; Bell 1985; Evans and Nelson 1993). McCann (1994: 53–58) notes that AFSCME's national leaders used pay equity litigation, especially publicity gathered by the favorable 1983 decision by Judge Jack Tanner in *AFSCME v. State of Washington,* as a tool for organizing and mobilizing members. Former national Committee on Pay Equity director Claudia Wayne credited AFSCME's legal victory with creating "a growing sense of inevitability" for the pay equity movement (quoted in McCann 1994: 56). The international union has been active in pursuing pay equity initiatives in state government employment, in such states as Washington, Oregon, Wisconsin, Connecticut, Hawaii, New York, Iowa, Illinois, New Jersey, Ohio, Rhode Island, and Massachusetts (AFSCME n.d., *AFSCME's Record*). Some AFSCME locals have used pay equity as an organizing tool, with great success (see Evans and Nelson 1989b; NCPE n.d.; Riccucci 1990; Shostak 1991). Although there have been fewer job evaluation studies or pay equity initiatives in the private sector, the UAW has had some involvement here. For example, the clerical workers at Boston University, represented by District 65 of the UAW, called for a study of pay equity at the university (Riccucci 1990: 152).

However, in Michigan the UAW sustained the drive for negotiated pay equity increases into the 1990s while AFSCME became preoccupied by cutbacks in civil service personnel. Both AFSCME and SEIU were affected by deep cuts in social programs, education, rehabilitation, services to patients in state psychiatric and other facilities, and similar state functions.[14] With the decline in numbers in the institutional unit, AFSCME's Council 25 membership decreased dramatically, from more than 10,000 in 1978 to 7,000 in 1980, and to 4,428 in 1991. A review of the Department of Civil Service's *Annual Work Force Report* indicates that only SEIU Local 31-M, representing human services support employees, lost more members, as a percentage, from 1981 to 1991. Thus, the state government's efforts to close state institutions or reduce their operations meant that AFSCME's presence in the Michigan civil service was waning.

In contrast, the decertification of MSEA by its two female-dominated bargaining units empowered these units, represented by the UAW, to pursue pay equity aggressively without fear of alienating blue-collar union brothers in the same local. Typically, male-dominated blue-collar unions and union locals (representing police, firefighters, state troopers, skilled crafts, etc.) have not supported pay equity (Gabin 1989: 56–57; Riccucci 1990: 159; Rhoads 1993: 105–10) either nationally or in Michigan. Further, the activist union culture the UAW developed in the Michigan private sector, dating back to its founding during the CIO sit-down strikes of the 1930s, was a stark contrast to the traditionally nonconfrontational style of white-collar public sector employee associations not affiliated with the AFL-CIO (see Snyder 1973; Zieger 1986; Troyer 1987; Murphy 1990). The UAW won certification from the two largest bargaining units in the same year the Comparable Worth Task Force issued its recommendation for pay equity increases. It is therefore not surprising that the UAW, in view of its tradition of advocating social justice, seized on the issue as a way to demonstrate its commitment to its new members.

Given the legacy of the representation and decertification elections, individual civil service unions had to be especially attentive to unique constituencies with divergent interests. These interests are reflected in the process of negotiating special pay increases. Although recommended by the Comparable Worth Task Force, workers' actual raises resulted from a complex collective bargaining process, in the context of changing state government political priorities. The next section will look at the process and the outcomes.

COLLECTIVE BARGAINING OVER PAY EQUITY

NARROWING THE DISPARITY IN 1985 AND 1986

Management, embodied by the Office of the State Employer, came to the bargaining table in 1985 prepared to grant special pay equity increases as recommended by the Comparable Worth Task Force. The UAW lawsuit created additional pressure to negotiate pay equity wage increases. The legal action was filed November 27, 1985, while negotiations between the UAW and the OSE, which had begun on November 19, were in progress. Winn Newman, the UAW's lead attorney in the unsuccessful case, told a *New York Times* reporter in 1989, "What typically happens in all these cases is that on the eve of the lawsuit, there's a show that he [the employer] is not a bad guy and he doesn't discriminate. The lawsuits, even if they lose, thus have been a conduit for change" (Lewin 1989). Newman specifically indicated that pay equity raises in Michigan would not have been forthcoming if it had not been for the lawsuit. In the resulting contracts, the UAW, AFSCME, and SEIU locals received two special increases over two years.

In order to implement the framework outlined by the CWTF, the Office of the State Employer based its initial bargaining proposal on an estimate of the wage disparity faced by female-dominated job classes. As described in chapter 3, the task force recommended comparing a salary line of female-dominated classes with the average salary line for all classes (male, female, and neutral) to calculate the disparity. To map these salary lines, regression techniques correlate pay to some other standardized assessment of the value or level of the job. In customary comparable worth techniques, points-to-pay regression lines are constructed using points from a job evaluation or classification system. This enables evaluators to measure whether female-dominated jobs are underpaid compared to jobs with comparable point values.

However, the pay adjustments recommended by the Comparable Worth Task Force were to begin in fiscal year 1985, rather than awaiting completion of the Equitable Classification Plan (ECP). Therefore, the unfinished classification plan could not be used for points-to-pay lines. Further, it was impossible for the Office of the State Employer to assess the wage disparity using the existing Benchmark classification system because point values were not comparable across highly gender-segregated service groups (clerical versus labor and trades, for example).

To provide a basis for comparisons, Joseph Slivensky, director of the Planning and Development Bureau in the Department of Civil Service, used Position Comparison Equivalency Levels (PCELs) to permit an analysis across the Benchmark service groups. At the time of the conversion from the Position Comparison System to the Benchmark in the 1970s, the civil service designated PCELs, 1 through 20, for each of the Benchmark classes corresponding to the existing Position Comparison System level for each class.[15] The PCELs were directly and positively related to the state's designation of skill and loosely associated with pay.

The majority of job classes at PCELs 14 and above were male-dominated; management chose to exclude these classes from an estimation of a salary line and therefore from possible pay equity wage adjustments. The Office of the State Employer calculated a weighted average of the maximum salary for all employees and for female employees at PCELs 13 and below. This decision especially concerned Women in State Government, whose membership was concentrated in the professional ranks. In their

November 1985 newsletter, WSG provided a criticism of this action: "In an odd twist of logic, OSE attributes a significant amount of the male/female wage differential to the fact that there are relatively few women at the 14 PCEL and above. So the 14 level and above classes were ignored . . . [and] disregarding the pay disparities that may exist at the 14 level and above is an insult" (WSG, *WIRE*, n.m. 1985: 3). Women in State Government asserted that gender-based wage disparities tend to widen at higher levels in organizational hierarchies. Therefore, excluding PCELs 14 and above artificially lowered the average disparity.[16]

Based upon the OSE's methodology, the differential between the salary lines, or gender-based wage gap, was estimated as $.80 per hour. In other words, a Michigan civil servant working in a female-dominated job was paid $.80 less per hour than the average wage of all employees at the same level. The amount of this discrimination varied, but averaged $.80 per hour across all measured jobs, according to the OSE. Women in State Government argued that this average disparity "masks the actual pay disparities that may range as high as $6,000 per year" (WSG, *WIRE*, November 1985: 3). Although the PCELs methodology, the use of the average disparity (rather than a class-by-class remedy), and other aspects of the OSE's formula were questioned by several unions and Women in State Government, this $.80 figure evolved into a target for labor negotiators. Unions interpreted the amount as a minimum commitment to eliminating gender-based wage discrimination.

In separate negotiations in 1985, civil service unions asked for pay increases for female-dominated classes where wages fell below the average wage line based upon this $.80 per hour figure. The state initially offered two $.10 per hour *across-the-board* increases for employees in female-dominated classes (defined as greater than or equal to 70 percent female) (UAW Local 6000 1991: 13). Setting the pattern for negotiations, the Office of the State Employer's opening offer did not differentiate the size of the wage adjustment by job class. The UAW, AFSCME, and SEIU locals ultimately each received two special increases of $.20 per hour in fiscal years 1985–86 (retroactive) and 1986–87, for a total adjustment of $.40 per hour over two years. This would close half of the aggregate disparity as calculated by the OSE. In their negotiations, the United Technical Employees Association was unsuccessful in obtaining a special pay increase for relatively well-paid dental hygienists, one female-dominated job class in their bargaining unit of mainly neutral job classes (Cohn 1992). Table 3 shows the approximate number of UAW, AFSCME, and SEIU employees receiving pay equity wage adjustments and the associated cost in each fiscal year by bargaining unit.

But the means to achieving this end were different for AFSCME on the one hand and the UAW and SEIU on the other. Both unions found

Table 3

Employees Receiving Pay Equity Raises by Bargaining Unit

Unit (Union)	# Employees	% of Unit	Cost FY 1985	Cost FY 1986
Administrative Support (UAW)	10,800	99.8%	$4,500,000	$4,500,000
Human Services (UAW)	5,400	53.8%	$2,250,000	$2,250,000
Institutional (AFSCME)	2,020	29.5%	$840,000	$840,000
Human Services Support (SEIU)	850	68.5%	$350,000	$350,000
TOTAL	19,070		$7,940,000	$7,940,000

Sources: Authors' calculations based on Department of Civil Service [Michigan], Annual Work Force Report, Fiscal Year 1985–86 and Thomas N. Hall, May 26, 1994, memorandum.

the 70 percent figure an arbitrary cutoff, but for AFSCME the impact of the reliance on this figure as a definition seemed worse. Since a majority of incumbents in the UAW and SEIU bargaining units were in female-dominated classes according to the 70 percent formula, most of their members (including almost the entire administrative support unit) were eligible for special wage increases (see table 3). The UAW and SEIU settled at the table in 1985. AFSCME did not.

The Michigan AFSCME News reported that a significant number of AFSCME members were excluded using the 70 percent definition. Only 2,250 employees (out of 6,841 in AFSCME's institutional unit at that time) were eligible under this threshold.[17] The definition was critical to AFSCME because the largest job class in the institutional bargaining unit was resident care aide, roughly 65 percent female; thus, about 2,800 workers narrowly missed qualifying for special pay increases.

In bargaining, AFSCME proposed a formula based on the methodology of the Equal Employment Opportunity Commission (EEOC) (Michigan AFSCME News, December 1985: 4; February 1986: 3–4). In the EEOC formula, a classification whose gender representation is 120 percent or more of their representation in the total workforce is regarded as dominated by the larger group. (The New York State Comparable Worth Study [1985] used a similar formula, 140 percent of representation.) With 53 percent of the total Michigan civil service classified workforce female, "female-dominated" would be: 1.2 x 53 percent or 63.6 percent female. When management rejected the EEOC formula, AFSCME brought the dispute to the Civil Service Commission-appointed Impasse Panel for resolution. The Impasse Panel's decision retained the 70 percent definition, as recommended by the Comparable Worth Task Force (CSC, ERB 1985). James Glass, Council 25 president, responded to the Impasse decision by saying that "The use of the 70% standard prevents the decision from adjusting the injustices done by the system to thousands of institutional unit workers" (*Michigan AFSCME News*, February 1986: 3).

AFSCME had to wait until another bargaining cycle (fiscal year) before it could negotiate special increases for their resident care aides. In 1986, special wage adjustments were allocated for low-paid or female-dominated classes which did not meet the strict 70-percent definition. The large category of resident care aides received $.15 per hour; child care workers received $.15 per hour; and activity therapy aides received $.15 per hour. One female-dominated class, practical nurses, received a $.10 per hour adjustment on top of the $.40 specified in previous negotiations. Reflected in AFSCME's 1986–89 contract, these special pay increases were negotiated (this time without the Impasse Panel) to become effective much later then other pay equity adjustments—in fiscal year 1990. However, these were the only increases received by the bargaining unit; other wages were frozen. Thus, the apparent AFSCME strategy was to trade across-the-board increases for pay equity adjustments for their largest group of employees. Under these conditions, the Office of the State Employer was willing to flex on the 70 percent demarcation. Although the state did not categorize the increases as pay equity adjustments (Hall 1994c), because they were targeted to female-dominated occupations under a less strict definition, we would do so.

Pay adjustments in 1985 and 1986 ($.40 per hour) were also given to non-exclusively represented employees in female-dominated classes. These were primarily employees in the same occupations as union members who are classified as "confidential" employees (those who have access to restricted financial records, for example) and are thus ineligible for union membership. Approximately 2,275 non-exclusively represented employees received $950,000 in each of fiscal years 1985 and 1986 (Hall 1994b).

In sum, most job classes defined by the state as female-dominated received special wage increases of $.40 per hour during this period. These adjustments were received by the UAW, AFSCME, and SEIU bargaining units, as well as by nonunion employees in confidential positions. Smaller increases were negotiated for specific job classes not strictly defined as female-dominated. These increases depended upon the bargaining strength and negotiating strategy of the unions representing each bargaining unit.

All of these increases were specifically linked to the gender composition of the occupation, and thus can be clearly labeled pay equity adjustments. However, they were not comparable worth adjustments since they were not based on a systematic effort to link compensation to an unbiased classification scheme. Further, most female-dominated job classes received exactly the same wage adjustment, rather than an amount equivalent to the disparity between the wages for each class and comparable jobs at the same level in the hierarchy.

MANAGEMENT STALLS FURTHER INCREASES, 1987–1989

Having negotiated the initial increases, the state used the bargaining agreements to argue that the plaintiffs in the UAW v. State of Michigan had no cause to seek remedy in the courts. "This agreement should constitute a full and final settlement and release of any and all pay inequity claims filed by employees who are represented by Plaintiffs UAW," the defendants argued in their January 1986 answer to the UAW's legal complaint (UAW v. State of Michigan 1985). The state subsequently cited the work of the Comparable Worth Task Force and various affirmative action efforts to refute the allegation that they had engaged in gender discrimination in employment.

Despite using the initial pay equity adjustments to defuse the litigation, once the threat was diminished by the lower court's finding for the defense, the state became obdurate. The strategy of the Office of the State Employer was to postpone further pay equity adjustments pending the outcome of the UAW's appeal of the 1987 district court decision and completion of the Equitable Classification Plan. Each fiscal year from 1987 to 1989, the UAW placed a proposal on the bargaining table for special wage increases based on the remaining disparity of $.40 per hour to be distributed among employees in female-dominated classifications. However, management argued to delay further increases. First, the Office of the State Employer was loathe to negotiate adjustments while the litigation based on the Benchmark classification system was pending at the appellate level, since a ruling favorable to the union would have meant back pay awarded as a remedy (see UAW Local 6000 1991: 13–14). Secondly, the state of Michigan was hesitant, even unwilling, to address any further possible wage disparities without the results of the new classification plan (see UAW Local 6000 1988; UAW Local 6000 1991). Although the OSE cited the forthcoming plan as a reason to delay consideration of further special increases, they also resisted a formal commitment to using the new ECP for comparable worth adjustments.[18]

Consequently, civil service unions deployed new strategies alongside the old. Successful strategies during the 1987–89 period targeted occupations perceived as historically underpaid whether or not they were 70 percent female. For example, UAW Local 6000, followed by AFSCME Council 25, and the United Technical Employees Association, requested raises be either in percentage terms or a minimum flat amount (in cents per hour), whichever was greater. This low-pay strategy avoided having percentage increases widen the gap between the highest and lowest paid members.

In 1987, the UAW spent considerable time and effort discussing possible payouts from an additional $2 million Pay Inequity Fund negotiated in 1986. Unlike the earlier pay increases, distribution would be in the form of one-time, lump sum payments not rolled into base salary (UAW Local 6000 1986–87: Art. 43, Sec. A). The stated purpose of the fund was "addressing pay inequities not addressed by the $.40 special increases for female dominated classes" (UAW Local 6000 1987: 1). The union had considerable discretion in selecting eligible job classes for receipt of these payments, although the allocations had to be approved by the OSE in negotiations. The UAW formed a Pay Inequity Committee to make recommendations for the distribution of the fund, a contentious issue throughout most of 1987.

The Pay Inequity Committee received requests from members, reviewed written submissions, and held hearings to allow members to present testimony and additional documentation in support of their request (UAW Local 6000, Pay Inequity Committee, 1987). In considering the requests and their recommendations, one of the key premises followed by the committee was: "The distribution of the two million dollar fund is not an extension of the comparable worth issue. As such, it can be used to address inequities created solely by market factors. However, we are not precluded from addressing inequities that may have arisen *as a result of the special increases granted,* nor from addressing sex-based wage inequities not yet addressed by the comparable worth increases" (UAW Local 6000, Pay Inequity Committee, 1987: 1, emphasis added). Why did the UAW suggest the possibility that the special increases may have led to new inequities? Comparable worth implementation does indeed have the potential to generate dissension within workplaces and bargaining units. This conflict occurs mainly across gender lines, as shown, for example, by Linda Blum (1991) in San Jose and Contra Costa County, Joan Acker (1989) in Oregon, and comparable worth opponent Steven Rhoads (1993) in Minnesota.

In Michigan, however, the manner in which the state chose to award 1985–86 special increases intensified the perception of inequity. Rather than bringing individual job classes up to an average pay for jobs rating comparable point scores, the Michigan Civil Service allocated lump sum increases to female-dominated job classes *regardless of their individual departure from the pay line.* The definition of female-dominated, the amount of the wage increases, and the exclusion of higher-skilled workers (in PCELs 14 and above) appeared arbitrary.

While the general recommendations in the UAW's Pay Inequity Committee report cover an extensive wish list for state government employees, from reaffirming the need for a single job evaluation system to suggesting a public relations campaign to boost the image of civil servants, the most significant decision was fund allocation. The committee chose *not* to use the payments to address gender-based wage discrimination, and recipient classes were not selected on the basis of their gender composition. The 2,830 employees receiving the lump sum payments were professionals in teaching and social service occupations (Hall 1994b). Most had been ineligible for pay equity adjustments because they were incumbents in integrated (or neutral) job classes which were not 70 percent female. Less than one-third of the seventeen class series designated for lump sum payments were close to the 70 percent female threshold, and one was male-dominated.[19] Although the UAW's $2 million fund may have addressed inequity, it was not what is traditionally considered "pay equity." Nevertheless, selecting these job classes sent a signal that the union acknowledged the undervaluation of female-concentrated professions emphasizing "feminine" nurturing skills.

Unsuccessful Attempts to Link Points and Pay in the 1990s

As the new Equitable Classification Plan for nonprofessional employees reached completion in 1990, the civil service unions, primarily the UAW, developed a two-tiered strategy for requesting pay adjustments: (1) using the plan to estimate a new differential between pay in female-dominated occupations and average wages and (2) pressuring the state to target the remaining $.40 of the PCELs-based disparity. However, the Office of the State Employer refused to accept the new methodology and denied that there was an implicit commitment to close the disparity completely. The state's earlier victory in *UAW v. State of Michigan* had been upheld on appeal in 1989, removing the litigation threat. A change of party affiliation in the governor's mansion at the end of 1990 also led to a policy of retrenchment in civil service industrial relations. No further special increases were awarded, and the new classification plan was never used as the basis for comparable worth adjustments.

The UAW brought a new calculation of the average salary line as an alternative to the PCELs methodology to the 1990 negotiations. The new salary line was based on a points-to-pay linear regression of the Group One Equitable Classification Plan. The UAW mapped salary lines corresponding to various point levels in the new classification system, then measured how much the female-dominated classes deviated from the expected salary for their point levels (see UAW Local 6000 1991: 15).

These negotiations took place following the election defeat of Democratic governor James Blanchard, but before Republican governor-elect John Engler assumed office. While the OSE did not explicitly accept or reject the UAW's methodology, they did agree to an additional $.03 per hour at each step of the base pay range for *all* Group One employees represented by the UAW, in addition to the 4 percent (or $.50 per hour, whichever is greater) across-the-board raise negotiated for the same year (UAW Local 6000 1991–93: Art. 43, Sec. A). Although, as noted earlier, most UAW members were in female-dominated occupations, it is significant that the increase was awarded to all Group One employees in the two bargaining units regardless of the gender composition of the job class (UAW Local 6000 1991: 16). The increase was also extended to non-exclusively represented employees on October 1, 1992.

While the OSE perceived the $.03 per hour increase as a pay equity adjustment that reduced the disparity to $.37, the UAW disagreed with this interpretation. Since the increase was not targeted to female-dominated job classes, the union continued to argue that these classes were entitled to an additional $.40 per hour based on the OSE's original calculation of the disparity utilizing PCELs (UAW Local 6000 1991; CSC, ERB 1991: 17). This disagreement was carried into 1991 negotiations.

Unfortunately, these negotiations were proceeding at a time when the new governor was advocating the need to reduce the state budget, "rightsize" state government, and increase subcontracting and privatization. The Michigan legislature was debating a bill to reject a 4 percent compensation increase already negotiated, authorized by the Civil Service Commission, and scheduled to go into effect on October 1, 1991. Governor Engler's Executive Budget did not include an increase in funding for civil servants, despite acknowledging the commission's approved raises. If the contract and budget were approved by the legislature, this meant that the pay raise would need to be absorbed by departments, probably through attrition and/or layoff; 2,900 additional layoffs were threatened.

Layoffs and planned layoffs had already affected more than 2,500 civil servants by April of 1991 (Whitbeck 1991a: 1). The Democratic-controlled state House of Representatives urged more negotiations between the unions, the Office of the State Employer, and the governor, and asked the parties to consider alternatives to offset the cost of the compensation increase. Meanwhile, the Republican-controlled senate rejected the pay increase. With additional political pressure, civil service employees did receive their commission-ratified 4 percent (or $.50 per hour, whichever is greater) general wage increase on October 1, 1991.

Layoffs and downsizing had an especially devastating impact on AFSCME's institutional unit, and their negotiations during this period centered on job security. Pay equity adjustments were placed on the back burner. On the one hand, the argument for pay equity wage increases came at a time of shrinking public budgets. However, Bell (1985: 294) argues that "pay equity represents an innovative wage strategy . . . offering a rationale for shaking loose money for higher wages from a tight-fisted state or local legislature coping with budget cuts." This was the strategy opted for by UAW Local 6000.

While the civil service unions, including the UAW, agreed at the bargaining table to an across-the-board compensation freeze in fiscal year 1992–93 to avoid further disemployment effects, the UAW continued aggressively to pursue additional pay equity increases. Given their membership, pay equity provided a justification for virtual across-the-board wage increases. In negotiations, the UAW again cited their linear regression of Group One employees overall and for individual bargaining units. The UAW argued that the relationship between pay rates and point values was stronger for classes in the male-dominated labor and trades unit and security unit (represented by MSEA) than for the classes in the female-dominated administrative support and human services units (see UAW Local 6000 1991: 20, 22).[20]

The UAW asked for equity increases ranging from $.07 to $1.05 per hour for seventeen mostly female-dominated job classes in Group One (such as assistant payments worker, library assistant, computer operator, and legal secretary) whose pay fell below the average wage line correlating ECP factor points with maximum pay. Management estimated the UAW-requested increases would cost about $11.5 million and argued that the state could not afford the pay equity adjustments. The issue went to an impasse proceeding in late 1991.

Documents from the Impasse Panel reveal quite a bit of disagreement between management and labor over whether a commitment existed to eliminate gender-based wage disparities completely. The UAW based its position on its interpretation of the task force recommendations as well as on prior Impasse Panel decisions (which supported the position that compensation should reflect job content) and a contentious "equal value" provision in Merit Principle 3 of the Pay Policy adopted by the Civil Service Commission in 1976: "Equitable compensation should be provided for work of equal value and incentives should be provided for excellence in performance" (CSC 1989: 4). Although the Pay Policy was written before comparable worth had been widely introduced into the political discourse over wage-setting, the UAW hoped to expand interpretation of the Merit Principle.[21]

The Office of the State Employer disagreed that the task force recommendations implied that the entire disparity should be eliminated. The adjustments already made complied with the task force direction to eradicate a "substantial" percentage of the difference between female-dominated wages and average wages. They also produced new statistics and questioned whether any disparity remained. Further, according to witnesses from the Department of Civil Service, the Equitable Classification Plan was not intended to dictate pay rates; the strong correlation between points and pay is not proof of an intent to link them causally (CSC, ERB 1991: 17).

The Office of the State Employer also insisted upon the importance of outside labor market rates and budget pressure in determining wages, and hired noted comparable worth opponent Mark Killingsworth, a labor economist, to testify. He argued that factor points in combination with market wages could explain current civil service salary levels (UAW Local 6000 1991; OSE 1991). The director of the OSE, William Whitbeck, argued that existing wage differentials were not based on gender, but rather reflected market wages—wages paid to workers in comparable private sector jobs ("Union to Negotiate with State to Increase Women's Salaries," *Ann Arbor News* 1992, January 14: A7). However, according to Sheila Strunk, former analyst and lobbyist for UAW Local 6000, the state is one of the largest employers in Michigan; it must affect market rates, and it is the market for jobs with no private sector comparators (Strunk 1992). OSE director Whitbeck summarized his perspective on the views of both parties: "The UAW's position was and is that there are continuing wage inequities manifest in the pay and classification systems. The Employer's position was and is that special wage adjustments have already been made which have addressed any inequities that may have existed. I believe it accurate to say that irreconcilable differences existed in September and continue to exist today with respect to this issue" (Whitbeck 1991b: 3).

In January 1992, the Impasse Panel decided against the equity increases sought by the UAW, pointing to a female-to-male wage ratio no lower than 95.17 percent for ECP levels 5–12, using maximum average pay for full-functioning or junior classifications within each level (CSC, ERB: 23). The Impasse Panel decision also maintained that the "wages paid to state classified employees compare favorably with those provided by other employers" (22).

Thus, the OSE, under political and economic pressures, appears to have backpedaled on its commitment to further pay equity increases, using "market factors" to justify different wage rates for job classes with comparable point values. While other civil service unions were preoccupied with job security and fighting wage freezes, the UAW (with the largest number of female-dominated job classes) maintained active pressure on management for additional pay equity adjustments.

As far as implementing pay equity through collective bargaining is concerned, the unions' success, temporarily at least, had run out. The reclassification was never used as the basis for comparable worth adjustments, the alignment of pay with evaluated points across female- and male-dominated job classes within a classification system. Pay equity claims in the 1990s have gone to the Impasse Panel and been denied. Reclassification, then, has become simply one instrument unions can try to use to persuade an unyielding Office of the State Employer and the Civil Service Impasse Panel to acquiesce to wage increases.

CONCLUSION

In sum, civil service unions have sought to follow up on the recommendations of the Comparable Worth Task Force and negotiate pay equity adjustments. The UAW, AFSCME, and SEIU successfully negotiated two special increases of $.20 per hour in 1985 and 1986 respectively, directly after the task force issued its report. Other, creative strategies were used to obtain pay increases for job classes which were not strictly female-dominated. In the fiscally and socially conservative climate of the 1980s and 1990s, success at the bargaining table was increasingly elusive.

Pay equity wage increases in Michigan, although not a direct result of the new classification plan, may have had an effect on raising the female-to-male median wage ratio within the civil service from 1985 to 1990 (see figure 3). The gender-based wage gap in the state of Michigan is on par with that of other pay equity states such as Minnesota, Iowa, Oregon, New York, California, and Washington (see Institute for Women's Policy Research 1993; Figart 1995). Michigan and these other states have wage gaps a few percentage points below the national average for state civil services. But a relative 12.5 percent reduction in the wage gap in the Michigan civil service from 1985 to 1990 is little more than the 10 percent decrease for the U.S. workforce as a whole for the same period (see Blau and Ferber 1992: 133).[22] In fact, the favorable trend reversed in 1991 and the wage ratio has stabilized, as displayed in figure 3.

It is more likely that occupational integration and affirmative action are responsible for the narrowing of the pay gap in the 1980s. The Department of Civil Service's *Annual Work Force Report* shows that the percent of women at mid-to-upper salary ranges has increased dramatically in the 1980s, reflecting the influx of women into middle management and the professions (see also Bass 1990). The state instituted affirmative action policies both before and after recommendations for affirmative action by the Comparable Worth Task Force. These gains, however, may have been undermined by cutbacks in state employment in the 1990s, as the wage ratio has fallen again since 1990. Pay equity advocates such as Heidi Hartmann, executive director of the Institute for Women's Policy Research,

Figure 3

Michigan Civil Service Gender-Based Salary Ratio and Gap

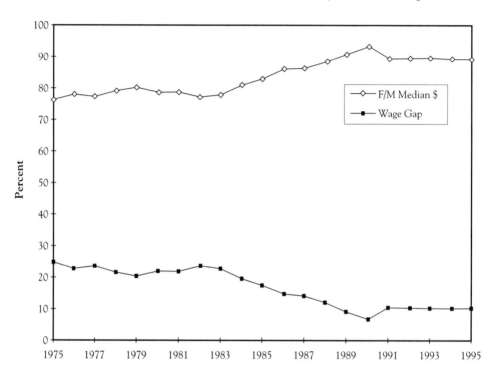

Source: Department of Civil Service [Michigan], *Annual Work Force Report*, various years.

have acknowledged that much of the decline in the wage gap nationwide is due to women's entry into nontraditional and integrated jobs as well as the decline in men's real wages (Hartmann 1993: 44–45).

The state of Michigan has spent between $19 and $26 million on pay equity wage adjustments between 1985 and 1990; not all wage adjustments were permanently added to base salary or directly related to the gender composition of the job class. The $26 million figure, an estimate made by Hartmann and Aaronson (1994) based upon information provided by the Michigan Department of Civil Service, includes a variety of pay increases. Nineteen million dollars is our more conservative appraisal of pay equity, encompassing only wage increases specifically linked to claims of gender inequity.

Clearly, the special pay increases targeted to incumbents in female-dominated job classes were pay equity increases: the two $.20 per hour increases to base pay in fiscal years 1985 and 1986. These increases, totaling about $18 million, were received by employees in four bargaining units represented by UAW, AFSCME, and SEIU, as well as by non-exclusively represented employees in comparable job classes. We would also classify as pay equity adjustments base pay increases for specific classes of employees in AFSCME's institutional bargaining unit who did not meet the strict 70 percent female definition. A rough estimate of the cost of this pay increase is about $1 million. Our estimate of state of Michigan expenditures on pay equity wage increases, only $19 million, is about .7 percent of payroll, less than many states which have implemented pay equity (see Hartmann and Aaronson 1994). We exclude those wage increases which were not linked to claims of gender inequity (including the one-time, lump sum Pay Inequity Fund of $2 million awarded to the UAW). Also omitted are what seem to be general wage increases (for example, a $.03 increase for all UAW members which the state counts as pay equity).

It is worthwhile to note that academic feminists and labor activists may have different notions of what constitutes pay equity. Jean Ross, a former SEIU national staffperson, views a broad pay equity approach as resulting in significant gains for women workers: "Much of the progress toward reducing the wage gap relied on . . . nontraditional bargaining strategies. . . . These victories are often inspired by the pay equity movement and have a similar impact, but receive little publicity and are often never termed 'pay equity,' due, in part, to employers' unwillingness to admit that they historically paid less for women's jobs than those jobs were worth" (1993: 50). This perspective suggests that we need to abandon a perception that pure comparable worth is somehow better or more feminist than diverse strategies to raise the pay of women's work and other low-paid work in the labor market.

Michigan civil service unions have attempted to negotiate broad strategies for achieving pay equity, as well as a technical comparable worth policy linking pay to points in the new Equitable Classification Plan. While unions were successful in negotiating limited pay increases for their members, they were less effective in challenging the fundamental wage-setting process, with its selective use of the market in setting relative pay. Management calculated the gender wage disparity, opted for across-the-board rather than class-by-class adjustments, used fiscal constraints to mitigate their responsibility to reduce the disparity, and refused to relate pay to the new classification system. The results did not take issue with (private) market interests. "Special" wage increases, as opposed to revaluing the work done in female-dominated jobs by consciously restructuring relative wage rates, were inconsequential in engendering demonstration effects in clerical and other labor markets. The negotiations process was overwhelmed by the constraints imposed by the political economy of Michigan in the 1980s and 1990s.

5

Points without Pay: The Reclassification Exercise

Both components of pay equity implementation in the Michigan civil service, reclassification and pay adjustments, followed from recommendations of the Comparable Worth Task Force. But implementation of pay equity was anomalous: reform was not done in the usual chronological order, where pay adjustments are derived from reclassification. In the previous chapter, we evaluated the limited pay equity wage increases won at the bargaining table, prior to the job reevaluation exercise. In this chapter, we investigate the reclassification exercise which began in 1986. Full implementation was completed ten years later. While civil service unions hoped that new job evaluation would be used to assess wage discrimination and adjust pay to correspond with new evaluated points, the civil service maintained the separation of pay from classification. According to the project director, Carol Mowitz, during the reclassification exercise the Department of Civil Service was careful "to educate people to the correct level of expectation, because pay was not involved" (Mowitz 1991).

The Comparable Worth Task Force found that the job evaluation and classification structure used in the civil service in the 1970s and 1980s, the Michigan Benchmark Evaluation System (MBES), had reinforced gender segregation of the workforce and contributed to wage discrepancies between women and men. The task force recommended that the Department of Civil Service remake the classification structure according to more gender-neutral principles. Specifically, the task force recommended that eleven gender-segregated Benchmark occupational service groups be consolidated into five non–gender-dominated groups. Gender-neutral factors of skill, effort, and responsibility should be used to evaluate all classes. The task force did not give specific instructions to the Department of Civil Service about the design of a new job evaluation system. However, from the beginning, the task force, rejecting the traditional route of conventional comparable worth implementation, made it clear that job evaluation and reclassification would not be an automatic basis for realigning pay.

Because the state separated classification points from pay, the reclassification exercise has been the aspect of pay equity most removed from pressures of the market and the Michigan political economy. As a result, the Equitable Classification Plan is the more creative and progressive part of Michigan's reform effort. The Department of Civil Service has been sensitive to issues of gender bias as it constructed factors and factor weights "in-house," breaking with the practices of leading job evaluation consultancies, like Hay Associates. The state did not evaluate the classification system for possible race bias (and the task force did not mention the racial composition of occupations) even though 20 percent of classified service employees were African-American. Further, while the five occupational groupings are not gender-segregated, they do maintain class distinctions in the sense of formal education and organizational authority.

This chapter begins by examining the limitations of classification systems in the civil service which preceded the new Equitable Classification Plan: the Position Comparison System, and the Michigan Benchmark Evaluation System. The new classification plan is then evaluated in some detail—including the group basis of reclassification, the choice of factors and factor weights, and the nature of position descriptions—in relation to women workers in the state. Despite the state's reluctance to link classification points and pay, we then assess Michigan's progress in achieving pay equity by correlating point scores with wages in male- and female-dominated job classes.

THE USE OF JOB EVALUATION IN PAY EQUITY

Job evaluation systems can be traced back more than one hundred years to the employment practices of the U.S. Civil Service Commission in 1871 and to the "scientific management" innovations of Frederick Taylor in the 1880s (Treiman 1979: 1). Their use in the private sector became widespread during World War II. A point-factor scheme marketed by management consultants Hay and Associates, probably the most widely used job evaluation system today, originated in the 1950s (Steinberg 1992). The major job evaluation systems, including Hay, were therefore developed in a historical period during which women's work was invisible and devalued. As late as 1980, job evaluation had not been studied by sociologists or psychologists and was practiced by consultants whose methodologies were viewed as "trade secrets" (Beatty and Beatty 1984: 59).

A decade of scrutiny of these systems by feminists and others has shown that these methodologies, far from being neutral technical tools, embody political choices that reflect, and have consequences for, the resources of women and men, manual and white-collar workers, labor and management. Feminists have identified discrimination in traditional job evaluation systems at various stages: in collection of position descriptions, in identification of compensable factors, in the weighting of factors, and in the establishment of pay policies. At all of these stages, women's work may be rendered invisible or undervalued (Feldberg 1987; Acker 1987, 1989; Evans and Nelson 1989a, 1989b; Haignere 1991; Blum 1991; Steinberg 1990, 1991; Neathey 1992). While contesting specific job evaluation practices, many feminists have accepted the general methodology of job evaluation, seen by personnel managers as a systematic method of job ranking, in order to reduce wage differentials due to occupational segregation by gender.

Traditional and comparable worth job evaluation both involve external wage comparisons with the labor market and internal wage comparisons within the organization. Job evaluation has customarily been used as one instrument in wage-setting to predict salaries for jobs for which sufficient market data is not available. "Benchmark" or key jobs for which market data are readily available are traditionally paid according to external market rates. Pay for related occupational categories is determined internally by point relationships to the benchmark jobs. Male and female job categories are rarely directly compared to each other. In contrast, the objective of comparable worth job evaluation is to assign similar pay to male-and female-dominated jobs—or job classes or classifications—with comparable evaluation points. A nondiscriminatory salary line is constructed by using existing pay rates for either the male, nonfemale, or average jobs in the organization. The salary line is likely to be influenced by market factors. The pay for female-dominated jobs is then ideally raised to the standard set by the salary line (see Sorensen 1994: 67–72).

When removing potential bias from classification systems, issues of appropriate technique are often controversial, driven sometimes by cost and policy containment. Employers who desire to minimize costs may seek to control or influence the selection of compensable factors and their weights during the job evaluation procedure. Costs can also be minimized in the process of linking points to pay, for example, in selecting a "bias-free" pay line or allocating funds for implementation. Ronnie Steinberg (1991) presents an excellent discussion of technical decisions and related strategies for containing pay equity by reviewing selected cases in the United States from 1972 to 1989. In Michigan, pay equity reform was contained less in the construction of the classification system than through the isolation of reclassification from pay-setting.

Michigan's Early Classification Systems

The Michigan Equitable Classification Plan (ECP) is the successor to two earlier state job evaluation and classification schemes. The Position Comparison System (PCS) was in place from 1938 to 1975. From 1975 to 1990, the Michigan Benchmark Evaluation System (MBES) determined job rankings.

The Position Comparison System was a single grading system with twenty-one grades. Classes and grades were delineated on the basis of ten factors, such as skill and responsibility.[1] However, there were no objective, standardized decision rules regarding the factors. Decision-makers conducted "whole job analysis," that is, considered overall job content in subjective rankings of jobs. Factors were not used consistently when personnel managers were asked to review existing assignments of jobs to grades, as George Minerick, a senior Department of Civil Service staff member, explained in a court deposition (*UAW v. State of Michigan* 1985).

Job classes were very specifically defined, with narrow experience and education requirements. In a system with approximately 50,000 employees, 800 of about 2,600 classes had between 1 and 3 incumbents. Twenty-one pay ranges were initially established for each of the 21 grades in the system; by 1972, there were 112 different pay ranges. Classification and compensation seemed in many cases to be departmentally and even individually driven. According to Minerick, the system relied upon "the squeaky wheel approach. Somebody hollered; you went in, and you did a patchwork job on it, but there was no comprehensive overall review" (*UAW v. State of Michigan* 1985, deposition August 12, 1986: 79). By comparing selected duties and responsibilities of one job with one of the less-skilled jobs at a higher level, individuals could manipulate the system. The growing unwieldiness of the PCS and a national shift to analytic point-factor evaluation and classification practices led to the adoption of the Michigan Benchmark Evaluation System (MBES).

Criticisms of gender discrimination by the Department of Civil Rights also contributed to the abandonment of the Position Comparison System. Job classes and grades were highly gender-segregated. Male classifications originally at the same grade or level and pay range as female classifications were moved into higher pay ranges over time.[2] The Michigan Department of Civil Rights argued that this classification and pay drift was one of several gender discriminatory practices (*UAW v. State of Michigan* 1985, plaintiff's findings: 3–13). These criticisms, however, preceded the broader, national comparable worth movement. Therefore, construction of the Benchmark system did not benefit from the feminist analysis of job evaluation.

Implemented between 1975 and 1981, the Benchmark system divided approximately 2,000 classifications into 11 separate service groups. Each service group consisted of from 41 to 461 separate classifications. The framework of the job evaluation varied from group to group, although similar general compensable factors were used across service groups. In a comment about the MBES in 1986, George Minerick said that the PCS was "a common ladder with 21 rungs while Benchmark was 11 different ladders, each with a different number of rungs, and those 11 ladders were independent of each other" (*UAW v. State of Michigan* 1985, deposition October 29, 1986: 6–7).

The Benchmark system reproduced previously existing bias against women's job rankings and pay in several ways. It separated men's and women's jobs into different gender-dominated service groups and applied different job evaluations and pay practices to the groups. The job evaluation instrument was flawed: it assigned fewer points to skills traditionally associated with women's jobs and could not pick up distinctions in skill levels associated with predominantly female classifications. Gendered pay ranges were carried over from the PCS system.

While six of the Benchmark groups were male-dominated, only two were female-dominated, and three were neutral. As shown in table 4, predominantly female classifications (and 88 percent of female classified employees) were clustered in four service groups: administrative support, human services support, human services, and institutional (domestic workers in state institutions). Over 40 percent of all female classified employees were in the administrative support group.

There is evidence that gender was a basis upon which these service groups were constructed. For example, while storekeepers and surplus property aides, mainly male, were initially assigned to the clerical service group because their work involved mainly record keeping, they were later moved to the labor and trades service group (*UAW v. State of Michigan* 1985, plaintiff's findings: 34). Liquor control clerks, a traditionally male class incorporating both heavy lifting and clerical tasks, were also all reassigned from the clerical service group to labor and trades. The separation of entry-level institutional workers from janitor-watchmen, of domestic service aides from janitor-watchmen, and of institutional attendant nurses from correction officers also maintained the gender segregation of service groups and the lower pay of female classes.

To rank job classes within each service group, the Department of Civil Service used Factor Evaluation Guides. The guides were used to evaluate job demands and assign point values. The Benchmark system point

Table 4

Occupational Segregation of MBES Groups and Average Hourly Pay in 1983

Service Group	Group Gender	% Female	Pay
Administrative Support	Female	94%	$7.92
Human Services Support	Female	77%	$9.26
Human Services	Neutral	67%	$12.03
Institutional (Domestic Workers)	Neutral	61%	$8.27
Business and Administrative	Neutral	29%	$14.75
Safety and Regulatory	Male	15%	$10.97
Security	Male	15%	$9.37
Scientific and Engineering	Male	14%	$13.50
Technical	Male	13%	$10.10
Labor and Trades	Male	9%	$9.60
Troopers and Sergeants	Male	3%	$12.61

Source: Department of Civil Service [Michigan], Occupational Segregation in the Michigan Classified Service, 1983, tables 2–4.

scores were used to determine each job's rank within a service group and to assign a pay range. Each job was evaluated on five compensable factors: knowledge (job) requirements; nature (difficulty) of work; responsibility; personal relationships; physical effort/work environment. There were also two subfactors for each of the five major factors (UAW v. State of Michigan 1985, plaintiff's findings: 21; DCS n.d.). The factor weights and maximum possible points for seven major service groups are depicted in table 5.

Factors were vaguely defined, with no uniform language across groups. Maximum point values attached to the five major factors also varied from group to group.[3] As implementation progressed, what seemed to be generic factor grids evaluating different service groups according to common criteria became more specific to each service group. The grids read more like arrays of particular job descriptions than like general factor definitions and degrees, according to the testimony of Norman Willis, a job evaluation consultant in the UAW's civil action against the state of Michigan (UAW v. State of Michigan 1985, August 3: 599–600). In view of this level of specificity, the evaluation system tended to recreate past gendered job hierarchies, rather than recasting these according to a gender-neutral evaluation of job demands.

Further, the Benchmark factors and their relative weights disadvan-

Table 5

MBES Factors and Weights for Seven Major Service Groups

Service Group	Knowledge	Nature Work	Responsibility	Personal Relations	Effort/ Env.
Business/Administrative:					
Factor weight	24.6%	35.4%	32.3%	5.8%	1.9%
Factor points	320	460	420	75	25
Total points = 1300					
Engineering/Scientific:					
Factor weight	24.6%	35.4%	32.3%	5.8%	1.9%
Factor points	320	460	420	75	25
Total points = 1300					
Public Safety, Security, Regulatory:					
Factor weight	31.7%	39.7%	20.6%	6.0%	2.0%
Factor points	400	500	260	75	25
Total points = 1260					
Human Services (Support):					
Factor weight	25.4%	36.5%	30.2%	6.0%	2.0%
Factor points	320	460	380	75	25
Total points = 1260					
Administrative Support:					
Factor weight	31.6%	36.8%	22.8%	6.6%	2.2%
Factor points	360	420	260	75	25
Total points = 1140					
Domestic Workers (later Institutional):					
Factor weight	37.2%	25.6%	25.6%	8.7%	2.9%
Factor points	320	220	220	75	25
Total points = 860					
Labor and Trades:					
Factor weight	37.2%	25.6%	25.6%	8.7%	2.9%
Factor points	320	220	220	75	25
Total points = 860					

Source: MBES factor grids; Alice Audie–Figueroa affidavit in *UAW v. State of Michigan* (1985).

taged the skills traditionally associated with women's work. For example, personal relationships could contribute only 75 maximum points to total scores, less than one-third to one-quarter of the maximum possible points for either the knowledge, nature of work, or responsibility factors (see table 5). Thus, human services workers dealing with difficult clients could command few total points based on their exercise of human relations skills. Supervision as a subfactor, on the other hand, seemed to be counted two or three times in most grids, under knowledge, nature of work, and level of responsibility factors (DCS n.d.; Audie-Figueroa affidavit, November 28, 1986; *UAW v. State of Michigan* 1985, plaintiff's findings: 24–26).[4]

Gender-based pay disparities remained evident in the late 1970s and early 1980s. Predominantly female classes were paid less than predominantly male classes, controlling for Benchmark scores, within the following service groups: human services support, engineering and scientific, human services, and business and administrative. An unequal points-for-pay relationship also applied across service groups according to both cross-evaluation on Benchmark grids by job evaluation consultant Willis and Associates and comparison on the basis of Position Analysis Questionnaire evaluation and point factor evaluation by Arthur Young and Company. Arthur Young's study of the MBES found a direct relationship between pay rate and gender composition of job, with male-dominated jobs receiving about $375 per month more than female-dominated jobs, and $225 per month more than mixed (neutral) jobs. These differences were not explained by differences in the jobs' evaluation scores (Arthur Young 1981: 105; *UAW v. State of Michigan* 1985, plaintiff's findings: 71–89). An internal study conducted by the Office of Women and Work (1981) found that gender composition of the service group was a statistically significant factor in pay. Also, as the percentage of females in the job class increased, average pay fell.

The Michigan Office of Women and Work also found that the Benchmark system's undervaluation of some skills and responsibilities was systematically related to the gender composition of job classes. Male jobs often received higher scores on responsibility, physical effort, and personal relationship factors than female jobs. Registered nurses (level VI), with responsibility for patients and evaluated at 500 points, were paid $1,636 monthly; groundskeepers (level V), a class rated at 455 points, were paid $1,665 monthly for being responsible for lawns (OWW 1980: 19).

An additional problem was that clerical workers were evaluated differently from all other service groups. Clerical support was the only service group differentiated in level and pay on the basis of work performed by the employee's supervisor. Workers who reported to clerical supervisors were allocated to lower skill levels and pay ranges than employees with similar duties who reported to nonclerical supervisors. The higher the position of the nonclerical supervisor, the more points a clerical worker could obtain for complexity and diversity under nature of work (*UAW v. State of Michigan* 1985, plaintiff's findings: 27; DCS n.d.).

Pay ranges for the Benchmark system were taken from the pay range under which most employees had fallen in the old position comparison system. Within the highly gender-segregated service groups—labor and trades, human services support, public safety, and administrative support—the previous rates were applied consistently to all classes in a skill level. But within relatively more integrated groups, such as human services and business and administration, the civil service maintained the previous distinctions between the pay of male and female job classes by assigning different pay ranges at the same skill levels (*UAW v. State of Michigan* 1985, plaintiff's findings: 28–36).[5]

The Karon Black/MSEA gender discrimination complaint filed with the Michigan Civil Rights Commission and Equal Employment Opportunity Commission and the subsequent class action suit filed by the UAW in federal district court called attention to the gender discriminatory practices of MBES. The legal case, the pressure of feminist insiders within the Office of Women and Work, and the work of the Comparable Worth Task Force set the stage for the development of a new classification and evaluation exercise in the state of Michigan, the Equitable Classification Plan.

THE EQUITABLE CLASSIFICATION PLAN

Development of the Michigan Equitable Classification Plan (ECP) began in 1986. The ECP involved collecting job data and updating position descriptions, developing new factors, assigning factor weights, testing the validity and reliability of factors, and rating job classes. Partly because of concerns about the suitability of Hay and other proprietary schemes for the public sector, the plan was designed internally. The first two phases (Groups One and Two) were the product of work by staff from the Department of Civil Service, with the assistance of an outside technical consultant familiar with job evaluation and potential sources of bias, Melissa Barker,[6] and labor-management advisory committees.

Each stage of the plan was developed first in "test classes" representing at least half of all employees.[7] The ECP only evaluated classes at the full-functioning level of each class series. Entry-level positions were automatically classified two levels below, apprentice or developing positions were classified one level below, and senior positions were classified one level above the full-functioning level. The process resulted in a job evaluation exercise which used relatively bias-free factors and factor weights, but within multiple job evaluation plans. Our assessment of the new classification plan, which follows next, discusses the issues of occupational groupings, factors and factor weights, and job specifications.

OCCUPATIONAL GROUPING AND SEQUENTIAL IMPLEMENTATION

Like the Benchmark system, the Equitable Classification Plan divides workers into groups and employs group-specific evaluation. However, the group structure of the plan is different from that of the Benchmark system. ECP planners, noting that occupations and jobs were gender-segregated in the Benchmark system, decided not to constitute the groups on the basis of occupational classifications but on the basis of education and supervisory responsibility. The Department of Civil Service specifically ensured, as the Comparable Worth Task Force requested, that Groups One and Two as a whole were not gender-segregated.

Group One is comprised of technical, office, paraprofessional, and service occupations. These classes are non-supervisory and do not normally require a bachelor's degree for entry. With more than 38,000 employees in 182 classes, Group One includes 60 percent of all civil servants. In descending order of size, the bargaining units in the group are: the United Automobile Workers (UAW), Michigan Corrections Officers (MCO, SEIU Local 26-M), American Federation of State, County and Municipal Employees (AFSCME), Michigan State Employees Association (MSEA), Michigan State Police Troopers Association (MSPTA), Service Employees International Union (SEIU), and the United Technical Employees Association (UTEA). Specific occupations in Group One are, for example, unemployment claims examiner, X-ray technician, word processing operator, police trooper, janitor, printing typesetter, and plumber. By combining predominantly female (e.g., secretary) and predominantly male (e.g., laborer) occupations, the state felt it would avoid the most obvious grounds for legal challenges of gender discrimination in evaluation, classification, and pay; that is, it would avoid the argument that it had used different bases of evaluation for predominantly male and predominantly female nonprofessional jobs.

Non-supervisory business and administrative, human services, scientific and engineering, and professional occupations comprise Group Two. These occupations normally require at least a bachelor's degree for entry. The group contains approximately 15,000 employees in 190 classes, including occupations such as dentist, building construction specialist, clinical social worker, registered nurse, facilities engineer, and parole officer. The business and administrative classes and most professional occupations do not have exclusive bargaining agents. Many of the other classes are represented by the Michigan Professional Employees Society (MPES), MSEA, UTEA, UAW, and AFSCME.

For Groups One and Two, reclassification was implemented in April 1990 and July 1993 respectively. As shown in figure 4, incumbents in these largest two groups represent approximately 84 percent of the civil service. Group Three combines nonprofessional supervisors without a four-year college degree (e.g., data coding supervisors, facilities managers) with professional managers. Reclassification of Group Three's 400 classes with 9,230 employees began in the fall of 1993 and was completed in March 1996. The smallest segment in figure 4, Group Four, contains more than 1,000 division directors and senior executives. Unlike Groups One and Two, no point factor evaluations were conducted for Groups Three and Four. Instead, positions were classified and ranked on the basis of internal managerial guidelines. A fifth group suggested by the Comparable Worth Task Force remains undefined and there is no current intention of assigning classes to it.

While the Benchmark System was highly gender-segregated, the groups in the Equitable Classification Plan were segmented by position in the formal organizational hierarchy: non-supervisory positions (Groups One and Two), supervisors (Group Three), and executives and administrators (Group Four). The civil service further differentiated non-supervisory jobs by education; the major distinction between Group One and Group

Figure 4

Distribution of Civil Service Employment in 1996

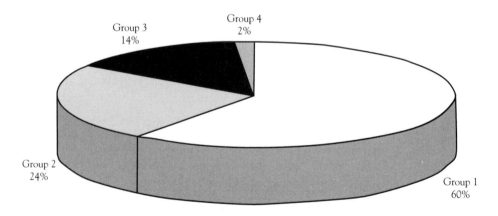

Source: Department of Civil Service [Michigan], Planning and Development Bureau.

Two is based upon possession of a bachelor's degree. Yet supervisory positions in Group Three and the most senior jobs in the civil service in Group Four, state executives, do not necessarily require a degree. State executives are defined strictly in terms of a reporting relationship with a politically appointed director or deputy director of a department.

In recommending multiple groups for evaluation, the Comparable Worth Task Force rejected an important comparable worth principle—using the same standard to evaluate all jobs within an organization. Most pay equity advocates argue that a single job evaluation system is vital for ensuring consistency in the evaluation of men's and women's jobs and for eliminating the devaluation of predominantly female jobs. According to the U.S. General Accounting Office, most states, and especially most pay equity states, have single job evaluation for their classified employees.[8]

Although Arthur Young and Company had successfully employed single job evaluation in a 1981 study of the Michigan Civil Service, high status, influential professionals such as physicians, psychiatrists, and attorneys rejected the idea of being compared with nonprofessionals.[9] Comparable Worth Task Force member Mary Brown, a senior Democratic state representative and advocate for women's issues, noted that "We also thought it would be easier to make equity adjustments within the three groups because you wouldn't have such a reaction against the idea of equity" (1993). Some job evaluation specialists saw multiple job evaluation as not only politically necessary, but as presenting administrative and methodological advantages. Michigan Civil Service officials, for example, thought that multiple job evaluation was a more manageable basis for gradually reclassifying two thousand Benchmark occupations (Slivensky 1992).

Technical consultant Melissa Barker (1994) reasoned that education (represented by knowledge or skill) is one of the primary factors in any job evaluation system. It would be, in fact, the major factor in a single job evaluation system. A skills factor would have to be sufficiently broad to allow for all possible levels of skill, types of education, experience, and abilities. The point range of the skills factor would be wide, and the number of maximum possible points very large. The factor would be heavily "loaded" and would possibly dilute the weight and importance of other factors. The emphasis on skill could severely diminish the responsibility factor for white-, blue-, and pink-collar workers such as nurses, corrections officers, state police, welfare case workers, and child care workers, for instance. Skill, as in the Hay system, would become not just the highest weighted factor, but the predominant factor.

Advocates of single job evaluation, including the Office of Women and Work in the Michigan Department of Labor, argue that compensable factors can be developed across all occupations, with appropriate levels or degrees of distinction (Remick 1984; Steinberg and Haignere 1987; Steinberg 1991; NCPE 1993). The Office of Women and Work, Women in State Government, and other supporters were satisfied that the Arthur Young system incorporated this sensitivity. However, because Groups One and Two are not gender-segregated, the Equitable Classification Plan does permit comparisons between the wages of female- and male-dominated job classes—unlike the Benchmark system. Therefore, for non-supervisory employees, the civil service averted most pay equity analysts' major criticism of multiple job evaluation plans (Treiman and Hartmann 1981: 78–80; England 1992: 204–5; Sorensen 1994: 66–68). Nevertheless, separate, group-specific job evaluation meant that the positions of highly-paid supervisors and executives (in Groups Three and Four) were not directly compared with the positions of those they supervise (in Groups One and Two). Since the ECP was not utilized to reform the state's pay policy, it could be argued that the classification plan's rankings are largely symbolic.

Factors and Factor Weights

Within each of the first two groups' reclassification exercises, the civil service has been attentive to feminist analysis of job evaluation in the selection of factors and factor weights. The general factor descriptions and their weights are virtually identical for Groups One and Two, yet the number and definitions of degree levels differ. Group Two classes are also assigned 1,000 unevaluated points, in addition to their job evaluation scores. Since the maximum possible point value in a Group One evaluation is 1,000, Group Two is thus loosely linked to Group One and designated as superior, perpetuating a symbolic class hierarchy.

To begin work on the compensable factors and their weights, the Department of Civil Service formed committees to seek involvement and input from interested parties, especially organized labor. A larger committee of approximately fifteen to twenty civil service staff, management, and labor representatives constituted the advisory committee (for Group One) to provide input on compensable factors. After two meetings of the full advisory committee, a smaller, six-member, technical subcommittee was formed for developing, reviewing, and refining proposals on factor definition and weighting. Labor and management were represented on the technical subcommittee, and worked closely with Department of Civil Service staff. From 1988 to 1990, the larger advisory committee met mainly to react to and approve the staff and technical subcommittee proposals.

On the recommendation of the Comparable Worth Task Force, the Civil Service Commission directed that the standard factors of skill, effort, and responsibility be used to evaluate jobs, be applied to all classifications within each group, and be bias-free and gender-neutral (CWTF 1985: 20–21). The ECP design team decided on factors and weights based upon surveys of other selected public jurisdictions—mostly state governments, such as Connecticut, Iowa, Wisconsin, and Ohio, that had revised their classification systems because of comparable worth initiatives—and internal discussion. They also reviewed the Hay and federal classification systems.

The civil service ultimately decided upon ten factors (without subfactors): knowledge and skill; judgment; responsibility (four factors); physical effort; mental/visual effort; work environment; and work hazards. The factors and their weights are arrayed in table 6 (see also appendix B for specific definitions of each factor). The weights vary from 27.5 percent for knowledge and skill to 5 percent for effort and environment. Each factor has at least three degrees of complexity. For example, degrees within judgment differentiate the extent to which employees make regular decisions without supervision.

However, Groups One and Two have different numbers of degrees within factors. Although the point spread between degree levels is constant within groups, it is variable across groups. The highest degree level is no longer ten times the weight of the factor in Group Two, as in Group One. There is no point overlap between Groups One and Two due to the 1000 unevaluated points assigned to Group Two classes. This creates a disjuncture in the classification system, although some classes in both groups occupy the same ECP levels and have comparable salaries.[10] These aspects of the plan contribute to its inconsistency and make skill comparisons across groups impossible.

While the Hay system has been criticized by feminists for relying upon three main factors and for emphasizing traditional, male-dominated responsibilities (see Acker 1989; Steinberg 1992), the Equitable Classification Plan seeks to assess and value a broader range of actual job behaviors. The Hay system depicted in figure 5, in contrast to the ECP, is based upon the three main factors of know-how, problem solving, and accountability. Each factor is divided into two or three subfactors; each subfactor is further divided into three to nine levels. Hay argues that this matrix covers the main factors that distinguish one job from another and gives sensible results. A fourth factor, (physical) working conditions, is sometimes used.

The main feminist criticism of Hay, and other traditional job evaluation schemes, is that "the factors measure as valuable the skills, responsibilities, effort, and undesirable working conditions differentially found in male work and treat job content traditionally found in female jobs as invisible, unskilled, and less responsible" (Steinberg 1992: 405; see also Wajcman 1991). Steinberg argues that Hay in particular treats the organizational dimensions of job complexity and responsibility as the only dimension of complexity and responsibility, severely limiting the scoring

Table 6

ECP Factors and Weights

Group One	Weight	Group Two	Weight
1. Knowledge and Skill	27.5%	1. Knowledge and Skill	27.5%
Degree 1 = 28 points		Degree 1 = 18 points	
Degree 2 = 89 points		Degree 2 = 73 points	
Degree 3 = 151 points		Degree 3 = 128 points	
Degree 4 = 213 points		Degree 4 = 183 points	
Degree 5 = 275 points			
2. Judgment	15.0%	2. Judgment	15.0%
Degree 1 = 15 points		Degree 1 = 10 points	
Degree 2 = 49 points		Degree 2 = 55 points	
Degree 3 = 83 points		Degree 3 = 100 points	
Degree 4 = 116 points			
Degree 5 = 150 points			
3. Responsibility: Financial and Material	10.0%	3. Responsibility: Financial and Material	10.0%
4. Responsibility: Well Being	10.0%	4. Responsibility: Well–Being	10.0%
5. Responsibility: Information	10.0%	5. Responsibility: Research and Analysis	10.0%
Degree 1 = 10 points		Degree 1 = 7 points	
Degree 2 = 40 points		Degree 2 = 37 points	
Degree 3 = 70 points		Degree 3 = 67 points	
Degree 4 = 100 points			
6. Responsibility: Communications and Public Relations	7.5%	6. Responsibility: Communications and Public Relations	7.5%
Degree 1 = 8 points		Degree 1 = 5 points	
Degree 2 = 30 points		Degree 2 = 28 points	
Degree 3 = 53 points		Degree 3 = 50 points	
Degree 4 = 75 points			
7. Physical Effort	5.0%	7. Physical Effort	5.0%
8. Mental/Visual Effort	5.0%	8. Mental/Visual Effort	5.0%
9. Work Environment	5.0%	9. Work Environment	5.0%
10. Work Hazards	5.0%	10. Work Hazards	5.0%
Degree 1 = 5 points		Degree 1 = 3 points	
Degree 2 = 20 points		Degree 2 = 13 points	
Degree 3 = 35 points		Degree 3 = 23 points	
Degree 4 = 50 points		Degree 4 = 33 points	
POINTS:			
Policy Band	100 - 1000		1300 - 1699
(Actual)	(176 - 828)		(1309 - 1626)
ECP Levels:	5 - 13		9 - 18

Source: Department of Civil Service [Michigan], Equitable Classification Plans, Groups One and Two.

Figure 5

The Hay Job Evaluation System

Factor 1: Know-how

Dimensions:

Technical (Knowledge)
Managerial Skills
Human Relations Skills

Range: from "Basic" to "Technical–Specialized Mastery"

Factor 2: Problem Solving

Dimensions:

Environment where Thinking occurs
Challenge presented by Thinking

Range: from "Strict Routine" to "Abstractly Defined"

Factor 3: Accountability

Dimensions:

Freedom to Act in organization
Job Impact
Magnitude (of program or budget in dollars)

Range: from "Prescribed" to "Strategic Guidance"

Factor 4: Working Conditions

Dimensions:

Physical Effort
Environment (exposure)
Hazards (risk of accident)

Range: from "Extremely Light" to "Strenuous"

Source: The Hay Guide Chart–Profile Method of Job Evaluation, Hay Group, 1986; Joan Acker, *Doing Comparable Worth*, 1989, Figure 3.1

of nonmanagerial jobs. In other words, Hay relies too much on formal position within organizational hierarchies and too little on direct assessment of actual job behaviors and tasks.

Knowledge and skills in the Michigan classification plan. In the Hay system, construction of the know-how factor contributes to gender bias. Know-how has three main subfactors: depth and range of technical know-how; breadth of management know-how; and human relations skills. Hay minimizes the importance of human relations skills, as it is a very minor subfactor of the know-how chart. Specifically, the subfactor depth and range of technical knowledge has eight major degrees of distinction with three levels within each degree. Breadth of management know-how is scored at seven different degrees, while human relations skills has only three degrees or levels. In addition, between the three levels of human relations skill there is just one 15-percent step, whereas between the central point of each level of breadth of management know-how there are two 15-percent steps (Trade Union Research Unit 1984: 11). The result is that the total possible point contribution of human relations skill is low compared to the point contribution of the other two subfactors of know-how (Acker 1987: 188–92; Feldberg 1987: 246–47; Acker 1989: 70–73; Steinberg 1992: 406–8). In addition, the Hay system magnifies the know-how scores and their biases by constructing its second factor, judgment or problem solving, as a percentage of know-how, rather than as an independent factor.

The Michigan Equitable Classification Plan, however, captures knowledge and skill directed toward care of others in the same general terms as other knowledge and skill. With five degrees, the knowledge factor for Group One differentiates carefully among different degrees of complexity. Unlike the Hay system, the ECP treats the factors of knowledge and judgment independently. The degree to which complexity of knowledge is assigned to nonmanagerial as compared to managerial jobs is difficult to assess without a comparison with Group Three.

In Michigan, there was spirited discussion between labor and management about the skills factor. The result was a factor which potentially better captures the content of female-dominated occupations. Initially, civil service staff proposed education and experience as two subfactors for skill. Labor representatives, acting as a coalition, proposed a single factor, such as knowledge and skill requirements, to replace the education and experience subfactors. They specifically suggested use of the state of Wisconsin's "knowledge required" factor. Knowledge and skill requirements would not tie a class to a specific educational level and would avoid "education labels." Labor argued that knowledge and skill would favor "behaviorally anchored [job] descriptions," claiming that these "protect against excluding people in the selection process who possess the KSA's [knowledge, skills, and abilities], but not the formal education" (Advisory Committee for Group One 1987, April 9: 4). Civil service staff favored education and experience as "more accurate." They argued that "education becomes a quantified label for the KSA's" (Advisory Committee for Group One 1987, April 9: 4), and that the experience subfactor should also be retained.

As adopted, the ECP defines the factor as skill and knowledge required to perform work assignments; the factor also refers to requisite education and experience. The wording appears to be a compromise between management and labor positions. It is difficult to ascertain the extent to which the two main terms of the factor definition (the term "skill/knowledge required" and the term "education/experience") may be in conflict, and, if they are, how such conflicts were resolved.

Responsibility in the Michigan classification plan. In developing the Equitable Classification Plan, the labor-management Advisory Committee for Group One was concerned about biases in evaluating responsibility (Advisory Committee for Group One 1987, June 12: 1). As a result, there are four responsibility factors: well-being, information, and communications/public relations, in addition to financial and material resources. In Group Two, the responsibility for information factor is replaced by a responsibility for research and analysis factor. Thus, the ECP diversifies the responsibility factor to include not only responsibility for financial and material resources but also responsibility for the well-being of others, for information, and for communications. This configuration of responsibility factors has been used increasingly in state employment since the 1980s. Alaska, Iowa, and Montana use similar systems. Responsibility for well-being appears to value client-centered work. However, in Michigan only one predominantly female job class, practical nurse, scores 100 points in well-being, while two male jobs, state police trooper and respiratory therapy technician, do so.

All four responsibility factors have four degrees of complexity. The first three responsibility factors carry weights of 10 percent, while responsibility for communications and public relations carries a weight of 7.5 percent (see table 6). According to Department of Civil Service technical consultant to the ECP Melissa Barker, responsibility for communications and public relations receives less weight because it is assumed that one mission of all state employees is to service the public and relate to citizens of the state (Barker 1994, May 18). However, an alternative would be to assign the factor a greater weight because the state particularly values service to the public. Many predominantly female job classes (such as receptionist, secretary, teacher, and human services worker) as well as some male classes (such as state trooper) might have benefitted.

The Hay system, on the other hand, tends to overlook the responsibilities associated with women's work. Steinberg (1992) argues that Hay defines autonomy only in terms of formal review relationships. Burton, Hag, and Thompson (1987) have also argued that another Hay subfactor, job impact on end results, tends to capture responsibility for money and supervisory responsibility for others, but to overlook direct responsibility for other people's well-being. A typical Hay guideline to evaluators is "If it can't be measured don't include it," yet much of women's work produces intangible, or at least not readily quantifiable, results (Burton, Hag, and Thompson 1987: 91-93).

Effort and work environment in the Michigan classification plan. Several of the other Equitable Classification Plan factors tend to render skills traditionally associated with women's work potentially more visible. For example, the plan includes not only a physical, but also a mental/visual, effort factor. Work environment as a factor mentions discomfort of dust, dirt, dampness, unpleasant odors, fumes. It does not mention cleaning dirt as equivalent to working in dirt, nor does it mention noisy, crowded offices. The work hazards factor measures threat of injury or illness, and conceives these threats as emanating from exposure to materials or substances which could result in injury or illness, from work with tools or equipment involving potential to cause significant cuts or injuries, and, at the highest degree, from violent and/or armed individuals. The wording of the hazards factor does not preclude attention to equipment requiring repetitive motion work or emissions from VDTs, although these equipment hazards are not listed explicitly. The SEIU expressed concern about whether the ECP recognized such job hazards. The union noted that prolonged operation of VDTs creates physical fatigue. While other classification systems have recognized this under a factor for physical effort, the ECP does not do so (SEIU Local 31-M 1991). It is also noteworthy that the hazards factor was developed and applied in a period of knowledge about and sensitivity to the HIV virus, and so could not overlook the sorts of hazards encountered by some women's health and human services occupations. However, in the Hay system, measurement of effort, environment, and hazards, though contributing limited points to total scores, is clearly biased towards traditionally male jobs (see Trade Union Research Unit 1984; Burton, Hag, and Thompson 1987; Acker 1989).

In sum, the construction of the ten *a priori* factors and factor weights in the Michigan Equitable Classification Plan made significant improvements over traditional classification systems such as Hay. Labor representatives succeeded in keeping the knowledge and skill factor broadly defined, although the quantifiable concepts of education and experience favored by management are incorporated into the factor definition. Judgment is treated separately. The four responsibility factors value accountability for people as well as objects. Ironically, responsibility for communications and public relations was weighted less than the other three responsibility factors, explicitly because service to the public is central to the state's overall mission. The effort factors for Groups One and Two include mental/visual as well as physical effort. The two working conditions factors, work environment (degree of comfort) and work hazards (risk of injury), are attentive to characteristics of women's health care and human services jobs, but less explicit about problems faced by clerical workers.

Job Specifications and Rating of Classes

Prior to evaluating jobs, the Department of Civil Service developed updated job specifications for the classes or occupations in Group One.[11] Burton, Hag, and Thompson (1987), Steinberg and Haignere (1991), and Neathey (1992) have called attention to the importance of bias-free position descriptions which describe behaviors, tasks, and functions of jobs accurately, comprehensively, and consistently. They have also noted characteristic problems in arriving at full and appropriate descriptions of women's jobs: women tend to under-describe their jobs, and supervisors and analysts tend to understate job tasks, often by using vague language.

For many job classes, it appears the Department of Civil Service relied upon old job specifications. For others, the department gathered new information in order to update position descriptions. They sent a job analysis questionnaire to a sample of employees in the test classes for Group One in 1987, a second job content survey to a sample of Group One test class employees and their supervisors in 1989, and conducted selected on-site interviews and observation.[12] The professional job analysts from the civil service staff who ultimately rewrote the job specifications based on the information gathered were trained in avoiding gender bias.

However, the use of the two questionnaires was in some respects problematic. The initial questionnaire had been developed without consulting the unions or the Advisory Committee for Group One and was sent to employees without notifying the unions which represented them. It was also not confidential, as employee responses were available to their supervisors. Finally, the sex of the respondents was known (Audie-Figueroa 1987). Several of the test classes, including corrections officer (MCO), fire and safety officer (MSEA), graphic arts designer (UTEA), practical nurse (AFSCME), resident care aide (AFSCME), and domestic care aide (AFSCME), had response rates below 40 percent (Advisory Committee for Group One 1988, May 20).

While the unions asked that the first survey be rescinded, management agreed only to supplement it with a job content survey for "verification." Worried that confidentiality might lead to employees' aggrandizing their jobs (Advisory Committee for Group One 1988, May 20), the civil service also surveyed supervisors separately. Although the (second) job content survey asked questions closely related to several factor degrees, it omitted any questions about responsibility and judgment, leaving supervisors and job analysts to define those characteristics. While the job content survey was detailed, there does not appear to have been any effort to guide or support employees in the completion of their questionnaires.

A job evaluation team composed of civil service staff used these job specifications to rate positions according to the ten factors.[13] That is, each position was awarded a specific degree on the factors, and this degree corresponded to a specific number of points (see table 6). Total point scores were then summed for evaluated job classes. Not all classes were factored, only the full-functioning or experienced level.

After job analysis and preliminary testing were completed for Groups One and Two, recognized employee associations and unions had the opportunity to appeal the factoring of evaluated job classes. The appeals procedure was put into writing by Joseph Slivensky, director of the Merit Systems Planning and Development Bureau within the Department of Civil Service (Slivensky 1990). The timeline for filing appeals seemed remarkably short. For example, the results of Group One were made available in March 1990 for implementation on April 1, and employees had to request review of their classification or level in writing by June 15. In contrast, after a new classification system was implemented in Tompkins County, New York, the appeals period was twenty months (Kates 1994b: 51).

The appeals process provides an indication of the politics, priorities, and bargaining strength of unions and Department of Civil Service managers. First, AFSCME filed no appeals in Group One, partly because of their longstanding frustration with the entire reclassification exercise. Their resources were also directed towards fighting privatization and preserving job security. UAW Local 6000 filed mostly unsuccessful appeals regarding the low factoring of over two dozen job classes. However, one of the UAW's largest classes, assistant payments worker, received a higher degree for mental and visual effort and thus more points after the appeals process; two other smaller job classes also had their points increased after appeal.

Aggressive appeals by SEIU Local 31-M, on behalf of eleven of twelve Group One classes in the human services support unit, included the most systemic critique of the ECP and its factors. Five of the appeals were successful. Among their arguments were that no factor existed for complexity of work, that continuous use of VDTs should be considered a work hazard, that there was little recognition and value placed upon difficulty or stress in communications, and that the entire system gave disproportional weight to some factors, causing male classes to outscore female classes (SEIU Local 31-M 1991).

Finally, the blue-collar units represented by MSEA appealed the factoring and/or ECP levels assigned in seventy-three job classes. One significant result of the MSEA appeals was that the four "licensed" skilled trades were awarded a higher degree on the communications and public relations responsibility factor, giving them enough points to be upgraded from ECP level 9 to ECP level 10. While none of the successful appeals had direct, immediate implications for pay, assignment to higher grades after appeal may have placed these predominantly male classes in better positions for future pay negotiations.

Assessment of the Equitable Classification Plan

What are the implications of the Equitable Classification Plan for gender equity in the Michigan Civil Service? The following discussion addresses this question from three perspectives. First, we summarize the state's own tests of the *a priori* factors and factor weights for gender bias. The results support the contention that the new classification plan represents progress in gender-neutral evaluation. Having established the relative equity of the ECP system, the points awarded within the system can be used to assess Michigan's progress in achieving the original goal of pay equity. We conduct our own regression analysis of Michigan's compensation system, constructing points-to-pay lines and testing for wage discrimination within Groups One and Two. We conclude that the pay equity adjustments negotiated in the 1980s have not fully remedied discrimination against female job classes. Finally, we briefly discuss the contribution of the reclassification exercise to administrative efficiency and career mobility. Reclassification has alleviated the problem of "topping out" for some employees, but has not been used to develop career mobility for women in dead-end jobs.

The State's Tests for Gender Bias

To assess possible gender bias in the new classification system for Group One, the civil service employed technical consultant Melissa Barker to help design tests of the validity and reliability of factors and any significant relationship between factors, evaluated points, and gender composition of occupations. Once testing procedures were developed and Group One reclassification was implemented, the civil service completed the tests for Group Two "in-house." The joint labor-management committees for Groups One and Two also continued to play advisory roles during testing. Statistical testing included comparison of underlying factor weights and policy weights, several difference-of-means tests, and multiple regression analysis.

One of the most important assessments was a comparison of the *a priori* policy-determined weights for each of the ten factors with their actual use by job raters. For instance, did points accumulated from the knowledge and skill factor, with an intended 27.5 percent weight, fall within a 25–30 percent band? Generally, Group One tests showed consistency between the policy weights and the underlying factor weights derived after job analysis. As shown in table 7, nine of the ten factors in the test classes were within the policy band. Three of ten factors did not fall within the policy range when all classes were ultimately factored. The greatest deviation was the high underlying weight of 33.4 percent for the knowledge and skill factor, a factor which received the highest weight in neutral job classes (see DCS, Merit Systems Planning and Development Bureau 1990c).

For Group Two, six of the ten factors had underlying weights which either exceeded or were less than the intended policy range. The underlying weights for two responsibility factors—research and information, and financial and material resources—were clearly greater than policy weights. While further review of these results would have been necessary to ascertain whether they indicate possible bias toward traditional professional and managerial responsibility, the civil service reported that the underlying and policy weights were nevertheless consistent and acceptable: "The relatively greater underlying weights for the responsibility factors appears [sic] to be appropriate for professional classes, and attributable to the [slightly] lower weight of the Judgment factor. This indicates that some of the significant ways in which job classes in Group 2 may be differentiated [from Group 1] is captured in the responsibility factors" (DCS 1992: 10).

For Groups One and Two overall, regression analysis and difference of means tests showed factors and their application to be bias-free in relation to gender (DCS, Merit Systems Planning and Development Bureau 1990c, 1993). Although few of the thirty-eight job classes in Group One with the highest scores on knowledge and skill are female-dominated, statistical tests found that the factor was not gender-biased.[14] However, statistical tests for Group One revealed that the two environment factors in the ECP, more than others, had some positive relationship with job gender, favoring male-dominated classes.[15] This association was present even before the two factors were altered to encompass four rather than three degree levels. The further differentiation of levels of complexity increased the relationship between these factors and gender. Since the aggregate relationship between factors, their weights, and gender was not significant, civil service staff and the advisory committee deemed this particular

Table 7

Results of Factoring for Group One Job Classes

| | | | Underlying Weights | |
| | | | Test Classes[a] | All Classes[b] |
Factor	Policy Weight	Policy Range	(n = 26)	(n = 171)
Knowledge and Skill	27.5%	25-30%	29.4%	33.4%
Judgment	15.0%	10-20%	13.4%	12.8%
Responsibility/Financial	10.0%	5-10%	9.6%	9.3%
Responsibility/Well-Being	10.0%	5-10%	9.8%	9.3%
Responsibility/Information	10.0%	5-10%	10.2%	10.1%
Responsibility/Comm. & PR	7.5%	5-10%	7.9%	7.1%
Physical Effort	5.0%	4-8%	4.5%	4.4%
Mental/Visual Effort	5.0%	4-8%	4.5%	3.6%
Work Environment	5.0%	4-8%	5.9%	5.4%
Work Hazards	5.0%	4-8%	4.8%	4.6%

Source: Department of Civil Service [Michigan], Merit System Planning and Development Bureau, *Summary of Testing of the Equitable Classification Plan for Group One Classes,* July 1990.

[a] Final underlying weights are listed. The weights changed slightly between approval of factors and weights and preliminary testing in February 1990 and final factoring in July 1990.

[b] Weights for 171 separate classes were derived from aggregating them into 55 "mega-classes" due to twice as many traditionally male as female job classes. The 171 classes were comprised of 92 male-dominated, 49 female-dominated, and 30 neutral classes. The 55 megaclasses included 19 male-dominated, 18 female-dominated, and 18 neutral job classes.

higher correlation acceptable. According to regression analysis performed by the Department of Civil Service, the relationship between percent female and each factor was even less for Group Two.[16] In particular, the relationship between the effort and environment factors and gender was less problematic than for Group One (DCS, Merit Systems Planning and Development Bureau 1993).

In discussing environment and hazards factors, it is important to keep in mind the distinction between the disparate impact of job evaluation factors due to bias in the classification scheme and other discriminatory employment practices. Women may be employed in jobs demanding less skill and responsibility or in jobs creating less environmental stress because of discriminatory recruitment and assignment practices (see for example, Roos and Reskin 1984; Reskin and Hartmann 1986; Burton, Hag, and Thompson 1987: 28; Reskin and Roos 1987; Tomaskovic-Devey 1993: 6). In fact, as discussed in chapter 3, the state of Michigan argued that its primary problem was not comparable worth pay discrimination but vertical as well as horizontal job segregation (CWTF 1985; Slivensky 1992). Thus, a correlation between environmental factors and gender of the job class may not be due to gender bias within the ECP, but to continued occupational segregation.

POINTS AND THEIR RELATIONSHIP TO PAY

The Equitable Classification Plan has not led to pay adjustments. Neither the civil service nor the Office of the State Employer has adjusted points-to-pay relationships after the Group One and Group Two reclassifications. During negotiations and hearings in 1991, the Office of the State Employer argued that the ECP was "never intended to dictate pay rates" (CSC 1991: 17). The pay equity wage adjustments negotiated between 1985 and 1992 were not related to the reclassification exercise.

One clear result of the separation of pay from the new ECP is that the gender neutrality of the state of Michigan's overall compensation system was never confirmed by a regression using evaluated points. Since analytic point factor job evaluation plans evaluate the worth of jobs to an organization by considering productivity-related factors such as skill, comparable worth advocates have argued that female- and male-dominated jobs with equal points should receive equivalent pay. The ECP can be used to assess whether wage discrimination in Michigan has been alleviated by special pay equity wage adjustments and other wage increases directed to lower-paid workers.

Group One points-to-pay. To assess possible wage discrimination against female jobs, a common technique in job evaluation is to analyze pay lines relating total points to pay (see, for example, England 1992: 206–

17). To plot points-to-pay lines and investigate possible discrimination, we utilized standard regression techniques described in appendix C. Figure 6 shows separate points-to-pay lines for female- and male-dominated job classes in Group One of the new Equitable Classification Plan. Classes were defined as male or female using the 70 percent definition. The maximum hourly wage is the dependent variable, and total factor points is the independent variable in a simple linear regression. We use the maximum hourly wage because the state used it for analysis of pay disparities, and roughly 80 percent of incumbents in each class are at the maximum pay rate for that class.

The male line lies above the female line, and the difference between the lines increases for jobs with higher point totals. The male and female job lines differ primarily in their slopes. When the male job line has a steeper slope and is above the female job line, this is evidence of discrimination against female jobs (England 1992: 209). A test of confidence intervals indicates that even though individual job classes vary from each line, there is a 95 percent chance that the male line is significantly above the female line.[17]

Figure 6

Group One Points-to-Pay, by Gender of Job Class

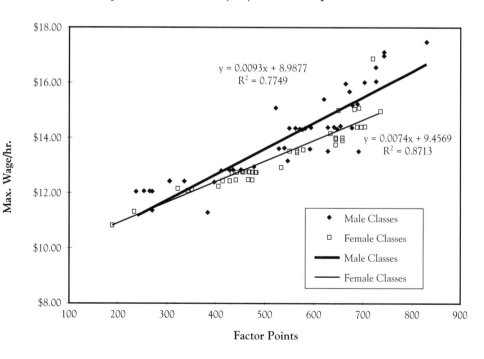

In figure 6, the different slopes indicate that the monetary return for each additional evaluated point is greater for male job classes (slope = .0093) than female job classes (slope = .0074). For each 100 additional evaluated points, male classes receive 93 cents whereas female classes receive 74 cents—a difference of 19 cents per hour. In short, male classes receive greater rewards for increased demands in the areas of knowledge, effort, responsibility, and working conditions. This indicates possible wage discrimination. Finally, the R^2 value for the regression on female job classes is higher than male job classes, demonstrating that points are relatively more of a predictor for pay in female than male jobs.[18] Considerations other than points are partly responsible for the relatively higher pay of male jobs. This is not surprising given the historical evolution of Michigan's compensation policy from the Position Comparison System where male classifications crept into higher pay ranges over time.

To further explore how gender is a factor in pay determination, we also estimated two multiple regressions using dummy variables for the gender of job classes (equal to one for female-dominated job classes) as well as ECP points. These procedures and tables of results are summarized in appendix C. Our results confirm that the gender of job class significantly affects pay. Specifically, the difference in monetary returns for female and male job classes is .002, or $.20 per hour for every additional 100 evaluated points. We find a significant negative correlation between female composition of the job class and pay.

Group Two points-to-pay. Figure 7 displays the points-to-pay lines for Group Two. The tests for Group Two seem ambiguous. Although the male line lies above the female line in figure 7, the lines are converging. Confidence intervals indicate that the slopes are not necessarily different. Visually, it appears that three male job classes with very high point scores (but lower returns for these additional points) are flattening the male line.

Among the professionals in Group Two, there is still evidence of a wage penalty associated with being employed in a female-dominated occupation. The female intercept is lower (a larger, negative number).[19] Because Group Two receives 1,000 unevaluated points, the difference in intercepts cannot be construed as a dollar measure of direct wage discrimination (see England 1992: 209). One result is clear: the R^2 value for the female line is much smaller than the male line, indicating that points are a much better explanation for pay in male, than female, job classes. For Group Two, it is likely that the market devalues female-dominated professions.

The effect of multiple job evaluation on classification and pay is most apparent when Groups One and Two are plotted on the same graph, as in figure 8. Group Two's negative intercept reflects the 1,000 unevaluated points. Although a comparison of job classes with the most points in

Figure 7

Group Two Points-to-Pay, by Gender of Job Class

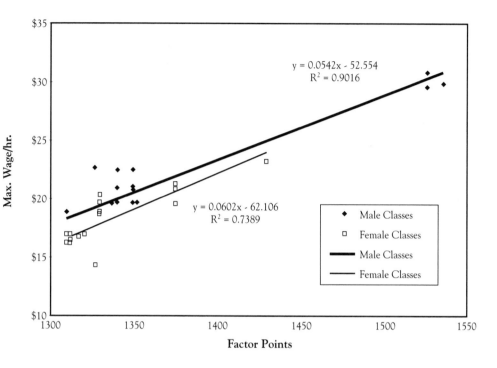

Group One and the least points in Group Two shows little difference in pay, more consequential is the nearly eight-fold difference in their slopes (.0089 versus .0696). The steeper slope for Group Two, compared to Group One, is indicative of the intrinsic value placed upon formal education. Such comparisons must be made with caution, however. A single pay line across all classes can not be constructed since Groups One and Two are incommensurate and pay is not consistently related to evaluated points.

It is not clear *a priori* whether female-dominated jobs, especially the lowest-paid jobs in Group One, would be helped or hurt by a single job evaluation system and a single pay line—provided the ECP were used for pay adjustments. Because the evidence of wage discrimination is unambiguous for Group One, the greater gender equality among professional workers could diminish estimated differentials if the groups were pooled. Additionally, the slope of a combined pay line for Groups One and Two would surely be steeper than the slope for Group One alone, but would the intercept be lower? What would this mean for hypothetical wage adjustments for jobs in the bottom of the organizational hierarchy?[20]

Figure 8

Groups One and Two Points-to-Pay

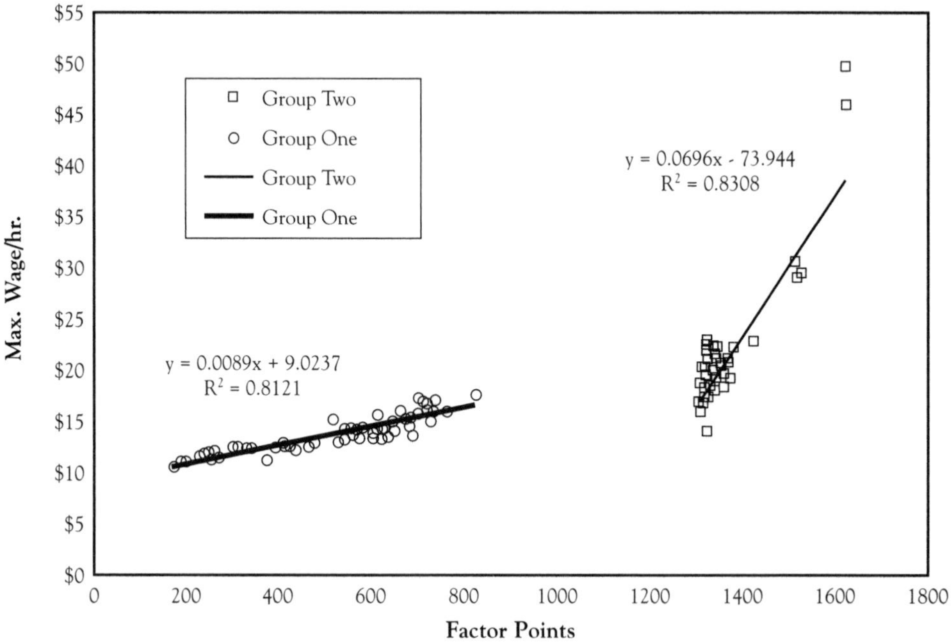

In sum, the reclassification exercise occurred in response to the documentation of the impact of occupational segregation by gender on wages. Although the Michigan Civil Service was careful not to link points and pay in a comparable worth context, it seems appropriate to use ECP points to evaluate the civil service wage structure. Our analysis indicates that wage discrimination still exists. Thus, even if the ECP truly reflects a classification scheme purged of gender bias, the lack of correspondence between ECP points and pay indicates that the civil service endorses the market's gendered pay practices.

ADMINISTRATIVE EFFICIENCY AND CAREER MOBILITY

If the new classification plan was not used for pay, it is worthwhile to explore whether it has had other tangible effects. In an April 1990 implementation announcement, the Department of Civil Service itself presented the Equitable Classification Plan as a mere simplification and rationalization of classification, emphasizing the benefits of administrative efficiency: "These classification system revisions will not change pay levels, seniority, benefits, or the makeup of employment units for collective bargaining purposes. The changes will make the classification system easier to understand, and more streamlined, with better identification of career ladders" (DCS, Merit Systems Planning and Development Bureau 1990b: 1).

The Equitable Classification Plan did standardize career ladders. Each class now has four levels: an entry position, a development position, a full-functioning position, and a senior position. Incumbents typically spend one year at the entry level and one year at the development level before being promoted to the full-functioning level. Under the Benchmark system, several nonprofessional classes (including public safety inspectors, investigators, and prison guards, predominantly male classes) had no senior track, stopping at the journey or full-functioning level. However, under the ECP, departments remain financially responsible for, and so must request, new senior posts.

In the clerical support classes under the Benchmark system, there were entry, journey, senior, and advanced levels, with a majority at the senior level. Under Benchmark the distinction between senior and advanced level was a reporting distinction—whether workers reported to a professional or supervisory clerical employee. This seemed an artificial barrier that created inequities. This distinction and the relevance of the reporting relationship to classification were eliminated in the ECP. Thus, ECP moved towards standards based upon skill levels and responsibilities rather than relationship to a boss as the basis for secretarial classification.[21] Also, in the ECP, a large number of secretaries, previously at the senior level, were reclassified as full-functioning. They thus receive the possibility of a further promotion to a senior level. However, the additional class represents not so much a career mobility program as a response to "grade creep," the tendency of large numbers of employees to reach senior grades relatively early in their careers and have no further promotion prospects. These new secretarial levels, like the other senior posts, also depend upon individual departments requesting them.

The attention to the actual content of jobs provided the Department of Civil Service with an opportunity to understand the content of and relationships among jobs more fully. The position description phase of ECP development, therefore, created a new potential for constructing more promotion opportunities for women and men. This potential could be acted upon by the Department of Civil Service (Barker 1994, May 31), as career progression opportunities have been developed and publicized in other public jurisdictions. However, the best example of a career development program for incumbents in female-dominated clerical jobs has nothing to do with the Equitable Classification Plan and, in fact, long preceded it.[22] In the early 1980s, the Michigan Department of Civil Service created a new job series entitled "department tech (trainee)." Clerical workers, for example, can obtain a two-year traineeship or apprenticeship to learn a professional job such as "analyst" in a particular department. Analyst jobs are currently in Group Two of the ECP. Michigan's effort is similar to several programs by public sector employers nationwide to advance employees within an internal labor market. Figart (1989) has summarized how public sector employers developed model programs to alleviate dead-end career ladders through labor-management cooperation. The cities of New York and Los Angeles and the states of Connecticut, Illinois, and New York State have implemented effective upward mobility programs.

CONCLUSIONS

While Michigan was a first-generation pay equity state in the sense that it carried out an early comparable worth study, it was a second-generation reclassification state. The earliest attempts at pay equity in state workforces focused on consistency, applying one job evaluation system to all job families and aligning the salaries of all jobs to one salary line, while underplaying gender bias in factors and factor weights (see Steinberg 1989: 14). Later reclassification efforts attended more to gender bias and the valuation of female-associated work demands in evaluation systems. The state of Michigan took into account limitations of the earlier state experiences and focused upon gender inclusivity, but more within than across groups. It has tried to ensure substantial consistency within broad strata of the workforce but only limited consistency across the workforce as a whole. Point factor evaluations were not even conducted for Groups Three and Four.

Michigan's Equitable Classification Plan has reduced gender bias within Groups One and Two, because it built upon new feminist knowledge of job evaluation and created a state-specific job evaluation scheme. ECP thus represents a considerable improvement over the Benchmark system, which was developed before the comparable worth movement drew attention to gender bias in job evaluation, classification, and resulting pay. The ECP also departed from some aspects of the proprietary Hay system, which incorporated gender bias.

However, the Equitable Classification Plan, like the Benchmark system, makes consistent job evaluation of the whole workforce impossible since it does not use a single job evaluation. By definition, workers in Group One cannot receive the same degree ratings on factors as workers in Group Two. As a union representative noted in a discussion of the judgment factor at an advisory committee meeting: "No matter what your experience, what you do, you're always going to be in Group I [One]"

(Advisory Committee for Group One 1987, April 9: 5). The message of multiple evaluation is that the knowledge, judgment, and responsibility of such predominantly female classes as executive secretary, legal secretary, paralegal, assistant payments worker, and unemployment claims examiner, for example, are incommensurable with the job demands of administrators and managers or professionals.

By employing multiple job evaluation plans and establishing four distinct groups based on education and supervisory and managerial responsibility, the ECP constitutes job hierarchies by means other than consistent job evaluation. The two bases of the group hierarchy—educational credentials and vertical position in the organizational structure—disadvantage women. A lower percentage of women than men in the Michigan labor force have college degrees (Sarri et al. 1987), although the gap is narrowing. This likely reduces the proportion of women with access to Group Two, a group designated as hierarchically superior to Group One. Furthermore, in the Michigan Civil Service, women were 23.3 percent of managers and administrators in 1992 (DCS, Management Services Division 1993), about 10 percent below the 1990 average for state and local government nationally ("Women Face Barriers in Top Management" 1991–92: 1). Except for supervisors of female-dominated job classes, many fewer women than men in Michigan government belong to Group Three. Insofar as the jobs hierarchy is based upon these groups rather than single gender-inclusive job evaluation, women are relatively disadvantaged. The group distinctions operate as hidden factors.

Michigan's reevaluation exercise may have been gender-balanced within non-supervisory groups, but it has had no direct implications for working women's pay. As in pay equity implementation in Tompkins County, New York, the state did not analyze the relationship between actual pay and the new classification system, "presumably because of the view that it was sufficient to check the new rating system for bias, leaving pay rates to be set through collective bargaining" (Kates 1994b: 57).

Would civil service administrators have aggressively pursued gender-neutral reclassification if cost containment had been a factor? Sorensen (1994) suggests that public personnel administrators generally seize on the pay equity issue as a means to enacting a new classification system and that they are relatively isolated from cost considerations. However, in the implementation phase, when pay is adjusted to point scores, political and economic factors intervene, resulting in "modified pay for points policies" (86). Job evaluators are often careful to distinguish, on the one hand, the points that a system arrives at for a particular job and, on the other, the wages allocated to the job. "What a job evaluation system tells us is what a job is worth to a company, not necessarily what the firm is going to have to pay for it" (Burton, Hag, and Thompson 1987: 7).

Thus, market rates, capacity to pay, seniority, and individual merit have traditionally intervened between point scores and wage rates. Similarly, the Comparable Worth Task Force of the state of Michigan argued simultaneously for non-discriminatory job evaluation and for the continued importance of market rates and ability to pay in wage-setting. The district and appeals court decisions in *UAW v. State of Michigan* reiterated that reliance on market wage rates rather than internal job evaluation for pay setting does not constitute unlawful gender discrimination.

Further, the Department of Civil Service has established a classification plan which seems to immunize it against the sort of legal challenges that were being brought in the early 1980s. Legal cases focused on the consistency of evaluation between predominantly female and predominantly male jobs within organizational strata (see Bureau of National Affairs 1984). The ECP, at least within groups, remedies such inconsistency. The 1981 legal complaint against the state of Michigan criticized the undervaluation of predominantly female as compared with equivalent predominantly male jobs in the state. In particular, the complaint made comparisons between secretaries and maintenance mechanics, typist clerks and laborers, domestic services aides and laborers, and registered nurses and physicians assistants (Black and MSEA 1981), occupational comparisons within the same ECP group. In addition, civil service staff have enacted state-of-the-art job evaluation and reclassification. They have rationalized the classification structure, incorporating equity considerations which are now an important part of public personnel practice.

Merely devising a gender-neutral system for evaluating the worth of jobs is not enough (Ames 1995: 723). Our statistical analyses show that systematic wage discrimination still remains. The policy containment of pay equity in the Michigan civil service partly derives from the explicit disjuncture of classification and pay policies. The legitimacy of market-based wage hierarchies was not effectively contested. In order to achieve monetary rather than symbolic gains for working women, feminist and labor activists decided to try to circumvent the civil service structure and bring their case through the political process. The next chapter discusses efforts to enact pay equity legislatively. These strategies shift the focus of pay equity implementation from comparable worth techniques to broad reform encompassing the private as well as the public sector.

6

The Pay Equity Network: Attempting to Deepen and Broaden the Reform

In 1985, activists in the Michigan Coalition of Labor Union Women (CLUW) established the Michigan Pay Equity Network (PEN) in response to perceived shortcomings of the Comparable Worth Task Force report. The Michigan Pay Equity Network was not influential in framing the Comparable Worth Task Force report, in winning wage gains for state employees, or in crafting the Equitable Classification Plan, though it made known its views on these developments. But beginning in 1986, the Pay Equity Network began to develop legislative strategies for achieving pay equity not only in the civil service, but also in the private sector.

The Pay Equity Network linked activists inside and outside state government and became a center of strategic thinking about how to strengthen reform. PEN attempted to draw upon organized labor's increasing attention to the needs of women workers, the Democratic Party's officially proclaimed support for pay equity, and the women's movement's concern for women's economic independence. Due to economic and political developments, however, labor, the Democratic Party, and the women's movement were focused elsewhere, on economic restructuring, fiscal pressures, and women's reproductive choice.

Focused mainly and doggedly on legislative reform for most of its history, yet without strong mobilization by its supporters, the Pay Equity Network failed to secure its proposed reforms of the Michigan Elliott-Larsen Civil Rights Act. Having never stood on the ground of grassroots organizing or consciousness-raising, PEN's impact on building a broad social movement was limited.

THE COALITION OF LABOR UNION WOMEN AND THE ORIGINS OF THE PAY EQUITY NETWORK

The Michigan chapter of the Coalition of Labor Union Women (CLUW) was instrumental in founding the Michigan Pay Equity Network. In the 1980s, CLUW was the largest national organization of trade union women in the United States and an inter-union organization with an agenda for women (Balser 1987; Milkman 1985). The increase in women's participation in the labor force increased activity among women in individual union organizations, and the rise of the women's movement contributed to CLUW's founding in 1974. The largest contingent at the founding conference was from the UAW, the international headquarters of which are at Solidarity House in Detroit. In some respects the founding of CLUW can be seen as a further development of struggles of union feminists within the UAW, who had fought gender discrimination by both management and unions in the plants. They had also identified and tried to overcome prejudice against women unionists at the highest levels of the UAW, and they had won union endorsement of the Equal Rights Amendment and interpretations of Title VII which declared protective legislation for women in violation of equal opportunities (Gabin 1990; Kates 1989).

While acknowledging the importance of organizing unorganized women, CLUW emphasized the empowerment of women trade union leaders, the advancement of an antidiscrimination agenda in the workplace, and the use of the electoral political process to advance the interests of women workers (Balser 1987; Milkman 1985). Its reliance on established union leaders and processes was quite different from that of 9 to 5, another feminist working woman's initiative, which stressed consciousness-raising and the diffusion of organizing skills among unorganized clerical workers (Milkman 1985).

Endorsement of comparable worth was implicit in many of the Coalition of Labor Union Women's early statements. In 1979, delegates to the CLUW national conference reaffirmed their commitment to comparable worth, calling for reevaluation of women's jobs according to their "real worth," and urging unions to adopt the concept of equal pay for work of comparable worth in all contract negotiations (Balser 1987: 194; Grune 1980: 141). Beginning in 1974, CLUW retained Winn Newman as its legal consultant. Newmann had pioneered comparable worth-type litigation against Westinghouse in the 1970s and continued to argue for comparable worth with an emphasis upon the illegal discriminatory nature of unequal wages for work of equal value (Madar 1992; Newman 1976; Newman and Vonhoff 1981).

Olga Madar, an early and forceful union backer of the Equal Rights Amendment, a former UAW vice-president, and a founder and first president of national CLUW, was a strong influence in the Michigan chapter of CLUW. Despite Madar's and Michigan CLUW's involvement with the comparable worth issue, coalition members had had weak links with even the trade unionists on the Comparable Worth Task Force. The preponderance of CLUW's membership was in private industry and the local public sector, to which most of their attention was directed. Several activists had also assumed that the task force would take necessary measures to remove pay discrimination because it was meeting during the tenure of a Democratic governor who once had strong ties to organized labor. In addition, three of the initial task force members—Paul Massaron, a UAW International representative, Barbara Roberts Mason, a Michigan Education Association (MEA) activist, and Mildred Jeffrey, a former UAW activist and longtime women's advocate—had been closely identified with labor. Task force members Yolanda Alvarado, Mary Brown, and Lawrence Glazer did not have direct union ties but were strongly connected to the state Democratic Party (Madar 1992; CLUW [Michigan] 1985d).

Coalition of Labor Union Women members were therefore surprised and distressed by what they saw as the shortcomings of the report issued by the Comparable Worth Task Force. First, the legal subcommittee and final report denied that illegal pay discrimination existed. Second, the report made no commitment to address discriminatory pay through immediate wage adjustments, and there was no recommendation that money be set aside for a pay equity fund. In addition, CLUW members were convinced that the report's failure to recommend a single gender-neutral job evaluation system was contrary to the accepted principles of comparable worth reform (CLUW [Michigan] 1985a). Finally, CLUW argued that the report implied that existing wage inequities were due to the collective bargaining process, though the Civil Service Commission itself was responsible. They read the report as a "false accusation against the collective bargaining process of the State," which could not go unchallenged. CLUW wanted to encourage the governor and citizens in general to put pressure on the Civil Service Commission to rectify gender-biased wage rates and establish single job evaluation (CLUW [Michigan] 1985c).

Because of these shortcomings, CLUW transformed what had been intended as a routine informational and educational conference on gender-based wage discrimination scheduled for August 1985 in Rochester, Michigan, into an advocacy and organizing conference. The Pay Equity Network was founded at this conference—only two months after the release of the Comparable Worth Task Force report. Sponsored by CLUW, in cooperation with the Ken Morris Labor Studies Center at Oakland University and with the Michigan AFL-CIO and affiliated unions, the conference was attended by about 150 trade union and other activists.[1] The concept of the Pay Equity Network was introduced at the last session and, following adjournment, about thirty-five organizational representatives met to establish PEN.

Nineteen people representing unions and other organizations, such as the Michigan chapter of the National Organization for Women, participated in the first organizing meeting after the conference on October 11, 1985. Participants established three categories of members: voting members, limited to officially designated representatives of membership organizations supporting the concept of pay equity (unions, non-union employee groups, women's organizations, civil rights organizations); supporting members (representing other organizations wishing to participate); and observers (individuals concerned with the issues). In maintaining an emphasis upon organizations as members, the Pay Equity Network reflected CLUW's orientation towards women already experienced in the labor movement and in organized politics (Milkman 1985: 314). In the emphasis given to organizational membership, the Pay Equity Network's structure resembled that of the National Committee on Pay Equity (NCPE), formed in 1979.[2]

The early concerns of the Pay Equity Network continued to be the fate of women in the Michigan Civil Service and the identified shortcomings of the Comparable Worth Task Force report. Consistent with the national position of the Coalition of Labor Union Women that unequal pay for work of equal value was illegal discrimination, the Pay Equity Network sought to hold the state of Michigan legally accountable for its classification and pay systems. PEN urged the MSEA and UAW to work together to continue to pursue Karon Black's lawsuit against the state of Michigan, and both the Pay Equity Network and the Coalition of Labor Union Women urged the UAW to pursue the case once it won the union recognition battle in 1985. PEN urged women in the legislature to press the Civil Service Commission to adopt a single job evaluation system. As its minutes and correspondence indicate, PEN tried to persuade the governor, the Department of Management and Budget, and the Civil Service Commission to set aside pay equity funds in the 1986 and subsequent budgets.

Meanwhile, the Pay Equity Network criticized the inadequacy of the pay equity wage adjustments negotiated between the UAW and Office of the State Employer in October 1985. Noting that the fragmentation of job evaluation systems made it difficult to assess the significance of the increases, PEN said that it would take eight years for women in entry-level clerical jobs to catch up to male laborers. If an increase of $.20 per hour were given to all women state workers each year, it would take nearly fourteen years for women's average pay to catch up with men's, the Pay Equity Network pointed out in an October 1985 press release. Polly Howe, an American Federation of Teachers activist and Pay Equity Network coordinator argued, "The Civil Service Commission ordered that comparable worth pay adjustments be completed in the next four years. It looks as though they are going back on their word right out of the starting gate" (PEN 1985, press release).

THE PAY EQUITY NETWORK'S LEGISLATIVE STRATEGY

Beginning in 1986, the Pay Equity Network began to canvass legislative strategies for achieving comparable worth for women not only in the civil service, but also in the private sector. PEN's legislative focus followed from several circumstances. First, the wage-setting processes internal to the civil service were inaccessible to Coalition of Labor Union Women activists, who were not civil servants. Michigan's labyrinthine and half-hidden civil service institutions had obscured pay equity developments from the view of activists and the general public. Legislative activity represented an attempt to make the debate about pay equity more public and more amenable to political pressure. Second, the legislative focus also seemed consistent with CLUW's general orientation of working systematically with existing organizations and within legislative systems to try to improve women's working conditions. The Pay Equity Network, like the Coalition of Labor Union Women, was something of an insiders' organization, a loyal opposition in the labor movement, and a legislative and lobbying network (Milkman 1985: 314). Olga Madar, who was prominent in both national and Michigan CLUW, had been closely involved with getting the Michigan legislature to ratify the ERA in 1972 (Madar 1992). Finally, other groups, such as the Democratic Party, the broad-based labor and women's movements, and official bodies like the Michigan Women's Commission, had failed to pursue legislative routes to broad pay equity policies for the state.

The Pay Equity Network, in fact, nearly single-handedly orchestrated the legislative effort for pay equity in Michigan. The organization began in 1987 to propose a series of legislative initiatives, altering their approach as employers and politicians resisted. Successive legislative strategies moved from placing heavier responsibilities for achieving wage equity on employers with somewhat less coverage of women workers towards limiting the onus on employers but formally covering more women. PEN's legislative strategies were serious attempts to define pay equity legislation that might be achievable and effective. Faced with an unfavorable political economy, the Pay Equity Network was unable to mobilize adequately its likely allies in the women's movement, organized labor, or the Democratic Party, and its efforts ultimately failed.

EARLY LEGISLATIVE EFFORTS

The Pay Equity Network began by examining the possibilities of amending the Wages and Fringe Benefits Act (1978) and the Minimum

Wage Act (1964) to require equitable job evaluation. Because of the limits of the two acts, however, both the Department of Labor and the Michigan Civil Rights Department suggested that PEN attempt to amend the Michigan Civil Rights Act.

In 1987 the Pay Equity Network instead embarked upon a strategy of drafting new pay equity legislation rather than amending existing labor legislation or amending the Civil Rights Act. Partly inspired by Canadian legislation, PEN's proposed act of February 1987 made employers responsible for using a single, gender-neutral job evaluation system; for eliminating wage disparities between female-dominated, male-dominated and balanced (neutral) classes; and for establishing equitable compensation relationships among covered employees. This "proactive" legislative proposal recognized the importance of a direct obligation upon employers to act to remedy gender-based wage discrimination. PEN proposed stronger legislation than the complaint-based equal-pay-for-work-of-equal-value provisions contained in the human rights legislation of (federal) Canada since the 1970s or the Equal Value Regulations of 1983 in the United Kingdom.

PEN's proposed act defined an employer as "a person, firm, corporation, or political subdivision of the state which employs 100 or more people in one or more establishments." Unlike the Manitoba legislation, which was limited to the public sector, the 1987 PEN draft, like the Ontario Pay Equity Act of 1987, applied to the private as well as public sector. However, small firms were excluded. The definition of employee was fairly ambiguous; there was no specification of whether part-time or temporary workers fell under the requirements of the act. The act would have established a Bureau of Equitable Compensation to oversee its implementation, an agency specifically responsible for and knowledgeable about pay equity.

By November 1987 PEN was working with a weaker draft that was more a job evaluation than a pay equity act, in that it did not include a requirement for pay adjustments. The act prohibited gender and race or ethnic discrimination in job evaluation systems; required employers to file a single, gender- and race-neutral job evaluation plan; and provided remedies and penalties for violations. The new draft provided fewer detailed requirements for employee participation in cases where there was no collective bargaining agreement and contained only a moderate penalty for failure to respond promptly and accurately.

Capitol Services, Inc., a legislative consulting firm with close ties to the Michigan labor movement, argued that reframing the act in this way would weaken employer objections while still maintaining pressure on employers to examine and correct their job evaluation and compensation practices. In particular they argued that apparently eliminating the goal of pay equity and requiring only that job evaluation plans be forwarded to the state would leave an employer objection to paperwork, but not to increased wage costs. Getting the evaluations done, however, would give the Pay Equity Network, unions, and other employee organizations data to use in contract negotiations and future legislative efforts. Because the courts by 1987 were unsympathetic to claims of comparable worth pay discrimination as sex discrimination prohibited by Title VII, a job evaluation showing discrimination in pay was not likely to expose an employer to legal penalties.

The November 1987 draft also moved enforcement responsibility from the Department of Labor to the Department of Civil Rights in order to reframe the issue as a civil rights matter. The Pay Equity Network hoped that while legislators might accept that compensation was a purely managerial prerogative, it would be more difficult for employers to convince legislators that their employees did not deserve civil rights. The new draft also incorporated language aimed at wage discrimination based on race and ethnicity.

AMENDING THE ELLIOTT-LARSEN CIVIL RIGHTS ACT

Work on a regulatory pay equity act was gradually abandoned, and in 1988 PEN began to work with legislators to introduce and pass amendments to the Elliott-Larsen Civil Rights Act and Michigan Handicappers' Civil Rights Act.[3] These amendments would define as violations of law an employer's failure to provide equal compensation for "work of comparable value in terms of composite skill, responsibility, effort, education or training, and working conditions." These amendments represented a complaint-triggered civil rights approach to pay equity, which shifted the onus of achieving equitable pay onto individual women workers. The amendments would require enforcement by the Civil Rights Department without, however, adding enforcement resources to the understaffed and underfunded department, which has traditionally been focused on race discrimination. Because of likely weak enforcement by the department, the amendments would in practice have been most helpful to unionized women with access to union legal resources. In view of the difficulties of unionized state workers in bargaining for pay equity, one of the amendment's main consequences might have been to give state workers another channel through which to press the Civil Service Commission.

However, the amendments to the Elliot-Larsen Civil Rights Act covered both the private and public sectors, defined "employer" broadly, and included many part-time employees. Amendments would have used the broad definition of employer under the Civil Rights Act, the persons or organizations responsible for setting employment conditions, a formulation that includes contractors and subcontractors, though not for "independent contractors."[4] The courts have also consistently held that regular part-time employees are covered under employment discrimination law, but there is some uncertainty as to how regularly or how many hours such employees must work to be covered (Larsen 1995). Like national civil rights law, the Elliott-Larsen Act also had limited exclusions based upon size, with firms employing fewer than fifteen workers not subject to the act.

In this legislative phase of its activity, the Pay Equity Network sought to mobilize its affiliated organizations and allies to support the amendments. PEN relied upon generating publicity through press releases, which it hoped would be picked up by the labor and general media; upon direct meetings with the governor's office and legislators; and upon writing letters to officials and official bodies. It tried to mobilize its affiliates and other labor organizations to do the same. As a labor women's network, PEN worked closely with organized labor and the women's movement, but also with members of the Democratic Party. However, representatives of the business community were well organized in their opposition to pay equity. Particularly in view of the economic and political developments in Michigan in the 1980s, both political parties generally deferred to business's proclaimed interest in unregulated wage-setting and lowered labor costs, which resulted in low wages for predominantly female work.

ORGANIZED BUSINESS AND THE AMENDMENTS

Private business interests in Michigan were well organized. Smaller business was represented by the Michigan Chamber of Commerce. The chamber contributed heavily to electoral campaigns and employed three full-time lobbyists. The U.S. Chamber of Commerce had voted in June 1984 to oppose "the theory of comparable worth." While it claimed to accept the concept of pay equity, it declared opposition to "any effort to implement into the workforce by government mandate the concept of 'comparable worth,' which would unnecessarily disrupt the labor market." It cited increased labor costs of $320 billion to employers and a 9.7 percent direct increase in inflation (Bureau of National Affairs 1984). The Michigan State Chamber of Commerce also issued an "Official Policy Statement Related to Comparable Worth" in April 1984, reaffirming its support for equal pay for equal work but "opposing any efforts which would establish as a matter of governmental policy or law a system of comparable worth for the compensation of employees" (Chamber of Commerce [Michigan] 1984).

At hearings on the Comparable Worth Task Force report in April 1985 the Chamber of Commerce, together with the Michigan Manufacturers Association and Michigan Merchant's Council, had spoken in favor of wage-setting according to market rates. After 1988, the chamber and other small-business groups opposed the amendments to the Elliott-Larsen Civil Rights Act. Their legislative analysis of the amendments labelled them, together with the increase in the state minimum wage, part of a pattern of "bashing the business community" to please organized labor in an election year. The chamber urged its members to inform legislators of their opposition.

Large employers in Michigan also opposed the amendments. Although the General Motors Corporation articulated no position on the amendments, it was a member of the Equal Employment Advisory Council, a group of large employers organized to oppose pay equity. Representatives of the Michigan Manufacturers Association and American Society of Employers (ASE) testified against the bills in November 1990. ASE argued that better pay in traditionally female jobs would institutionalize male and female jobs, that women could achieve higher pay by entering traditionally male jobs, that jobs have no inherent worth, and that employers should remain free to set wages as they see fit within the limit of existing antidiscrimination law (ASE 1990). In an interview in 1995, David Zurvalec of the Michigan Manufacturers Association stated his organization's opposition, emphasizing that the MMA was totally opposed to government involvement in wage-setting. "We took the view that the government could come in and do points, that the courts could end up imposing wages" (Zurvalec 1995). As market wage-setters with high wage costs and less labor intensivity than small business, large manufacturers were less concerned about increases in total wage costs than about interference with their freedom to set wages.

The Pay Equity Network organized support for the Elliott-Larsen amendments from women's organizations, organized labor, and the Democratic Party. However, as we argued in chapter 2, the priorities of these groups lay elsewhere, as women's reproductive choice remained under attack, as the core male constituency of organized labor and increasingly the feminized public workforce were threatened, and as the Democratic Party competed with Republicans as advocates of a deregulated business climate and reduced state.

WORKING WITH THE WOMEN'S MOVEMENT

Michigan members of the National Organization for Women supported pay equity in the 1980s but did not identify it as an organizational priority. According to the current president and long-time activist, Gloria Woods, "NOW did not have the luxury of defining its priorities in the 1980s, its priorities were thrust upon it" by the anti-abortion movement (Woods 1993). The organization continued to work on economic issues, but its economic priorities were poverty in female-headed households, child care, and health care, all issues affecting large numbers of poor women. Ironically, pay equity was not seen as a reform that could address poverty.

NOW was, nevertheless, affiliated with and active in the Pay Equity Network. It did not, however, testify at the November 1990 hearings on the amendments to the Elliott-Larsen Act. In 1993, with the recent election of the Clinton administration and what it hoped would be the end of the siege on reproductive rights, the conference of Michigan NOW listed economic justice issues, including pay equity, as their first priority after passage of the ERA (Woods 1993).

NOW was the largest and most general women's organization in Michigan supporting pay equity. But other women's organizations, such as the Michigan Federation of Business and Professional Women and the American Association of University Women, advocated pay equity in general and the amendments to Elliott-Larsen in particular. The Pay Equity Network succeeded in building support for pay equity in the Michigan Women's Assembly, an organization of the heads of most of the women's organizations in the state, and tried to increase the support of the Michigan Women's Commission.

ENLISTING THE SUPPORT OF LABOR

By the early 1980s, Michigan's AFL-CIO unions showed some limited interest in organizing women workers and capturing organized women workers for AFL-CIO unions. Women, however, were seen more as members for labor's battalions rather than as workers with distinctive gender-based concerns, such as pay discrimination and working time issues. However, under the influence of the Coalition of Labor Union Women, the increased entrance of women into the workforce, and changes in gender consciousness in society as a whole, the Michigan AFL-CIO became more sensitive to issues of women workers over the course of the 1980s. Overall, the Michigan AFL-CIO played a secondary role and tended to work behind the scenes rather than on the front lines of the Michigan pay equity movement.

In the early 1980s, the Coalition of Labor Union Women and others prevailed upon the Michigan AFL-CIO to support pay equity. In March 1983 the Michigan AFL-CIO listed among its Human Rights legislative objectives a recommendation to "amend the Michigan Equal Pay Act to extend its authority to unequal wages paid in traditional women's occupations where skills and responsibilities are comparable to occupations primarily held by men. At the present time, women benefit from the act only if their work is 'substantially similar' to men's work in the same establishment. The law should require equal pay for comparable work" (5). In every subsequent year, pay equity has been listed as a legislative goal, though legislation to make unequal pay for work of equal value illegal was not introduced until the Pay Equity Network took action in 1988.

From their first introduction in 1988, the AFL-CIO supported amendments to the Elliott-Larsen Civil Rights Act, and its lobbyist devoted some time to working with the Michigan Pay Equity Network and other groups on the amendments. In April 1990 the AFL-CIO supported the amendments to Elliott-Larsen in hearings before the House Labor Committee. In testimony, the state federation argued

> all discrimination is wrong, but wage discrimination is the most unjust because it robs those who need it most of fair treatment in the economic marketplace. Some claim that those who promote the concept of pay equity are interfering in the free market by telling an employer how much they have to pay their employees. This is not the case at all. Pay equity still allows the employer to determine the pay scales. All that it does is guarantee that when an employer sets those pay scales, the pay is based on the job itself and not on the race or sex of the people in the job. (Michigan House of Representatives 1990)

Three individual unions representing large female constituencies—AFSCME, the Michigan Federation of Teachers, and the Michigan Education Association—and the Pay Equity Network, testified in support of the amendments. The UAW, while not testifying, also officially endorsed the amendments.

However, the Michigan AFL-CIO conveyed few of the issues surrounding pay equity in general or the amendments in particular to member unions through its paper. The *AFL-CIO News* reported none of the pay equity developments for state employees, not even the large class-action suit undertaken by the UAW against the State of Michigan. Beginning in 1983, after the initial decision in the Washington state case, the *News* discussed pay equity approximately once a year, mainly in columns on the inside pages by national guest contributors. The Michigan AFL-CIO endorsed and publicized schools for women workers, including pay equity schools, run by labor education programs and the Pay Equity Network.

Working with the Democratic Party

Like organized labor, the Democratic Party, under the influence of the women's movement, had made organizational and policy commitments to women over the course of the 1980s. The state party had a women's caucus. For the state central committee and for policy committees the party had a rule mandating that men and women should be equally represented. The policy committee on Human Rights and Social Welfare regularly addressed a limited number of women's issues (Michigan Democratic Party 1980–88).

The Democratic Party at various levels also acknowledged the merit of pay equity. On the one hand, the party platforms on "Human Rights and Social Welfare" from 1981–82 indicate the party's endorsement of pay equity (Michigan Democratic Party 1981–88). However, the party's embrace of pay equity meant little to the behavior of individual Democratic legislators in an undisciplined, nonprogrammatic party system. The platform was not specific enough to be a policy statement, was not ordered to represent a list of priorities, and was not binding on individual legislators or the governor, the policy leader of the party.

The proposed amendments to the Elliott-Larsen Act and the Michigan Handicappers' Civil Rights Act consequently went down to a series of defeats in House committees with Democratic majorities and in the Democratic House as a whole, as well as in the Republican-controlled Senate. Representative Mary Brown, a member of the Civil Service Commission's Comparable Worth Task Force and a senior woman in the Democratic Party, was for a time Democratic caucus leader in the state House. In an interview in 1993, she recalled that there were not enough votes within the Democratic Party to pass the amendments in the late 1980s and early 1990s (Brown 1993). Even in the 1987–88 legislative session, when the Democrats had a substantial majority in the House and were strengthened by Blanchard's reelection, the amendments failed to be reported out of a Civil Rights Committee with a Democratic majority. Even efforts to introduce the amendments through the civil rights and judiciary committees rather than in labor committees failed. The retention of Trish Elms, previously a lobbyist for the Michigan Women's Assembly, also generally failed to pull the bills out of committees and onto the legislative floors. Democratic as well as Republican legislators were affected by the politically organized efforts of business, as well as the prevailing view that business needed market incentives rather than regulation to create prosperity (see Lindblom 1977, 1988).

In 1991 and 1992 PEN stepped up pressure on the Democratic Party and Democratic legislators. A resolution affirming the general principle of comparable worth and recognizing the specific need to pass the amendments was adopted by the Democratic Women's Caucus, but was not adopted by the August 1991 State Democratic Convention. In 1992 Millie Hall, president, and Olga Madar, legislative chair of Metro-Detroit CLUW, wrote to Lewis Dodak, the Democratic House leader, that the Democratic majority should act favorably on the amendments, partly in the hope that the party could show itself to be a supporter of women's rights and so appeal to moderate Republican, independent, and Democratic women in the forthcoming state and national elections. Their view was based upon the polling results of the *Women's Voices* study, commissioned by the Ms. Foundation for Women and the Center for Policy Alternatives. The poll had shown equal pay to be a high priority of women. However, in the months before the election the House Democratic leadership seemed to be more focused on enacting legislation requiring parental consent for abortion. The Coalition for Labor Union Women saw this as an example of Michigan Democratic legislators responding to and helping to create a conservative social climate by giving in to conservative notions of family values rather than working to create economic and social conditions under which women and men could better raise families and women as individuals would be treated equitably (Hall and Madar 1992).

Despite PEN's efforts, neither many Michigan Democrats nor Republicans in the late 1980s and early 1990s were willing to pass legislation which would have required private business to ensure pay equity. More precisely, the amendments would only have provided recourse for those women with legal resources who felt they were denied equal pay for work of equal value. The most politically organized constituencies of the Democratic Party did not demand action. The concept of comparable worth seemed to contravene "common sense" notions about both business freedom and gendered hierarchies at work. Business was careful not to frame the issue merely in terms of cost, but also in terms of justice, arguing that women should be treated equally and with dignity, but that comparable worth was not the right means of doing so. But Democrats as well as Republicans no doubt saw pay equity reform as driving up the cost of labor and inhibiting capital investment and job creation in an economy recovering from recession and undergoing major economic restructuring. Politicians depended upon private business to create jobs for the voters.

CONCLUSION

The Michigan Pay Equity Network, established by women active in the Coalition of Labor Union Women, took as its initial objective remediation of the serious flaws in the report of the Comparable Worth Task Force. Beginning in 1986 it devoted its energy to a broader legislative strategy for pay equity. But legislative efforts were not bolstered by successful mobilization that could maximize the prospects of legislative enactment, and the preoccupations of PEN's affiliates and allies made the issue a marginal one.

PEN's legislative formulations were a serious attempt to think through what sort of pay equity legislation would be most helpful to work-ing women in and beyond the state bureaucracy. The successive legislative strategies indicated a move from a heavier onus on employers with some-what less coverage of women workers to less onus on employers with some-what broader coverage. In the letter of the law and its symbolic or cultural impact, therefore, the amendments to Michigan's Elliott-Larsen Civil Rights Act would have carried pay equity beyond the well-organized state bureaucracy into the private sector. But as a complaint-based remedy, the amendments to Elliott-Larsen required individual women workers to be familiar with the law and initiate complaints, and the amendments might have provided additional legal pressure on the Civil Service Commission itself.

In 1990 Pat Curran, then director of the Office of Women and Work in the state of Michigan and a Pay Equity Network activist, reflected on four years of PEN activity: "The legislative efforts of the members of the Pay Equity Network have been likened to a roller coaster—a great many highs and lows. The lows have been the slow progress that has been made, and the highs have included the wonderful educational conferences and the . . . House Labor Committee hearing on [the bills]" (WSG, *WIRE*, December 1990: 3). In fact, the Pay Equity Network undoubtedly had an educational impact upon its own activists and upon those it reached through its three conferences. While we have not focused our study on the impact of the Pay Equity Network and other pay equity movement activity on the consciousness of women workers and labor activists, McCann (1994) and Blum (1991) conclude that an important impact of the pay equity movement was its ability to change the way women workers and labor activists thought about "the market," hierarchy at work, and the importance of unions in relation to women's labor market position. While the Pay Equity Network's legislative initiatives did not result in policy en-actment, they did keep the issue of gender-based pay inequity before the legislature and sections of the public. PEN also represented a network through which activists could exchange information and resources.

Nevertheless, PEN's legislative strategy was an "insider" strategy, reflective of some of the Coalition of Labor Union Women's traditions of thinking about change. Its confidence in the political power of insiders, displayed in its initial optimism about the Comparable Worth Task Force and the governor and in its legislative strategy, indicated an instrumental view of the state, a view that the right insiders could use the state to make radical reforms, rather than a more structural view that reform would be constrained by capitalist economic relationships and the power of orga-nized business. It was undeterred by the increasingly negative views of labor market regulation and "high" wage costs that won more representa-tion in the legislature and governor's office in the 1980s and 1990s. PEN did not focus on the uses of pay equity in organizing drives in the public or private sectors, as an informal demand in collective bargaining, or as a way of changing consciousness of the value of women's work within the union rank and file.

In seeking a more general version of comparable worth reform, a version that relied upon amending a civil rights statute, PEN undertook an ambitious pay equity strategy which encountered strongly articulated and well organized opposition from business, as well as unstated opposition or disinterest from other organized forces in the context of the politics and economics of the 1980s and 1990s. A small group of advocates—bureaucratic insiders, state civil service union leaders, and other union and feminist activists—was not enough to secure support for a bill with ramifications for the workforce of the private, as well as public, economy.

7

Michigan and the Future of the Pay Equity Movement

THE CONTRADICTORY MOMENT AND THE CONTAINMENT OF THE MICHIGAN REFORM

We have argued that the political economy—the political articulation of the interests of capital and labor, the interests of male and female workers, and the appropriate roles of the state and the market—have limited pay equity reform in the state government of Michigan. Along with other states, Michigan set up a task force, effected some structural reforms, and relied on collective bargaining agreements to adjust wages. Pay equity was constrained by an autonomous Civil Service Commission, political priorities which placed measures to improve the business climate over equality policies, and the downsizing of state government. The withdrawal of the state from its role as model employer and regulator of nondiscriminatory employment had a similar impact. The turn toward the market in both discourse and institutional arrangements reinforced the subordination of women through the market wage. As a movement which challenges the neutrality of market wages and the beneficence of market forces, pay equity thus contradicted dominant political and economic trends.

Implementation decisions also contributed to containing the Michigan reform. Other studies have focused upon intra-organizational dynamics and the administrative processes of pay equity containment. They have demonstrated how gender and class are recreated in organizations; they have called attention to the politics of technique within comparable worth reform (see, for example, Feldberg 1987; Acker 1989; Evans and Nelson 1989b; Blum 1991; Steinberg 1991). While acknowledging the importance of this pathbreaking work and using its insights, we have also argued that the state, the location of most pay equity reform in the United States, is a particular type of employer. On pay equity, the state's decision-making was related to a broader politics of the economy, of political parties, and of political debate about the state and the market.

Pay equity in Michigan developed at a contradictory moment in the broader political economy. On the one hand, women of all ages were entering and remaining in the labor force in the 1970s and 1980s. By 1980, women comprised 42 percent of the total U.S. workforce and their labor force participation rate was 52 percent and still rising. Women were increasingly responsible for supporting families and men's real wages were declining, rendering pay equity vital to working-class families as well as to women's own economic independence.

On the other hand, ending wage discrimination and revaluing women's work directly contradicted contemporary capital accumulation strategies. An economic order which had institutionalized relatively high wages for certain groups of men in Western nations was being replaced by a global economic system reliant upon a new international division of labor and feminization of labor (Standing 1989). Feminization of labor is both a strategy to use low-paid and contingent workers and an outcome of deindustrialization (Nash 1983; Jenson, Hagen, and Reddy 1988; Ward 1990; Parker 1994). The issues facing white male workers—wage concessions and unemployment—were not the same as those facing low-paid women in the service sector. The collapse of manufacturing employment displaced gender and race equity in political debate about the economy.

Equal opportunities policies and the women's movement raised women's expectations of their rights at work even as the Reagan administration deregulated the social relations of gender and race, as well as abandoned traditional economic stabilization and regulatory measures. The pay equity movement developed most fully in state government, reflecting the increased organization of state workers, the presence of advocacy agencies for women within state government, and the election of feminist politicians. But the movement developed in state government just as these employers were facing a fiscal squeeze. In the longer run, state governments and their workers were met with antistate politics.

Michigan represents an interesting and instructive case through which to explore this confrontation between the gathering forces of reform, the restructuring economy, and state politics. Extending from the late 1970s through the early 1990s, the state's reform was long-running. Michigan underwent a deep recession in the early 1980s and longer-term economic restructuring throughout the decade, focused largely on loss of market share in auto production. With an antitax insurgency, a moderate Democratic governor for much of the 1980s, and a growing conservative movement within the Republican party, Michigan politics reflected the widely diffused movement away from views of the state as a positive economic and social instrumentality toward the idea that an active state disrupts the benign, efficient, wealth-creating, and freedom-protecting market. It is particularly interesting that the Michigan economy was highly dependent on the automobile industry and that the long-serving Democratic governor had close ties to industry executives and labor. The industry itself was structured along rigid gender hierarchies and job segregation, a result not only of managerial strategy but of male workers' protection of their own higher-paying jobs (see Milkman 1983; Gabin 1990).

While some features of the Michigan political economy and industrial relations are unique, the broader issues raised by restructuring are not particular to this case. Economic restructuring is an international trend not confined to the industrialized Midwest. Michigan exemplifies the general tendency toward deindustrialization in the United States and other Western nations. Thus, Michigan's pay equity efforts illuminate the fate of reform over time, as national economies and politics change.

In emphasizing the politics of pay equity, we reject arguments that Michigan, due to fiscal constraints or a depressed economy, was unable to fund pay equity reform. During the period when the Civil Service Commission was considering pay equity, the Michigan economy sustained positive income growth. Though the economy as a whole was undergoing restructuring, it did recover from the 1980–82 recession. The unemployment rate was often higher than the national average, but employment grew at a rate slightly higher than the national average from 1982 to 1989. Real income per capita was above the national average each year from 1985 to 1989 (Department of Commerce [Michigan] 1991).

Most obviously, the political process often involves purposive and contested resource allocation not captured by measures such as income growth, per capita GDP, or similar macroeconomic measures. A policy-neutral measure—a fiscal capacity index constructed for American states—shows that Michigan was no more economically constrained from financing pay equity than other state governments which instituted significant pay equity reform. Table 8 presents the comparative fiscal capacity indices for twenty states that have undertaken major pay equity reform in state government.[1] Slightly below the national average, Michigan's index is higher than some states and lower than others. In 1984, Michigan's index was close to Oregon's, an early and nationally recognized pay equity state, and states with a wide range of fiscal capacity have undertaken pay equity.

In fact, fiscal capacity does not appear to correlate with expenditures from a pay equity fund. Relative to other major state pay equity reforms enacted in the 1980s, Michigan transferred neither the least nor the

Table 8

Fiscal Capacity Indices in Major Pay Equity States
(U.S. average = 100)

State	Year 1984	1986	1988
California	118	118	115
Connecticut	126	137	142
Florida	102	102	103
Hawaii	113	109	111
Illinois	98	97	100
Iowa	87	84	84
Maine	86	91	97
Massachusetts	110	121	131
Michigan	**93**	**96**	**96**
Minnesota	100	101	103
New Jersey	118	125	126
New Mexico	121	100	88
New York	100	108	110
Oregon	92	92	91
Pennsylvania	89	91	95
Rhode Island	91	100	100
South Dakota	83	77	78
Vermont	92	97	102
Washington	98	97	98
Wisconsin	89	86	90

Source: Advisory Commission on Intergovernmental Relations, *State Fiscal Capacity and Effort*, Report M-170, August 1990, table B-13. Reprinted with permission from Deborah M. Figart, Evaluating Pay Equity in Michigan: A Strategic Choice Perspective," *Industrial Relations* (April 1995): 273.

Note: The measure of fiscal capacity is the Representative Revenue System (RRS). RRS estimates statutory bases commonly taxed by state and local governments, as if each used the same (average) mix of tax instruments and using national average tax rates as weights.

most resources to underpaid workers in predominantly female job classes. Reallocating about 0.7 percent of payroll to pay equity, Michigan disbursed fewer resources than Vermont (11.8 percent), Oregon (9.8 percent), or Iowa (7.5 percent), three states with comparable or lower fiscal capacity indices in 1984 and 1986, but more than New Jersey (0.4 percent), a state with robust fiscal capacity (our payroll estimate for Michigan; Hartmann and Aaronson 1994 for other states).

The peculiarities of Michigan's civil service industrial relations give rise to another possible explanation for the containment of pay equity reform: institutional structure. The relative obscurity and independence of Civil Service Commission decision-making made it difficult to mobilize women's advocates for participation in agenda-setting and implementation. However, changing the institutional structure would not be a sufficient condition for generating a different policy outcome. It is unlikely that stronger legislative powers over the civil service would have ensured a different result unless there had also been strong mobilization by feminists, unionists, and Democratic leaders.[2]

Our argument is that while the pressure of the national pay equity movement and specific women's organizations inside state institutions moved Michigan to enact pay equity reform for state employees, strong class and gender interests in the larger political economy served to limit the reform. There is little evidence that pay equity was a priority for larger political forces in the state—the Democratic party, organized labor, or the women's movement—or that these forces held the balance of power in the legislature. Civil service unions pressed for pay equity in relative isolation from the male-dominated labor movement, which was preoccupied with plant closures and wage concessions in the auto industry. The Michigan women's movement was relatively weak and focused on reproductive rights issues.

Further, pay equity was undertaken reluctantly by the Michigan Civil Service Commission. The commission appointed its own task force to undertake political decisions about pay equity. The Comparable Worth Task Force, chaired by a former auto executive, included representatives of companies which employed large numbers of clerical and health-care workers. Union influence was marginalized, and members who were eager to defer to the market were a strong presence. Much of the limitation of reform took place at this early stage, when the task force's recommendations were officially adopted by the Civil Service Commission and set the framework for pay equity reform. The task force report rejected the comparable worth principle that pay for both male- and female-dominated job classes be consistently related to evaluated points. The task force invoked the state's "ability to pay" and the importance of market rates in determining wages. The final report, however, made some recommendations that drew upon debate and activity created by the pay equity movement.

The task force's technical choices were really political ones. For instance, it recommended a combination of affirmative action, special pay equity wage increases targeted to female-dominated occupations (to be negotiated by management and civil service unions), and a reclassification exercise to eliminate gender bias. The selection of the pay line, the conventional definition of predominantly female jobs, and the exclusion of an analysis of racial composition had significant implications for civil servants. Finally, pay adjustments and reclassification were separated, delegated to different agencies and assigned different time scales.

Class and gender interests continued to operate throughout implementation of the task force recommendations. Across-the-board special pay increases were awarded to female-dominated job classes in most bargaining units in 1985 and 1986, but these preceded and were separate from reclassification and had relatively little impact on gender-based wage differentials. While civil service unions sought additional increases for their lowest-paid members through a variety of low-pay strategies, the civil service maintained the separation of pay from the new Equitable Classification Plan. By 1990, it became clear that the reclassification exercise remained essentially a paper reform, incorporating feminist criticism of traditional job evaluation and recognizing women's previously devalued skills, but entirely separated from wage-setting policies. Once a relatively unbiased evaluation of the value of job classes within the organization was available, the refusal to link pay to points can be construed as a decision not to correct gender-based wage discrimination.

Michigan's pay equity reform did have limited positive material consequences for women working in the civil service. Although management's conservative estimate of the wage penalty against female-dominated job classes was an average of $.80 per hour, pay increases specifically targeted to these classes totaled only $.40 per hour, or an extra $7.00 to $8.00 per week, for the bargaining unit members who received them. As noted in chapter 4, the gender-based wage gap in the Michigan civil service narrowed during the implementation period; however, this reduction was only slightly greater than in the United States labor force as a whole. Regression analysis of evaluation points and pay rates indicate continued wage disparities between male- and female-dominated classes in nonsupervisory jobs. Thus, the wage adjustments did not eliminate measurable gender discrimination. The constraints on the negotiated wage increases clearly bear the imprint of political ideas that, given the general condition of the economy and fiscal circumstances of government, the state should not rectify identified gender discrimination.

The reclassification proceeded with somewhat more insulation from the politics of the economy, but was still conditioned by what sociologists have pointed to as the political tendency of job reevaluation to reproduce the administrative status quo. Unlike the pre-existing Benchmark Evaluation System and other traditional job evaluation systems, the Equitable Classification Plan valued skills associated with predominantly female jobs and occupations, giving significant weight to knowledge and responsibility related to caring work; to knowledge about and responsibility for communication; to mental and visual effort; and, to a more limited degree, to women's hazardous working conditions. However, while addressing feminist concerns in factors and factor weights, the civil service rejected the pay equity principle of using a consistent standard of analysis for all job classes. Employees were segmented by education and supervisory responsibility, and so the job evaluation presumptively maintained organizational class hierarchies.

The Michigan Pay Equity Network, an organization founded by activists in the Coalition of Labor Union Women, initially lobbied to correct the shortcomings of the Comparable Worth Task Force report. They subsequently attempted to amend the state's civil rights act, Elliott-Larsen, to create legal remedies for complainants who were not paid equally for work of equal value. In a long-running legislative effort, they faced the limited interest and capacity of their likely allies and the hostility of organized business. Especially in volatile economic times, legislators were less than eager to approve legislation bitterly opposed by business interests.

The discourse that justified the task force recommendations, pay negotiations, the reclassification exercise, as well as the rejection of broader legislative initiatives was that of the market: the market was argued to be the most efficient arbiter of wages and to necessitate conventional wage hierarchies. State managers and politicians also resorted to arguments about fiscal constraint, a concern that the state reduce spending and limit taxation, partly by privatizing state services. In a state economy historically linked to the fortunes of the auto industry, the power of corporate ideology in restricting the pay equity agenda is not surprising. In Michigan, the state has been the third largest employer after General Motors and the Ford Motor Company (Crain's Detroit Business 1994), and the potential demonstration effects of civil service wage policies, especially on private sector clerical labor markets, were great.[3]

THE FUTURE OF THE PAY EQUITY MOVEMENT IN THE U.S.

The case of pay equity reform in Michigan draws attention to the importance of thinking about the political economy in relation to the future of pay equity reform in the country as a whole. In a restructuring political economy, with the state under attack as diverting resources from the market and corporate strategies often emphasizing lower labor costs and labor flexibility, does pay equity have a future?

The large-scale, systemic, relatively technocratic efforts to create true comparable worth in state government will probably have limited usefulness. These efforts have always tended to exclude large numbers of women who are not employed in the state civil service sector or other large bureaucratic organizations. With few exceptions, the pay equity movement in the United States has had difficulty in expanding from public sector to private sector initiatives. In industrialized countries generally, the practice of comparable worth, at least through job reevaluation, does not seem to have been applied extensively. For the member countries of the European Union, the European Court has upheld the principle of equal pay for work of equal value written into the Equal Pay Directive of 1975. Yet in Britain, for example, individuals must take complaints through a cumbersome process, and large-scale job reevaluation is rare. For establishment- or economy-wide applications, the province of Ontario, Canada, remains an example of comprehensive legislation. Its 1987 act requires public and private employers to implement pay equity, even though implementation has entailed compromises and containment.[4]

Nevertheless, pay equity, broadly understood as addressing inequities in predominantly female jobs and occupations and as drawing upon the history of the undervaluation of women's work, remains an indispensable part of strategies for improving workers' economic status. Studies have repeatedly documented the existence of a gap between average or median full-time male and female earnings. Paradoxically, some of the recent reduction in the wage gap is in fact due to a decline in men's average earnings. Part of the remaining gap can only be explained by the gender composition of jobs. In addition, recent studies show increasing class divisions among women, with some professional women advancing, but more and more women overrepresented in the lowest paid jobs in the economy (see, for example, Kuhn and Bluestone 1987; Wagman and Folbre 1988; Danziger and Gottschalk 1993).

The pay equity strategies most closely allied to comparable worth, however, ought not to be seen as single solutions to the problems of low-paid workers in predominantly female jobs. The pay equity movement must be understood as one solution to the more general problem of securing a living wage for women and men in the restructuring economy, as well as a means for challenging gender inequity. Pay equity strategies need to become more informal and decentralized, to reach beyond the state sector, and to invoke powerful social arguments rather than technical and economistic ones. There are powerful arguments that increasing the minimum wage, restructuring women's work and their career ladders, and extending the coverage of employment legislation such as the Family and Medical Leave Act are also integral to alleviating wage discrimination. In the long run, national legislation that applies to both the public and private sectors would serve to strengthen local efforts both by setting standards and by making a cultural statement supporting equal pay for work of equal value. In the current political climate, the strategy of pursuing national pay equity legislation must be understood at least temporarily as a mainly educational one.

Restructuring and the Difficulties for Traditional Pay Equity

Economies enter periods of restructuring when sustained crises generate "major structural changes in the organization of work and the structure of labor markets" (Gordon, Edwards, and Reich 1982: 2). One aspect of contemporary economic restructuring has been a process of feminization. As previously noted, women's work, the jobs targeted by pay equity reform, predominate in the expanding sectors of the economy. However, there are other aspects of the structural reorganization of work which, while gender neutral on the surface, have implications for gendered employment practices and the future of the pay equity movement. Bakker (1991: 254) argues that these structural changes "may undermine the goals of current pay equity policies or, at the very least, dramatically challenge their effectiveness." Among the specific aspects of restructuring identified by Bakker as having implications for pay equity are the expansion of competitive product markets, privatization and contracting out, and functional flexibility.

Increasingly competitive markets and pay equity. As the case of Michigan shows, arguments for pay equity in the 1990s face objections that reform raises costs and renders U.S. industry uncompetitive by introducing labor market inefficiencies. Pay adjustments in the state sector, it is argued, increase taxes and the cost of labor in certain labor markets such as clerical work. Such arguments against state intervention (and demonstration effects) in private sector markets can be found in other jurisdictions. Writing from a Canadian standpoint, Bakker (1991) points out that a free-trade environment allows business to use competitiveness as a rationale for opposing pay equity regulations. However, Sorensen (1994) and others have demonstrated that pay equity reform has neither demanded large payroll shares in most organizations that have implemented it, nor has the adoption of equal value legislation rendered national or state economies uncompetitive (Kahn 1992; Gunderson 1994; Hartmann and Aaronson 1994).[5] Powerful social arguments dictate that wage discrimination must be rectified despite its costs, and we discuss economic equity arguments below.

Privatization and contracting out initiatives. While the state's interest in the profitability of the private sector has always blurred the boundaries between public sector and private sector labor markets, privatization and subcontracting of public services further clouds the distinction. Initiatives to restructure the state by diminishing its functions and separating state responsibility from delivery of services have occurred not only in Michigan, where they have intensified under the Engler administration, but also in many other states and localities. In the United States, where mainly state and local workforces have benefitted from pay equity, these initiatives remove some workers from coverage of the instituted pay reforms and suggest that progressively fewer women will be covered by pay equity reform located in the state government. In fact, a majority of public service jobs contracted out during the 1980s were jobs at the bottom of wage hierarchies, where women and people of color are concentrated. The state functions which most rely on contracting services—corrections, health, mental health, and data processing—employ the highest percentage of women and people of color (Schneider 1993; SEIU n.d.).

A recent British case illustrates the problem that contracting arrangements may pose for pay equity. School lunch workers in North Yorkshire recently won an appeal of an equal value claim in the House of Lords. Yet the victory may be a Pyrrhic one. The North Yorkshire local authority (the workers' employer) has argued that an internal bid incorporating equal value rates is bound to lose the competitive tendering round and that the women have essentially "priced themselves out of a job." Since 1983, local governments and the National Health Service have been required to contract certain services to the lowest bidders after compulsory competitive tendering.[6] The case therefore illustrates how, even when pay equity reform is secured in the public sector, new pressures on the state can claw back improved pay.

In Ontario and Canada generally as well as in Britain, where the private sector is held to a comparable worth standard, corporate restructuring and contracting out create similar possibilities of erosion and evasion. Employers may implicitly deregulate labor, as they shift employment to small firms not covered by pay equity law and/or to part-time, temporary, and home workers. They may also reorganize work so as to make location of a comparator, key to Canadian and British equal value claims, difficult.

Skill diversification and functional flexibility. Recent employer attacks on pay equity have stressed the trend toward greater flexibility in internal employment policies, including multifunctional jobs with rotating responsibilities and open job descriptions. Opponents charge that comparable worth job evaluation introduces rigidities into the internal labor arrangements of the workplace. And in the 1990s, flexibility has become ideologically linked to the concept of competitiveness. Open job descriptions, outsourcing, antiunionism, and increased use of contingent labor are all justified by the need to succeed in global competition. Opposition to pay equity based upon labor flexibility requirements adds a different substantive argument to previous objections that comparable worth would increase the role of government in the private economy and that pay equity policies would generate disemployment and inflationary effects (see

O'Neill 1984; Clarke 1984; Spigelmyer 1985; Lorber 1985; Killingsworth 1985, 1990; Paul 1989; Rhoads 1993).

Bakker (1991) argues that the trend toward skill diversification may contradict job classification and evaluation based on clearly defined job descriptions. While open job descriptions or descriptions which do not provide any clear delineation of responsibilities and tasks certainly pose problems for comparable worth job evaluation, it is not entirely clear that multiskilled jobs cannot simply be described in broad terms and properly evaluated. Rapid job reprofiling (rearrangement and redefining of job tasks), rather than multiskilling, may be more of a deterrent to use of timely job evaluation, though sound job evaluation involves reassessment of jobs at regular intervals. Yet job reprofiling also presents an important opportunity for women workers to demand compensation based on carefully and consistently assessed skills—if they are able to exercise power in the workplace.

TOWARD A BROADER, MORE DECENTRALIZED PAY EQUITY MOVEMENT

A number of these challenges suggest the importance of conceiving pay equity in broader, more decentralized, and less formal terms. The severe constraints on state employment make it vital to expand pay equity into other employment sectors. In addition, intensified global competition and public and private managerial strategies have decentralized labor relations and pay determination. As management pursues labor flexibility, it institutes local arrangements that address hours of work, job descriptions, and pay (Golden and Pontusson 1992; Hyman and Ferner 1994). Therefore, smaller scale efforts outside the large state jurisdictions are likely to assume greater relative importance in the pay equity movement.

There has, of course, always been a steady, only partly documented, stream of efforts to pursue pay equity on a smaller scale outside the large state jurisdictions. Many of these have occurred in cities and towns: San Jose, California (Blum 1991; Johnston 1994); Philadelphia, Pennsylvania (see McCann 1994); Contra Costa County, California (Blum 1991); Los Angeles (NCPE n.d.); and Tompkins and Nassau Counties in New York (Kates 1994b), for example. Others have occurred across the country in hospitals, schools, county social service departments, universities, newspaper offices, and manufacturing plants (see Kahn and Meehan 1992; NCPE *Newsnotes;* NCPE n.d.).

Although we have criticized the Michigan Civil Service for not utilizing its new classification plan for wage adjustments, we do not believe that job reevaluation is a necessary precursor to pay increases. Pay equity advocates need to abandon the perspective which views any deviation from traditional comparable worth as a compromise and uncover and encourage creative strategies at the grassroots level. Within individual work-places, jobs can be appraised on the basis of any crucial compensable factor (such as education), or some index of easily measured factors appropriate to the organization, rather than formal job evaluation points. For example, pay lines can be constructed in order to compare the wages of female-and male-dominated jobs with similar education requirements. This simplified procedure avoids the diversion of time, money, and other resources while permitting active employee involvement.[7]

Efforts to recognize the value of predominantly female jobs may or may not identify themselves as comparable worth or pay equity campaigns. Low-pay campaigns based on nontechnical appeals to justice and equity are not dependent upon employer cooperation in job reevaluation and may have greater mobilization potential than technocratic reform. Karen Brodkin Sacks (1988), for example, describes how data terminal operators at Duke University Medical Center, mostly African-American women, succeeded in getting their work reevaluated without job evaluation technology. Newspaper Guild members in Manchester, New Hampshire, and Eugene, Oregon, successfully launched "wage parity" campaigns to raise the pay of classified-advertising jobs closer to (historically male) sales occupations in the external labor market; job content factors were only one part of an aggressive bargaining strategy (NCPE n.d.). In chapter 4, we referred to a low-pay strategy utilized by three Michigan civil service unions. These unions negotiated flat-rate increases for the lowest paid workers since across-the-board percentage wage increases accentuate the gap between low-wage and high-wage workers.

One way of making pay equity more informal and decentralized is for advocates and negotiators to focus on the equal value claims of particular job classes in relation to others. This kind of practice is common in Great Britain, where the Equal Value Regulations require an individual (or group of individuals) to name a comparator (or comparators) rather than requiring employers to evaluate their entire workforce. Advocates in Britain are pressing for more collective remedies, as the equal value procedures are slow, time-consuming, and overly individualizing (Jarman 1994). Johnston's analysis of comparable worth campaigns in California also suggests that job or occupational exclusivity in comparable worth efforts might be divisive (1994). But outside public personnel or other large bureaucratized job evaluation systems and especially in the absence of legal requirements, less aggregated reforms that fall short of whole-workforce reevaluation may represent one of the few ways forward. For example, two successive contracts between the UAW, representing clerical workers, and Columbia University corrected internal pay inequities between clerical workers and maintenance and security-guard staff based on job comparisons (NCPE *Newsnotes*, Fall 1992, Fall 1995). Pay disparities between workers of color and white workers were also addressed. Similarly, office workers represented by the Office and Professional Employees International Union at Hofstra University in Long Island, New York, compared their jobs to the mostly male custodians, grounds keepers, painters, drivers, and locksmiths represented by the International Brotherhood of Teamsters. After a brief strike, cashiers, computer operators, secretaries, and mail room clerks received both general and "equity" wage increases (NCPE n.d.; NCPE *Newsnotes*, December 1989).

The argument for diffusion of pay equity outward and downward presupposes, however, an organizational infrastructure outside the public sector that can help carry such efforts forward. Most pay equity initiatives have relied on unions to assist women in developing a collective identity and marshalling collective resources to carry through pay equity demands.[8] In order to advance their pay in female-dominated jobs, women need unions and other organizations which take their particular issues as women workers seriously.

The debates about the causes for and solutions to low levels of unionization in the service sector, where women work disproportionately and many predominantly female jobs and occupations are located, have been well rehearsed and remain urgent (see Green and Tilly 1987; Shostak 1991; Cobble 1993; Hurd 1993). One set of arguments—that unions and union culture have marginalized women—is currently being addressed by the labor movement. Since the election of John Sweeney, former president of the Service Employees International Union, as president of the AFL-CIO in 1996, resources targeted to organizing women and low-paid minorities in the service sector have increased significantly. Also addressing this issue, Cobble (1994) recommends a postindustrial unionism, which would organize workers not tied to one employer or location (including temporary workers and home workers) and negotiate multi-employer contracts (see also Carré, duRivage, and Tilly 1994). Such unionism might emphasize occupational identity, control over labor supply, peer determination of performance standards, and portable rights and benefits (as many skilled craft unionists have). Fudge (1993), also interested in extending women's organizing networks beyond traditional workplace bargaining units, recommends changing structural elements of labor law to permit "new forms of broader-based bargaining and inclusive unionism" (244). Her formulation, however, suggests more national, industry-wide and less occupationally based organization of bargaining units. In the short run in the United States, a drive toward aggregated representation may submerge the interests of women in predominantly female jobs. Predominantly female unions with female leadership and female union culture are more apt to advance issues such as pay equity. However, in the long run, Fudge's inclusive union model might overcome "the deeply fragmented, gendered, and hierarchical labor market which currently exists" (1993: 244).

One future possibility for the pay equity movement is the development of occupationally-based national networks supportive of local initiatives. The 9 to 5 (National Association of Women Workers) model of pre-union organizing, which emphasizes the realities and skills associated with clerical work and empowering women at the grassroots level, remains relevant. The association has educated workers and put pressure on employers in local communities to improve pay and working conditions.

Child-care work also provides a strong basis for such an occupational network. The devaluation of child-care workers has been a continuing concern of the pay equity movement. In 1975, Witt and Naherny noted that the third edition of the *Dictionary of Occupational Titles*, a standard reference produced by the U.S. Department of Labor, rated the skill and complexity required by dog-pound attendants and zookeepers more highly than nursery-school teachers or day-care workers. Pay equity advocates have subsequently repeated Witt and Naherny's observation that evaluators had confused the responsibilities and demands of a paid job with stereotypical notions about women's nature; child-care workers' wages reflect the association of women's paid and unpaid work. The pay of child-care workers is also of concern to childrens' advocates, who have used pay equity language in some of their publications and launched a Worthy Wage Campaign. Here, the relationship between women's pay and the public need for services is clear, providing a potential for worker-child advocate and other coalitions (see Strober, Gerlach-Downie, and Yeager 1995).

The Child Care Council of Westchester County, New York, for example, is in the process of rewriting detailed and evaluative job descriptions for child-care workers in a manner that highlights levels of skill, responsibility, and knowledge, mental demands, and working conditions. This represents an attempt to use comparable worth "talk" and job descriptions structured on comparable worth categories to further the goals of upgrading child-care workers in the absence of a formal job evaluation (Power 1994).

Broadening the pay equity agenda beyond comparable worth should also encompass less static approaches to raising women's wages. Traditional comparable worth techniques base pay equity adjustments on the average wages or maximum wages in specific job classes in an organization. However, even if work is revalued in the short run, many women and people of color are employed in dead-end jobs. Thus, women's pay over the life cycle is also affected by wage mobility within and between occupational categories. A career development program involves identifying dead-end jobs within an organization and awarding longevity increases, providing employee training, or establishing elongated career ladders through job restructuring. In contrast to affirmative action, which seeks to improve women's economic status by facilitating individuals' access within existing job structures, career development programs seek to recognize and reward skills in traditional women's work. Initiatives can range from formal reviews of personnel systems to informal labor-management agreements.[9] Although economic restructuring has led to the decline of job ladders in traditionally male manufacturing industries, career development programs targeted to female-dominated occupations in individual workplaces provide a decentralized approach to pay equity and are an important component of a broad-based strategy in the long run.

A ROLE FOR NATIONAL PAY EQUITY LEGISLATION IN THE UNITED STATES?

The historic relationship between law and the pay equity movement in the U.S. is dichotomous. Legal language and legal hopes have catalyzed national and local pay equity movements, yet comparable worth cases have tended to fail in the federal courts. The introduction of the new Fair Pay Act in the U.S. Congress by Representative Eleanor Holmes Norton is a recognition of the limits of Title VII of the Civil Rights Act of 1964 and an attempt to reinvigorate a labor-feminist-civil rights coalition behind a reassertion of rights at work by joining a variety of possible provisions involving employer obligations and complaint-based remedies. Its introduction and possible passage are compatible with informal, decentralized pay equity strategies.

McCann (1994) has shown that the visibility of legal cases and the use of the language of rights at work had a catalytic impact on local pay equity movements in the early 1980s. Early legal decisions opened the door to claims of intentional gender-based wage discrimination that fell outside the scope of equal pay for equal work. By the mid-1980s, litigation based on the belief that an equal pay for work of equal value standard was implicit in Title VII was failing. While legal decisions such as *Gunther* motivated Michigan and other state employers to investigate their compensation systems, less favorable court decisions subsequently minimized public and private employer perceptions that they were at legal risk. It was on this downward slope of legal support for comparable worth that the UAW case in Michigan failed as a Title VII claim. It is unlikely that the courts will now read a prohibition against unequal pay for equivalent work into Title VII.

The new Fair Pay Act, therefore, attempts to amend the Fair Labor Standards Act of 1938 with explicit comparable worth language.[10] (The

Fair Labor Standards Act created a federal minimum wage; the Equal Pay Act of 1963 was an amendment to this act.) The Fair Pay Act would prohibit different pay for "equivalent jobs" on the basis of gender, race, or national origin. Equivalent jobs is defined to mean "jobs that may be dissimilar, but whose requirements are equivalent, when viewed as a composite of skills, effort, responsibility, and working conditions" (H.R. 1507: Sec. 3 [4] [B], 104th Congress).

The Fair Pay Act does not require, as did a Michigan Pay Equity Network proposal, the filing of nondiscriminatory job evaluation plans, nor the filing of nondiscriminatory pay plans, as does Ontario law. Rather, it would allow individual complaint-triggered litigation on the basis of comparable worth principles, with technical assistance provided to employers, labor organizations, and the public by the Equal Employment Opportunity Commission (EEOC). Most importantly, the act would require employers to file annual reports with the EEOC; the reports would disclose wage rates by occupation or job title as well as the gender, race, and national origin of employees within those positions. In a move similar to Michigan's 1982 amendment to its Wages and Fringe Benefits Act of 1978, it would forbid retaliation against anyone who inquires, discloses, compares, or otherwise discusses wages with any other person.

Unlikely to pass in a Republican-controlled Congress, certainly in its entirety, the variety of strategies embedded in the act make it a useful educational tool. Passage of even some of these provisions would also serve local organizing purposes. For example, the mere stipulation that wages ought to be public would allow workers to investigate wage scales and make internal and external wage comparisons. In the private sector, where employers often attempt to keep wages secret and present pay as an individual matter, the obfuscation of pay rates for predominantly male and female occupations contributes to inactivity on pay equity. Similarly, regular access to wage information can ensure that pay equity wage adjustments are not a one-time fix. Any pay equity reform needs ongoing review of both classification and pay so that wage drift doesn't erode hard-won gains. By demystifying internal wage hierarchies and shedding light on employer pay policies, the law might therefore be an important catalyst for local action. The national legislation also suggests another local strategy: state-level initiatives to pass such pay-disclosure laws.

Future legislative efforts on pay equity should expand the definition of employer to ensure that workers in small firms, home workers, part-time workers, temporary and other contingent workers, geographic floaters, and subcontractees are covered. Too often employers elude and employees are excluded from coverage under existing legislation such as the Fair Labor Standards Act, the National Labor Relations Act (NLRA or Wagner Act), the Family and Medical Leave Act, and Title VII of the Civil Rights Act.

Under current labor law the definition of a bargaining unit best fits workers employed permanently by one medium- or large-sized employer in a fixed location. Although we do not explore possible revisions to labor law here, any successful effort to amend the NLRA, such as models of representation that have been discussed and proposed by the Commission on the Future of Worker-Management Relations (the Dunlop Commission) would certainly assist the pay equity movement (Commission on the Future of Worker-Management Relations 1994, 1995). To complement changes in labor law, Carré, duRivage, and Tilly (1994) propose regulatory change in the short run, mandating wage and benefit parity between full-time and part-time and contingent workers coupled with adoption of universal key benefits such as health care (see also duRivage 1992).[11]

LINKING PAY EQUITY TO OTHER ECONOMIC EQUITY ISSUES

Six out of ten of all working women are employed in female-dominated occupations, a potentially broad constituency for social change. According to a poll for the National Committee on Pay Equity, 77 percent of U.S. voters would support a pay equity law. The responses in a recent Ms. Foundation and Center for Policy Alternatives *Women's Voices* project and the U.S. Department of Labor Women's Bureau *Working Women Count!* questionnaire show that equal pay is one of the top priorities of concern for women in the United States. Nevertheless, for pay equity movements to be revitalized, it is essential to link the issue to other campaigns for economic equity. Fundamentally, this entails addressing the perception that pay equity is primarily an issue benefitting white, middle-class women in female-dominated professions.

One basis for redefining the pay equity movement is linking the issue to antipoverty and welfare rights struggles. Women in female-dominated occupations find it difficult to support families; the percentage of women earning less than the official poverty level for a family of three ranges from 15 percent in administrative support to 54 percent in the category of "other services" (Lapidus and Figart 1994). Case studies in the United States and the United Kingdom suggest that pay equity reforms, especially those targeted to the lowest paid or most undervalued grades, contribute to the alleviation of household poverty (Acker 1989; Evans and Nelson 1989b; Blum 1991; Hastings 1992; Kautzer 1992; Sutton 1992). Lapidus and Figart (1994) have calculated that comparable worth wage increases mandated nationwide in the U.S. and implemented at the establishment level would reduce women's poverty significantly. Still, recent welfare reform initiatives are based on the spurious assumption that movement from welfare to the labor market will move women and children out of poverty.

General economic policy which targets poor, low-paid workers, such as an increase in the federal minimum wage, could also help achieve the goal of pay equity. Because it targets low-wage workers, many of whom are employed in female-dominated jobs, raising and maintaining the real value of the minimum wage would go a long way toward helping the economic status of working women and reducing the gender-based pay differential (see Figart and Lapidus 1995). However, discussions of minimum wage policy generally overlook the gender of the breadwinners, even though roughly 60 percent of all minimum wage workers are women, and many are working year-round, full-time (Mellor 1987).

Further, as women's work becomes the economic base of a restructured economy, the importance of pay equity for working families, both dual-earner and female-headed, can form the basis for political alliances. Stronger labor, feminist, and other community alliances need to be constructed through local mobilizing and through national efforts by organizations such as the National Committee on Pay Equity. Kautzer (1992) and Ladd-Taylor (1985) have argued that the Yale University clerical and technical workers' strike in 1984 succeeded partly because union organizers identified the issue of women's low pay and built intra-workforce and community alliances around it. The reaffirmation of the importance of human services—such as child care, health care, and social services—can also be the basis for such alliances. Johnston (1994) has shown that the women of San Jose, who struck successfully for comparable worth in 1981, formed inter-occupational alliances and mobilized for public needs associated with traditionally female public service jobs.

Efforts to create a fair and living wage for workers in predominantly female jobs and occupations, therefore, remain critical in the 1990s and beyond. The positive potential for the pay equity movement lies in broadening the approach, both in terms of location and strategic content. Strategies that demand equal pay for work of equal value are essential, but need not be predicated on technical job evaluation exercises. Equally imperative are attempts to raise the pay of traditionally female jobs through low-pay campaigns, career development programs, and regular minimum wage increases. Political mobilization to extend the coverage and improve the substance of national and state employment legislation is difficult in the current climate, but can form the basis of education and organizing campaigns. New, decentralized, more creative approaches in a broad-based pay equity movement can further women's efforts to contest the gendered labor markets at the core of economic restructuring.

Appendix A

The Civil Service Bargaining Process

The trilateral bargaining process, as well as the method for approving collective bargaining agreements in the civil service, is outlined in figure A.1. The state typically demands one-year wage packages. First, proposed increases in compensation are negotiated by unions and the Office of the State Employer. If an agreement is reached at the bargaining table that is ratified by a majority of the membership, recommendations on pay and benefits are then submitted to the Civil Service Commission for final approval. For contracts applicable to the succeeding fiscal year, agreement is necessary by August 15.

When negotiations reach an impasse by this deadline, the process is more involved and cumbersome, as shown in figure A.1. If collective bargaining talks fail, unresolved issues are submitted for mandatory mediation. The Labor Relations Bureau within the Department of Civil Service assigns a mediator, who is a civil service employee. Any remaining disagreements are referred to an Employee Relations Board (ERB), a three-member board appointed by the Civil Service Commission for three-year terms. The ERB then acts as the "Impasse Panel" for issues not resolved by mediation. The Impasse Panel's findings are not ratified by the union's membership; rather, they are imposed on both parties, subject to Civil Service Commission approval.

Any pay increases are approved or disapproved by the CSC, which ratifies collective bargaining agreements. The commission also reviews any findings of the Impasse Panel and decides whether to authorize them. As shown in figure A.1, pay increases approved by the Civil Service are transmitted to the legislature as part of the governor's budget. The Michigan

Figure A.1

The Collective Bargaining Process for Civil Service Employees

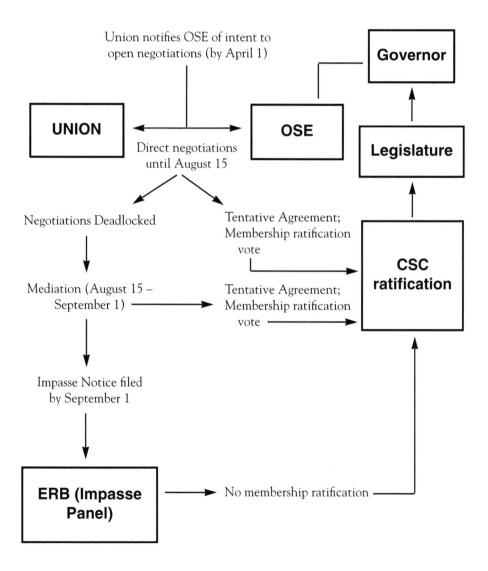

legislature may reject or reduce increases in compensation authorized by the commission in a two-thirds vote. As a result, the bargaining agents must wait until both the Civil Service Commission and legislature approve negotiated pay increases. Commission-approved wage increases have never been vetoed by both houses of the legislature. The governor has the constitutional power to approve, disapprove, or line-item veto individual appropriation bills.

Within sixty days after the commission approves the primary agreement, secondary negotiations on non-compensation issues can occur at the department level in consultation with the Office of the State Employer. Such negotiations would concern conditions which are special to one bargaining unit or department. Examples might include items such as safety and reimbursement, although these are almost always included in the bargaining agreement. These negotiations, including mediation and impasse, if necessary, must be completed within sixty calendar days from the initial negotiation date.

The Office of the State Employer also has the authority to develop a plan for compensation and conditions of employment for nonunionized employees for presentation to the Employee Relations Board. The board then recommends to the Civil Service Commission a compensation plan for nonunionized workers. In this role, however, it acts as and is called the "Coordinated Compensation Panel."

Appendix B

Factor Definitions in the Michigan Equitable Classification Plan (Group One Employees)

Factor 1—Knowledge and Skill:
This factor ranks the knowledge and skills required to perform work assignments typical of the class at the experienced level, which are acquired through education and work experience.

Factor 2—Judgment:
This factor ranks the judgment required to make decisions and take actions of increasing complexity, importance, and consequence in order to carry out work assignments.

Factor 3—Responsibility for Financial and Material Resources
This factor ranks the degree of responsibility and accountability for financial and material resources of the state, including responsibility for: the control and disbursement of funds and other budget items; management of accounts; the safeguarding, use, or maintenance of property, natural resources or equipment of significant value; or the efficiency of operations.

Factor 4—Responsibility for the Well-Being of Others
This factor ranks the degree of responsibility for the well-being of others, including responsibility for the protection of people, the provision of health care, educational, rehabilitation and related services, and for assuring the rights or safety of others.

Factor 5—Responsibility for Information

This factor ranks the degree of responsibility for information, including responsibility for obtaining, recording, organizing, processing, and analyzing data and information.

Factor 6—Responsibility for Communications and Public Relations

This factor ranks the degree of responsibility for communicating with others orally or in writing, the importance of such communications, and the difficulty of the interpersonal relations required to carry out work assignments.

Factor 7—Physical Effort

This factor ranks the strength and stamina required to do the job considering the work position, the amount of standing, walking, carrying, etc., required; the weight of materials handled; and the continuity of effort.

Factor 8—Mental/Visual Effort

This factor ranks the extent and frequency of concentration and attention to detail needed to complete tasks. It does not consider the analytical or reasoning ability required to do the job.

Factor 9—Work Environment

This factor ranks environmental conditions which are inherent to the work site. It does not consider temporary or incidental fluctuations which may be caused by accident, mechanical failure, or remodeling.

Factor 10—Work Hazards

This factor ranks the degree of hazard involved in the work and the probability of incurring work-related illness or injury in the normal conduct of work, assuming the observance of all health and safety regulations.

Source: Guide to the Job Evaluation Factors (Lansing: Michigan Department of Civil Service, March 1990).

Appendix C

REGRESSION METHODOLOGY

Using Ordinary Least Squares (OLS), we ran three linear regressions to assess the relationship between evaluated points, pay, and gender of the job class. Results appear in Tables A.1 and A.2.

EQUATION (1)

$$Pay = \alpha + \beta_1 (POINTS)$$

where α is the intercept and β is the slope of the points-to-pay line.

β_1 represents the additional pay for each additional evaluated point in the classification plan. Equation (1) is estimated separately for male and female job classes.

EQUATION (2)

$$Pay = \alpha + \beta_1 POINTS + \beta_2 GENDER$$

where GENDER is a dummy variable that $= 1$ if female job class and 0 if male job class.

To include a dummy variable for gender, Equation (2) pools the data on male and female job classes. β_1 is as defined in Equation (1). β_2 is called an intercept dummy variable and measures the vertical distance between the male and female regression lines. The regression coefficient represents the impact of gender on pay by asking: do incumbents in female classes earn less on average then incumbents in male classes? If female job classes continue to have lower pay for comparable points, then β_2 will be negative. Whereas β_2 can evaluate *whether* female job classes are underpaid, we need an additional equation to estimate *how much*.

EQUATION (3)

$$Pay = \alpha + \beta_1 POINTS + \beta_2 GENDER + \beta_3 (GENDER \times POINTS)$$

where (GENDER x POINTS) is an interaction term.

Equation (3) also uses the pooled data and β_1 and β_2 are as defined in Equation (2). The interaction term evaluates the difference in the slope of the male and female regression lines. It tests the hypothesis that the returns for additional points in female classes are less than for male classes. Using just the interaction term (slope dummy) without the gender dummy would incorrectly constrain the model because female classes would have to have the same intercept as male classes. Therefore, using both dummies is better than using either separately.

For female-dominated job classes:

$\text{Pay} = \alpha + \beta_1 \text{ POINTS} + \beta_2 \text{ GENDER} + \beta_3 \text{ (GENDER x POINTS)}$

Since GENDER = 1, (GENDER x POINTS) = POINTS.

$\text{Pay} = \alpha + \beta_2 \text{ GENDER} + (\beta_1 \text{ POINTS} + \beta_3 \text{ POINTS})$

$\text{Pay} = \alpha + \beta_2 \text{ GENDER} + (\beta_1 + \beta_3) \text{ POINTS}$

Define $\beta_4 = \beta_1 + \beta_3$:

$\text{Pay} = \alpha + \beta_2 \text{ GENDER} + \beta_4 \text{ POINTS}$

For male-dominated job classes:

Since GENDER = 0,

$\text{Pay} = \alpha + \beta_1 \text{ POINTS}$

β_4 is the return to points for female job classes; β_1 is the return to points for male job classes. Therefore, $\beta_4 - \beta_1$, or β_3, is the *monetary difference in the returns to points for female and male job classes.*

Table A.1

Estimated Coefficients from Group One Pay Equations

Variable	Eq. 1		Eq. 2	Eq. 3
	Male	Female		
Intercept	8.99	9.46	9.35	8.99
	(30.0)	(44.8)	(42.4)	(34.0)
Points	.0093	.0074	.0086	.0093
	(18.2)	(18.2)	(23.4)	(20.6)
Gender	—	—	−.484	.469[a]
			(4.3)	(1.1)
(Gender x Points)	—	—	—	−0.002[b]
				(2.4)
Adjusted R^2	.77	.87	.82	.82
n	98	51	149	149

Source: Based on data from the Michigan Department of Civil Service.

Note: With the exception of [a] and [b], all results are significant at the 1% level; [b] is significant at the 2% level. The absolute value of t-statistics appears in parentheses.

Table A.2

Estimated Coefficients from Group Two Pay Equations

Variable	Eq. 1		Eq. 2	Eq. 3
	Male	Female		
Intercept	− 52.55 (12.2)	− 62.11 (5.7)	− 53.67 (13.3)	− 52.55 (12.1)
Points	.0542 (17.1)	.0602 (7.3)	.0550 (23.4)	.0542 (17.0)
Gender	—	—	− 1.45 (4.4)	− 9.55[a] (0.8)
(Gender x Points)	—	—	—	.0060[a] (0.7)
Adjusted R^2	.90	.73	.88	.88
n	34	21	55	55

Source: Based on data from the Michigan Department of Civil Service.

Note: With the exception of [a], all results are significant at the 1% level. The absolute value of t-statistics appears in parentheses.

Notes

CHAPTER 1. INTRODUCTION

1. According to economists, wage discrimination exists when two groups of workers are paid differently although they are equally productive. After accounting for all possible productivity-related measurable characteristics that affect wages, a remaining wage gap between two workers could partly be due to discrimination. In a multiple regression, institutional characteristics such as industry, union status, and firm size are often included as independent variables along with productivity characteristics. Used together with as many non-gender biased characteristics as possible, variables such as race or gender can help detect the possible presence of discrimination.

2. States where pay equity for state employees was enacted through legislation include Connecticut, Iowa, Minnesota, Oregon, and Wisconsin. Collective bargaining and class-action litigation have also been an important means for pay equity wage adjustments in states such as California, Illinois, Massachusetts, New Jersey, New York, Ohio, Pennsylvania, Vermont, and Washington (see NCPE 1989; Hartmann and Aaronson 1994).

3. Traditional business opponents of comparable worth still hold on to the simplistic view of labor markets with tenacity. This becomes clear each time a comparable worth bill or even a proposal for a pay equity study is introduced in the U.S. Congress or any state legislature. The U.S. Chamber of Commerce, the National Association of Manufacturers, the National Federation of Independent Businesses, and other business groups line up to testify against pay equity. But business is not alone. Conservative social scientists, lobbyists, and other political opponents also join the queue.

4. For excellent discussions of the experiences of black and white women in clerical and service occupations, see Power and Rosenberg (1993, 1995).

5. The four major job evaluation methods are ranking, grade description, factor comparison, and point factor.

6. Unlike *a priori* point-factor job evaluation, the policy capturing approach derives factors and their weights empirically by using the organization's existing
pay structure.

7. Sorensen (1994) explains this latter approach as a linear points-to-pay regression for all jobs within an organization that includes the gender composition
of the job as an additional explanatory (dummy) variable. The *corrected* average line eliminates the estimated wage depreciation based upon gender composition of job classes. In Sorensen's words, it "measures the relationship
between pay and evaluation points after controlling for the sex composition
of the occupation" (70). The estimated coefficient for points then represents
the monetary value to the employer of an additional evaluation point in the
absence of discrimination.

8. In conventional Marxist usage, class structures refer to both property relations
and to the organizational and ideological forms that accompany them (Marglin 1974; Edwards 1979). In usage derived from non-Marxist sociological
theory and integrated into some recent neo-Marxist accounts, class also refers
to patterns of inequality of organizational authority and reward (Wright 1978;
Ehrenreich and Ehrenreich 1979; Aronowitz 1979; Salaman 1981). We use
the term *gender* to refer to the classifications that society constructs to exag-
gerate the differences between females and males and to maintain a system of
gender inequality (Reskin and Padavic 1994: 2–7). Gender domination involves both male control of more material resources and various ideologies
which legitimate or obscure male power (see Acker 1990; Cockburn 1991).

9. Steinberg (1991) has also made the point that labor unions have had to choose
to accept compromise or possibly lose any funds disbursed for pay equity.

Chapter 3. (Not) Above Politics

1. The broad exclusions from the classified service include elected officials; persons in the armed forces of the state; members of boards and commissions;
and employees of the legislature, courts of record, and state institutions of
higher education. The other exclusions are quite narrow: (1) the principal
executive officer heading principal departments, except for the Civil Service
Commission; (2) when requested by the department head, two other positions, one of which shall be policymaking; and (3) eight positions in the office
of the governor (CWTF 1985).

2. The Department of Civil Service had come in for especially harsh criticism in
the 1971 review. Quoted by Daniel Byk, UAW staff member, in his affidavit
in *UAW v. State of Michigan* (1985), the review noted, "It is apparent that a
substantially altered merit system must be implemented successfully within
the department before the department can be looked upon as competent to
fulfill the same responsibilities on a state-wide basis" (7). In 1980, women
were 8 percent of Department of Civil Service administrators and officials
and 98 percent of office and clerical workers. At level 17 and above, in a 21-
grade structure, Civil Service, a small department, had one African-American
woman and twelve men. Between January 1971 and September 1980, the

representation of women in the department workforce declined to 7.86 percent; it was the only agency in which the percentage of women had declined (DCS, Management Services Division 1980: 61, 79, 110; Massaron 1992).

In September 1971, in response to the Employment Practices Review, Republican governor William Milliken issued the first of a series of affirmative action orders to heads of departments in the state (Milliken 1971). A second directive was issued in 1979. Governor Blanchard issued a new affirmative action order in 1983.

3. Even after the Employment Practices Review in 1971, departments recruited and fired on the basis of gender. For example, in the 1980s the Department of Mental Health claimed that more men than women needed to be retained in a period of dismissals, because being male was a bone fide occupational qualification for working with developmentally disabled clients in its facilities (AFSCME Local 567 1993). The Department of Corrections continued to advertise for policewomen with duties distinct from those of policemen.

4. The Civil Rights Commission and its administrative arm, Department of Civil Rights, were responsible for enforcing the state's civil rights legislation in the private and public sectors. In a series of cases culminating in *Department of Civil Rights ex rel Jones v. Department of Civil Service* (101 Mich App 295, 1980) the Civil Service Commission insisted it had full jurisdiction over its employment practices and was not subject to Civil Rights Commission review. The court held that the Civil Service Commission's constitutional power over state employment was not without limit and that the Civil Rights Commission did have jurisdiction. The Elliott-Larsen Civil Rights Act, which the court ruled the Civil Rights Commission had rights to enforce in the civil service, did not, however, have explicit comparable worth language written into it, and so an under-resourced Civil Rights Commission would play little role in developing pay equity policy in Michigan. The tradition, among commissioners and staff, had, in any case, been to focus on race matters (Haener 1993; Cooper 1993). In 1983, two thousand women filed claims under a settlement agreement which brought to a close long-standing claims involving the denial of long-term disability insurance benefits for pregnancy-related absences from work between June 1973 and October 1978 (WSG, *WIRE*, August 1983: 3, March 1984: 1–4, August 1984: 1).

5. The August 1981 complaint filed by the Michigan State Employees Association and Karon Black on behalf of all female employees in the state classified service alleged violations of the Civil Service Rules, the Michigan Elliott-Larsen Civil Rights Act, and Title VII of the Civil Rights Act of 1964. The complaint argued that in instituting the Michigan Benchmark Evaluation System the civil service had intentionally undervalued positions primarily held by women, both where women performed jobs substantially similar to those performed by men and where the actual tasks performed by women were different but job demands were similar. After four years of inaction, in 1985 the U.S. Department of Justice issued a notice of Right to Sue within ninety days. In November 1985, therefore, the UAW, which had recently won a certification election over MSEA, sued in federal court. In 1987 the district court

dismissed the complaint, finding insufficient evidence to prove that the state's wage system constituted intentional discrimination. In 1989 the U.S. Court of Appeals affirmed the lower court's ruling.

6. As a voluntary group but not a union, Women in State Government could make a presentation to the Coordinated Compensation Panel, but not within the collective bargaining arena. The Coordinated Compensation Panel heard presentations from various employee associations, and recommended pay adjustments for those classes not represented by unions. At this stage, WSG urged that six measures be adopted. First, they argued that labor market wage survey data should not be considered valid for wage-setting for any occupations which had more than 70 percent of one gender. Rather, single job evaluation should be used as the basis of pay for these classifications. Second, the state should not use labor market wage survey data from any employer currently charged with gender discrimination in wages, an employer who ever settled a gender discrimination in wages complaint, or an employer found guilty of wage discrimination. Third, the state's single job evaluation should be gender-neutral. Fourth, the state should aim to achieve pay equity within five to ten years. Fifth, the state should gradually increase the proportion of pay determined by gender-neutral criteria and decrease the proportion of pay based upon the labor market. Sixth, the state should establish a pay equity fund. The Coordinated Compensation Panel argued that the WSG demands were "premature" until research of a recently appointed Interdepartmental Committee on Comparable Worth was concluded.

7. Also testifying at the public hearing were Women in State Government (WSG), the Michigan State Employees Association (MSEA), the American Federation of State, County, and Municipal Employees (AFSCME), the National Organization for Women (NOW), the Michigan Manufacturers Association (MMA), the Office of Women and Work (OWW), the Michigan Department of Civil Rights, the League of Women Voters, and the Michigan Nurses Association (MNA) (WSG, *WIRE*, February 1984: 1–2).

CHAPTER 4. CONFLICT AT THE BARGAINING TABLE

1. When AFSCME, for example, began to raise the issue of pay equity wage adjustments at the bargaining table in 1984, the OSE resisted, and discussion was deferred until the CWTF issued its report in 1985.

2. For example, although the Department of Civil Service had an established practice of conducting salary surveys to ascertain market rates for comparable jobs among a mixture of public and larger private-sector employers, the surveys were not used in wage negotiations every year, and were not statistically reliable. In his 1986 deposition in *UAW v. State of Michigan* (1985), Joseph Slivensky, director of the Planning and Development Bureau in the Department of Civil Service, related that each year only fifty of the roughly twenty-four hundred job classifications under the Benchmark evaluation system were surveyed.

3. Across the U.S., more than half of the growth in labor union membership since

1960 has been due to organization in the public sector (McLaughlin 1970). By 1990, three out of ten union members worked in the public sector (Horowitz 1994: 170). Public sector organizing has increased the rate of unionization among working women in particular. Female public sector workers are as likely as their male counterparts to be unionized; 40 percent of female and male workers in the public sector are organized (Bell 1985: 282).

4. When public employees did unionize, however, they were generally not permitted to strike. Michigan banned strikes by public employees in the Hutchinson Act of 1947; in fact, it called for an automatic discharge of strikers (McLaughlin 1970: 148). The Public Employment Relations Act (PERA) has gradual penalties for strikes, up to and including automatic discharge.

5. Vallette and Freeman (1988: 406, table 3; 416, table 9) identify Michigan as a state "all probargaining" for the public sector, although not an "early" one, and as one of the states with an overall strong bargaining environment. In reality, bargaining is stronger in municipal government, where employees are covered by PERA, than in the civil service.

6. Many Michigan officials, including the Civil Service Commission, perceived a conflict between the merit system and unionization. Unionization emphasizes seniority and wage uniformity while, in theory, a merit system rewards increased productivity or skill. The civil service instead granted official recognition of employee associations that could meet informally to discuss working conditions. This policy was referred to as "meet and confer" and fell short of unionization. Employees also had the right to grieve against management and could be represented in their grievance by their recognized employee association (DCS 1964).

7. In developing a collective bargaining system, there were tensions between the civil service and the executive branch over how personnel functions would be divided and who would have authority to negotiate with employee associations. For example: Should the Office of the State Employer, an agent of the governor, negotiate tentative agreements or should a new bureau be established within the Department of Civil Service? The ultimate decisions made by the Civil Service Commission enabled them to maximize control over state personnel and labor relations issues. The Office of the State Employer (under the governor) is considered "management" for purposes of labor relations, while the civil service maintains oversight of the merit system (including classification and promotion), approves all collective agreements, and arbitrates grievances. The CSC recognized the authority of the OSE to conduct, coordinate, and administer negotiations with exclusive employee representatives in areas of collective bargaining, contract administration, unfair labor practices, improvement of work performance, and administrative efficiency.

8. The troopers and sergeants ballot "Proposal G" passed on November 7, 1978 with 57 percent of votes in favor (*Michigan Report* 1978, Election Results: 1).

9. The CSC's own internal Staff Task Force on Employee Relations (STAFER) had recommended changing from meet-and-confer systems to full collective bargaining in 1975, as New York, Wisconsin, and Minnesota had already done (STAFER 1975: 2, 6).

10. An agency shop arrangement requires employees to either join the union or pay a servicing fee (roughly equivalent to the union dues). This contrasts with an open shop, which allows individual employees to decide whether to join the union. In both cases, a collective bargaining contract covers them regardless of whether they become dues-paying members.

11. The independent MSEA won the right to exclusive representation of the safety and regulatory unit in 1978 (*Michigan Report* 1978: no. 178). Yet MSEA lost out to AFSCME to become the exclusive bargaining agent for the ten thousand institutional workers in October 1978 (*Michigan Report* 1978: no. 191). The next election was for the labor and trades unit. MSEA, the representative before "meet and confer," filed first, and AFSCME followed (*Michigan Report* 1978: no. 191). MSEA won a relatively close election with 1,518 votes; AFSCME received 1,188 votes and there were 222 votes against any representation (*Michigan Report* 1979: no. 52). MSEA also won a runoff election against AFSCME to represent the 10,400 human services workers in August 1979 (*Michigan Report* 1979: no. 159). The MSPTA was officially certified by the CSC on February 29, 1980 (*Michigan Report* 1980: no. 41). Local 31-M of the SEIU was certified as the bargaining representative for about 2,230 employees in the human services support unit on April 10, 1980 (*Michigan Report* 1980: no. 70). Employees in the scientific and engineering unit chose the Michigan Society of State Engineers and Professional Affiliates to be their exclusive bargaining agent in October 1981. It was a runoff election against "no exclusive representative" (*Michigan Report* 1981: no. 191). Civil service "associations" independent of the AFL-CIO and "unions" affiliated with the AFL-CIO, such as AFSCME and SEIU, also vied for statewide employees in California (see Crouch 1978). In the late 1980s, MSEA chose not to remain independent and became affiliated with AFSCME as MSEA, AFSCME Council 5, AFL-CIO.

12. The intra-labor movement division between the UAW and AFSCME runs deep. For example, a grassroots organizing campaign at Harvard University affiliated with the UAW in 1981. UAW District 65 then assumed responsibility for organizing the university's clerical (and technical) employees, until leading staff members left in 1985 to form an independent Harvard Union of Clerical and Technical Workers, which ultimately affiliated with AFSCME in 1987 (Hurd 1993: 320–321).

13. In *White-Collar Workers and the UAW*, Carl Dean Snyder (1973) discusses the history of the UAW's Technical-Office-Professional Department and its struggle to organize office workers in the private sector.

14. Nationwide, working women were also deeply affected by long-term reductions in public and social services. While much of the budget-cutting in the 1970s was due to reduced local revenue and thus services (police and fire, sanitation, highways) were cut, the budget cuts in the 1980s starting with the Reagan administration primarily affected health, education, and social services employees (Bell 1985: 288–289).

15. Since a one-to-one PCS to PCEL correspondence was impossible for newly combined or newly expanded classes and class series, the DCS had to choose

among existing PCS levels. For example, to determine the appropriate new PCEL level for a combined class, DCS typically chose the level where the greatest number of employees were classified. Since the choices resulted in new designated levels that were not a match with the PCS, DCS added the term "equivalency level" to the phrase "position comparison" to yield the new abbreviation PCEL (Slivensky 1994).

16. Women in State Government was correct that the *average* disparity was lowered when higher-level positions were excluded from the analysis. However, there are two factors affecting the relative deviation of *individual* job categories from a pay line: the intercept of the line and the slope of the line. The level of the intercept has the greatest impact on the lowest paid job classes. By excluding the higher paid jobs, the pay line's intercept would be higher, especially if the gender-based wage differential were extremely wide at the bottom. The Office of the State Employer's methodology might actually have benefitted the female-dominated classes in the lowest PCELs. On the other hand, if gender-based wage differentials were wider at higher PCELs, the OSE's methodology may have served to lower both the slope and the intercept of the pay line, limiting women's wage gains. Nevertheless, since the OSE's position at the bargaining table was based upon the average disparity (rather than the deviation of individual job categories from the pay line, as is typical in points-to-pay comparable worth implementation), Women in State Government's focus on the average disparity seems appropriate.

17. These eligible job classes included: barber cosmetologist; client resident affairs advisor; dental aide; domestic services aide; housekeeping supervisor; institutional worker; launderer; practical nurse; and seamster (*Michigan AFSCME News* 1986, February: 3–4).

18. For example, collective negotiations between the UAW and OSE went to impasse in 1988 (for fiscal years 1989 and 1990). At issue was not only a general wage increase, but the request of the UAW to reopen wage negotiations to correct any remaining gender-based wage discrimination upon completion of the first phase of the reclassification exercise. The UAW based its reopener request on a prior impasse panel decision to put off further pay equity wage negotiations with AFSCME in 1985 until completion of the ECP (AFSCME 1986–89: Art. 22, Sec. O; CSC, ERB 1988: 16). While specific language requesting a reopener never successfully appeared in UAW Local 6000's 1988–1990 collective bargaining agreement, it was understood that the OSE, the UAW, AFSCME, and additional interested parties were awaiting the new ECP to reevaluate claims of gender-based disparities. For example, in 1985 the OSE had referred to the $.40 special increases as "only the first phase of what is required," and signaled their intention to review pay equity claims once the ECP was completed (cited in CSC, ERB 1988: 19–20). Negotiations between the Michigan Corrections Officers (MCO) and the OSE also went to impasse in 1988 over special pay adjustments for corrections officers who thought they were underpaid relative to state troopers. OSE's position was consistent: it maintained that when the ECP was implemented, it would allow precisely the kinds of comparisons which MCO sought (see UAW Local 6000 1991: 15).

19. The seventeen class series (with one or more job classes within the series) were: adult foster care consultant; camp consultant; child welfare consultant; communications clerk; developmental disabilities programmer; institutional social worker; music therapist; radio operator; recreational therapist; school psychologist; school teacher; social services specialist; social services worker; special education teacher; trades instructor; welfare services specialist; welfare services worker.

20. Even the regressions by the OSE-hired expert, Mark Killingsworth, a labor economist, showed a significant positive relationship between points and pay, but that at the maximum-wage rate, the percentage of females in a job class is negatively correlated with pay (see UAW Local 6000 1991: 49).

21. The UAW's impasse brief pointed out that Joseph Slivensky, director of the Department of Civil Service Bureau of Classification, had previously argued that job evaluation points measure job value in testimony in an impasse with the Michigan Corrections Organization in 1988; the union relied on Merit Principle 3 to argue that if points measure value, the state must remunerate equal points comparably. However, the state had long denied that the concept of equal value in Merit Principle 3 implied comparable worth. In his testimony for the state in the UAW v. Michigan lawsuit, Slivensky had explained the principle as meaning equal pay for employees with the same or similar jobs across departments, an improvement over departmental differences in pay under the old Position Comparison System. In an interview with the authors, state personnel director Martha Bibbs suggested Merit Principle 3 derived from federal standards (Bibbs 1992).

22. In absolute terms, the decline in the wage gap nationwide is probably larger. A 10 percent decline in a wage gap near 30 percent nationwide is 3 cents on the dollar. In Michigan, the 12.5 percent decline in the 17 percent wage gap amounts to just over 2 cents on the dollar. Wage gaps in the female-concentrated public sector tend to be lower than the national average for all men and women in the workforce because of greater discrimination in male-dominated sectors.

Chapter 5. Points without Pay

1. Each job was ranked by comparing its attributes with predefined descriptions of categories in the hierarchy (and with the attributes of other jobs). The ten factors used to assign jobs to classes and classes to grades were: public contacts; policy determination; work conditions; supervision exercised; supervision received; place in organization; difficulty and variety; qualifications required; judgment; and consequences of error.

2. The state argued not entirely convincingly that this wage drift was dictated by market rates.

3. The specification of subfactors was also inconsistent across service groups. For example, under the knowledge factor, the female-dominated administrative support service group had "complexity" as a subfactor while the male-dominated safety and regulatory service group had "purpose of work" as a subfactor

(OWW 1980: 10). Even semantically similar and logically related subfactors appeared under different major factors among the service groups.

4. Physical effort/work environment was weighted toward risks with correctional residents and toward heavy lifting rather than exposure to illness or repetitive motion. In fact, the two factors of personal relations and working environment were generally not measured and simply assigned a minimum point value, even where the job (such as registered nurse) warranted a much higher rating.

5. This practice of creating openly gendered salary structures is not unique to Michigan. According to Kim (1989), the California Civil Service maintains a relative wage structure based on gendered pay practices established in the 1930s.

6. Melissa A. Barker, Ph.D. in sociology, had been involved in the comparable worth movement in the state of Oregon, and had presented seminars throughout the state of Michigan on classification, job evaluation, and gender and cultural bias. At the time of her work with DCS, she was an assistant professor at Michigan State University.

7. In Groups One and Two, 26 and 34 test classes respectively were chosen to represent a broad range of civil service occupations, occupations with large numbers of incumbents, and occupations in all bargaining units. The test classes represented 60 percent of all employees in Group One and about half of all employees in Group Two.

8. Arguments for consistency and uniformity have led many pay equity states other than Michigan to opt for single job evaluation across all education or skill levels. Minnesota, Wisconsin, New Jersey, Maine, and Massachusetts successfully use single point factor methods of job evaluation. States which have used the grading method of single job evaluation to implement pay equity include New York, Oregon, and Illinois (U.S. GAO 1986; *Report of Wisconsin's Task Force on Comparable Worth* 1985).

9. In the MBES, incumbents in such occupations as lawyer, judge, physician, and psychiatrist had negotiated special pay ranges.

10. The highest ranked position in Group One is airline pilot, garnering 828 total points and a maximum hourly wage of $17.52 in 1990. Seven classes (three male, two female, and two neutral) tied for the lowest Group Two point score of 1,309. The maximum wage for these jobs ranged from $15.71 to $18.86 per hour.

11. Job specifications included position descriptions, examples of duties and tasks, and minimum qualifications and educational requirements for the job.

12. A job or position analysis questionnaire is only one of many job analysis methods. Ten different methods used by a variety of employers are described by Bemis, Belenky, and Soder (1983).

13. Their evaluations were tested for "inter-rater reliability," to ensure consistency between evaluators.

14. When the knowledge and skill factor was applied by job raters to the classes in Group One, the overall operational weight was 29.8 percent for female-dominated classes, 33.5 percent for neutral classes, and 31.9 percent for male-

dominated classes (DCS, Merit Systems Planning and Development Bureau 1990b: 15).

15. The coefficient of determination, R^2, between percent female in the job class and these two factors was much higher than on the other factors (DCS, Merit Systems Planning and Development Bureau 1990b: 17–21).

16. The highest R^2 was .05 for responsibility for financial and material resources; as the percentage of females increased, points declined significantly (DCS, Merit Systems Planning and Development Bureau 1993).

17. Confidence intervals are generally used to assess whether estimated coefficients derived from a sample accurately reflect the population. In this case, we have the actual values of the population, but we do not have a regression that specifies every possible independent variable which could affect pay. Therefore, the coefficient of ECP points, the slope or $\hat{\beta}$, is still estimated. The formula for a confidence interval is: $\hat{\beta} \pm SE_{\hat{\beta}} t_c$ where t_c is the critical t value for the desired level of confidence (Studenmund 1992: 583). Since a confidence interval around the slope value for female classes did not include the slope value for the male classes, the two regression lines are statistically different.

18. As discussed in chapter 4, the UAW developed a similar correlation between pay rates and point values in the new ECP for classes in the male-dominated labor and trades unit and the security unit and compared it to the correlation for their classes in the female-dominated administrative support and human services units. They argued that the relationship was stronger for the male-dominated classes than female-dominated classes and sought additional pay equity wage increases.

19. Confidence intervals for the intercept terms suggest a possible overlap for male and female job classes. An additional regression run with an intercept dummy variable for female job classes indicates a significantly negative relationship between pay and female composition of the job class. However, when both the slope and intercept dummy variables are included, results were insignificant (see table A.2 in appendix C).

20. Katz and Krueger (1991) have found that an increase in college/high school wage differentials during the 1980s was largely confined to the private sector. Formal education has become less valued in the public sector relative to the private sector. Earnings distribution in the public sector is also more equal than in the private sector (see also Blank 1994a). Thus, for an employer such as the Michigan Civil Service, the effect of pooling Groups One and Two would likely be modest.

21. The job class of executive secretary, primarily consisting of confidential employees excluded from collective bargaining, retains ECP level assignments based on the rank of their supervisor (WSG, *WIRE*, October 1990: 2).

22. A career development program is generally a commitment to internal promotion as opposed to outside recruitment. It involves identifying and establishing career ladders that enable employees in dead-end jobs to advance and defining the education and experience required to move up the career ladder (Figart 1989). To help women, career development sometimes involves restructuring

the work that women do or building new "bridge" positions between existing jobs.

Chapter 6. The Pay Equity Network

1. CLUW had previously taken the Michigan AFL-CIO to task for not publicly opposing either the preliminary or final Comparable Worth Task Force reports. CLUW had sent the state federation the civil rights section of the handbook material distributed at the 1985 AFL-CIO regional conference, which listed pay equity as a top priority. On grounds of this prior organizational commitment and reasserting the importance of bringing more women into the halls of labor, CLUW asked the AFL-CIO to cosponsor the conference, contribute $500 towards PEN's administrative costs, and "use the Michigan *AFL-CIO News* to offset the management press in Michigan as they cheer for the market rates to prevail at the workplace" (CLUW 1985b).

2. On the National Committee on Pay Equity (NCPE), only organizational members in good standing are eligible to vote at annual membership meetings and run for the board of directors, which makes a great many of the organization's decisions. The NCPE designates categories of organizations, among which it maintains a balance of representation on its board: trade unions, women's groups, and civil rights/minority groups. The same types of groups were affiliated to the Michigan Pay Equity Network, but PEN did not promulgate formal rules about the balance of representation among types of organization. The emphasis on organizational representatives, the location of activity mainly in Washington, D.C., and the lobbying focus of the organization make the National Committee on Pay Equity something of an "insider" organization. However, it has worked hard to disseminate the idea of pay equity in more popular and accessible forms by working with affiliated unions. Similarly, the Michigan Pay Equity Network has relied upon its trade union members to reach the rank and file with information about pay equity. The Michigan Pay Equity Network also ran occasional weekend conferences which attempted to reach rank-and-file union and feminist activists.

3. The Elliott-Larsen Civil Rights Act and the Michigan Handicappers' Civil Rights Act are "tie-barred." An amendment to one is necessarily an amendment to the other.

4. "Independent contractors" are defined in civil rights law as contractors who set their own timetables, bring their own tools, and engage in like work for other organizations.

Chapter 7. Michigan and the Future of the Pay Equity Movement

1. A fiscal capacity index measures the impact of macroeconomic performance on fiscal capacity with the assumption of policy neutrality. It measures a governmental unit's potential ability to raise revenue from tax and non-tax sources.

It assesses this capacity relative to a national average. Variations in the fiscal capacity index signify differences in underlying tax bases rather than variations in political climates or public officials' attitudes. The Representative Revenue System (RRS) is the fiscal capacity measure we use. It includes all potential state revenue sources, including residents' earnings on out-of-state assets, user fees, and sales taxes from tourists.

2. Determining the relative importance of institutional structure and political mobilization is nearly impossible, as the two are closely connected. For example, the political priorities of feminists and labor may have been influenced by institutional, as well as political and economic, factors.

3. The direct relationship between corporate agendas and state priorities is especially strong in Michigan. For example, the first use of eminent domain by a government on behalf of a private corporation (instead of for a public good such as highways) took place when a neighborhood (Poletown) in Detroit was confiscated to construct a General Motors plant (Jones and Bachelor with Wilson 1986).

4. Summaries of equality policies and comparable worth endeavors in Europe, Australia, and Canada include Ames (1995), Gunderson (1994), Miller (1993), Kahn and Meehan (1992), Fudge and McDermott (1991), *Equal Remuneration* (1986), and *Equality for Women at Work* (1985).

5. However, the limited demands on resources by pay equity reform is partly related to the compromised nature of implementation.

6. The legal case in the House of Lords was *Ratcliffe and others v. North Yorkshire County Council.* The employer's claim was complicated by the operation of the Transfer of Undertakings Protection rules which (somewhat ambiguously) oblige new employers to maintain the pay, working conditions, and representation of employees who transfer from the public sector. The protection of employment regulations in 1981 was a response to European Community Directive 77/187, Acquired Rights Directive—On the Approximation of the Laws of the Member States Relating to the Safeguarding of Employees' Rights in the Event of Transfers of Undertakings, Business, or Parts of Businesses (see Labour Research Department 1993).

7. Patricia McDermott, of York University in Canada, made this point when speaking at a conference, "Equal Pay in a Deregulated Labour Market," at Middlesex University, United Kingdom, June 1996.

8. The union wage premium for women workers is still large and positive, controlling for other variables including occupation and industry (see Spalter-Roth, Hartmann, and Collins 1994).

9. Job restructuring changes the work that people do so that dead-end jobs include new duties and responsibilities utilized for career advancement. For instance, employees can move directly from dead-end positions and "cross-over" to an entry-level job on a better career track. Personnel administrators could also create permanent "bridge positions" between dead-end (paraprofessional, technical, or clerical) jobs and occupations with advancement potential. If a workplace such as a hospital has highly technical occupations with a smaller nontechnical support staff, bridge positions could help lower-paid support staff advance (see Figart 1989).

10. H.R. 1507 was introduced in the House of Representatives of the 104th Congress on April 7, 1995. On that date, it had twenty-one cosponsors; by the summer of 1995, the bill had over forty cosponsors. It was referred to the Committee on Economic and Educational Opportunities.
11. Suggestions for reversing labor's decline must go beyond reforming labor law. Among industrial relations scholars and practioners, recommendations of the Dunlop Commission are perceived as modest. For an overview of the issues involving union strategy, organization, structure, and government regulation, see, for example, the special issue of *Industrial Relations* on law reform (July 1995), especially articles by Strauss (1995), Kochan (1995), Rogers (1995), and Wachter (1995); Wial (1994) is also relevant.

References

Note: Michigan documentary materials and interviews can be found beginning on p. 207.

GENERAL REFERENCES

Aaron, Benjamin. 1988. "The Future of Collective Bargaining in the Public Sector." In *Public Sector Bargaining*, 2d ed., edited by Benjamin Aaron, Joyce M. Najita, and James L. Stern, 314–26. Washington, D.C.: BNA Books.

Aaron, Henry J., and Cameron M. Lougy. 1986. *The Comparable Worth Controversy.* Washington, D.C.: The Brookings Institution.

Acker, Joan. 1987. "Sex Bias in Job Evaluation: A Comparable Worth Issue." In *Ingredients for Women's Employment Policy*, edited by Christine Bose and Glenna Spitze, 183–96. Albany: State University of New York Press.

———. 1989. *Doing Comparable Worth: Gender, Class, and Pay Equity.* Philadelphia: Temple University Press.

———. 1990. "Hierarchies, Jobs, Bodies: A Theory of Gendered Organizations." *Gender and Society* 4 (2): 139–58.

Advisory Commission on Intergovernmental Relations. 1990. *State Fiscal Capacity and Effort.* Report M-170, August. Washington, D.C.: ACIR.

AFSCME. n.d. *AFSCME's Record on Pay Equity.* Washington, D.C.: AFSCME.

———. n.d. *Fact Versus Fiction: Debunking the American Legislative Exchange Council's Report Blaming Public Employees for Government's Fiscal Problems.* Washington, D.C.: AFSCME.

Albelda, Randy, and Chris Tilly. 1994. "Towards a Broader Vision: Race, Gender, and Labor Market Segmentation in the Social Structure of Accumulation Framework." In *Social Structures of Accumulation: The Political Economy of Growth and Crisis*, edited by David M. Kotz, Terrence McDonough, and Michael Reich, 212–30. Cambridge: Cambridge University Press.

Albert, Michael, and Robin Hahnel. 1979. "A Ticket to Ride: More Locations on the Class Map." In *Between Labor and Capital*, edited by Pat Walker, 243–78. Boston: South End Press.

Aldrich, Mark, and Robert Buchele. 1986. *The Economics of Comparable Worth.* Boston: Ballinger.

Ames, Lynda J. 1991. "Legislating Equity: A Comparison of Provincial Legislation in Manitoba and Ontario Requiring Pay Equity." *International Journal of Public Administration* 14: 871–92.

———. 1995. "Fixing Women's Wages: The Effectiveness of Comparable Worth Policies." *Industrial and Labor Relations Review* 48 (4, July): 709–25.

Amott, Teresa. 1993. *Caught in the Crisis: Women and the U.S. Economy Today.* New York: Monthly Review Press.

Armstrong, Pat, and Hugh Armstrong. 1991. "Limited Possibilities and Possible Limits for Pay Equity: Within and beyond the Ontario Legislation." In *Just Wages: A Feminist Assessment of Pay Equity*, edited by Judy Fudge and Patricia McDermott, 110–21. Toronto: University of Toronto Press.

Aronowitz, Stanley. 1979. "The Professional-Managerial Class or Middle Strata." In *Between Labor and Capital*, edited by Pat Walker, 213–42. Boston: South End Press.

———. 1984. "Labor Is the Key." In *Beyond Reagan: Alternatives for the '80s,* edited by Alan Gartner, Colin Greer, and Frank Riesmann, 256–70. New York: Harper and Row.

Badgett, M.V. Lee, and Rhonda M. Williams. 1994. "The Changing Contours of Discrimination: Race, Gender, and Structural Economic Change." In *Understanding American Economic Decline*, edited by Michael A. Bernstein and David E. Adler, 313–29. Cambridge: Cambridge University Press.

Bakker, Isabella. 1991. "Pay Equity and Economic Restructuring: The Polarization of Policy?" In *Just Wages: A Feminist Assessment of Pay Equity*, edited by Judy Fudge and Patricia McDermott, 254–80. Toronto: University of Toronto Press.

Balser, Diane. 1987. *Sisterhood and Solidarity: Feminism and the Labor Movement in Modern Times.* Boston: South End Press.

Baron, Ava, ed. 1991. *Work Engendered: Toward a New History of American Labor.* Ithaca, N.Y.: Cornell University Press.

Barrow, Clyde W. 1993. *Critical Theories of the State: Marxist, Neo-Marxist, Post-Marxist.* Madison: University of Wisconsin Press.

Beatty, Richard W., and James R. Beatty. 1984. "Some Problems with Contemporary Job Evaluation Systems." In *Comparable Worth and Wage Discrimination: Technical Possibilities and Political Realities*, edited by Helen Remick, 59–78. Philadelphia: Temple University Press.

Beechey, Veronica. 1987. *Unequal Work.* London: Verso Press.

Beechey, Veronica, and Tessa Perkins. 1987. *A Matter of Hours: Women, Part-Time Work and the Labour Market.* Cambridge: Polity Press.

Bell, Deborah E. 1985. "Unionized Women in State and Local Government." In *Women, Work and Protest: A Century of U.S. Women's Labor History*, edited by Ruth Milkman, 280–99. New York: Routledge and Kegan Paul.

Bemis, Stephen E., Ann Holt Belenky, and Dee Ann Soder. 1983. *Job Analysis: An Effective Management Tool.* Washington, D.C.: Bureau of National Affairs.

Berger, Brigitte. 1984. "Comparable Worth at Odds with American Realities." In *Comparable Worth: Issue for the 80's*, 65–74. Washington, D.C.: U.S. Civil Rights Commission.

Bergmann, Barbara. 1986. *The Economic Emergence of Women*. New York: Basic Books, Inc.

Bergren, Orville V. 1984. "A Business Viewpoint on Comparable Worth." In *Equal Pay for UNequal Work*, edited by Phyllis Schlafly, 209–17. Washington, D.C.: Eagle Forum Education and Legal Defense Fund.

Best, Michael H., and William E. Connolly. 1976. *The Politicized Economy*. Lexington, Mass.: D.C. Heath and Company.

Blank, Rebecca M. 1990. "Are Part-Time Jobs Bad Jobs?" In *A Future of Lousy Jobs? The Changing Structure of U.S. Wages*, edited by Gary Burtless, 123–64. Washington, D.C.: The Brookings Institution.

———. 1994a. "Public Sector Growth and Labor Market Flexibility: The United States versus the United Kingdom." In *Social Protection versus Economic Flexibility: Is There a Trade-off?* edited by Rebecca M. Blank, 223–64. Chicago: University of Chicago Press.

———, ed. 1994b. *Social Protection versus Economic Flexibility: Is There a Trade-off?* Chicago: University of Chicago Press.

Blau, Francine D., and Marianne A. Ferber. 1992. *The Economics of Women, Men, and Work*. Englewood Cliffs, N.J.: Prentice Hall.

Block, Fred. 1987. *Revising State Theory*. Philadelphia: Temple University Press.

Bluestone, Barry, and Irving Bluestone. 1992. *Negotiating the Future: A Labor Perspective on American Business*. New York: Basic Books.

Bluestone, Barry, and Bennett Harrison. 1982. *The Deindustrialization of America*. New York: Basic Books.

Blum, Linda M. 1991. *Between Feminism and Labor: The Significance of the Comparable Worth Movement*. Berkeley: University of California Press.

Blumrosen, Ruth G. 1979. "Wage Discrimination, Job Segregation, and Title VII of the Civil Rights Act of 1964." *University of Michigan Journal of Law Reform* 12: 397–502.

Bowles, Samuel, and Herbert Gintis. 1987. *Democracy and Capitalism: Property, Community, and the Contraditions of Modern Social Thought*. New York: Basic Books.

Brenner, Johanna. 1987. "Feminist Political Discourses: Radical Versus Liberal Approaches to the Feminization of Poverty and Comparable Worth." *Gender and Society* 1 (4, December): 447–65.

Bridges, William P., and Robert L. Nelson. 1989. "Markets in Hierarchies: Organizational and Market Influences on Gender Inequality in a State Pay System." *American Journal of Sociology* 95 (3, November): 616–58.

Buffa, Dudley. 1984. *Union Power and American Democracy: The UAW and the Michigan Democratic Party*. Ann Arbor: University of Michigan Press.

Bureau of National Affairs. 1984. *Pay Equity and Comparable Worth*. Washington, D.C.: BNA.

Burton John F., Jr., and Terry Thomason. 1988. "The Extent of Collective Bargaining in the Public Sector." In *Public Sector Bargaining*, 2d ed., edited by Benjamin Aaron, Joyce M. Najita, and James L. Stern, 1–51. Washington, D.C.: BNA Books.

Burton, Clare, Raven Hag, and Gay Thompson. 1987. *Women's Worth: Pay Equity and Job Evaluation in Australia*. Australian Government Publishing Service.

Callaghan, Polly, and Heidi Hartmann. 1991. *Contingent Work: A Chart Book on Part-time and Temporary Employment*. Washington, D.C.: Economic Policy Institute.

Cappelli, Peter, and Robert B. McKersie. 1985. "Labor and the Crisis in Collective Bargaining." In *Challenges and Choices Facing American Labor*, edited by Thomas A. Kochan, 227–45. Cambridge: MIT Press.

Carré, Francoise J., Virginia duRivage, and Chris Tilly. 1994. "Representing the Part-Time and Contingent Workforce: Challenges for Unions and Public Policy." In *Restoring the Promise of American Labor Law*, edited by Sheldon Friedman, Richard W. Hurd, Rudolph O. Oswald, and Ronald L. Seeber. 314–23. Ithaca, N.Y.: ILR Press.

"The Chastening of Public Employees." 1993. *Governing* (January): 26–30.

Chi, Keon. 1986. "Comparable Worth in State Government: Trends and Issues." *Policy Studies Review* 5 (4): 800–814.

Clarke, Edwin R. 1984. "The Relationship of Wages to Profits." In *Equal Pay for UNequal Work*, edited by Phyllis Schlafly, 199–208. Washington, D.C.: Eagle Forum Education and Legal Defense Fund.

Cobble, Dorothy Sue. 1993. "Remaking Unions for the New Majority." In *Women and Unions: Forging a Partnership*, edited by Dorothy Sue Cobble, 3–23. Ithaca, N.Y.: ILR Press.

———. 1994. "Making Postindustrial Unionism Possible." In *Restoring the Promise of American Labor Law*, edited by Sheldon Friedman, Richard W. Hurd, Rudolph O. Oswald, and Ronald L. Seeber. 285–302. Ithaca, N.Y.: ILR Press.

Cockburn, Cynthia. 1991. *In the Way of Women: Men's Resistance to Sex Equality in Organizations*. Ithaca, N.Y.: ILR Press.

Cole, Richard T. 1989. "Michigan Governor Blanchard: Managing through Messages." *The Journal of State Government* 62 (July/August): 147–52.

Commission on the Future of Worker-Management Relations. 1994. *Fact Finding Report*. Washington, D.C.: U.S. Department of Labor, May.

———. 1995. *Final Report and Recommendations*. Washington, D.C.: U.S. Department of Labor, January.

Corcoran, Mary, and Gregory J. Duncan. 1979. "Work History, Labor Force Attachment, and Earnings Differences between the Races and Sexes." *Journal of Human Resources* 14 (winter): 3–20.

Crouch, Winston W. 1978. *Organized Civil Servants: Public Employer-Employee Relations in California*. Berkeley: University of California Press.

Cuneo, Carl J. 1990. *Pay Equity: The Labour-Feminist Challenge*. Toronto: Oxford University Press.

Dahl, Robert. 1985. *Preface to Economic Democracy*. Berkeley: University of California Press.

Danziger, Sheldon, and Peter Gottschalk, eds. 1993. *Uneven Tides: Rising Inequality in America*. New York: Russell Sage Foundation.

Davies, Margery W. 1982. *Woman's Place Is at the Typewriter: Office Work and Office Workers, 1870–1930*. Philadelphia: Temple University Press.

Dean, Virginia, Patti Roberts, and Carroll Boone. 1984. "Comparable Worth under Various Federal and State Laws." In *Comparable Worth and Wage Discrimination: Technical Possibilities and Political Realities*, edited by Helen Remick, 238–66. Philadelphia: Temple University Press.

Donohue, John D. 1989. *The Privatization Decision: Public Ends, Private Means.* New York: Basic Books.

Dresang, Dennis. 1984. *Public Personnel Management and Public Policy.* Boston: Little, Brown and Company.

duRivage, Virginia, ed. 1992. *New Policies for the Part-Time and Contingent Workforce.* Armonk, N.Y.: M. E. Sharpe.

Edsall, Thomas Byrne. 1988. "The Reagan Legacy." In *The Reagan Legacy*, edited by Sidney Blumenthal and Thomas Byrne Edsall, 3–50. New York: Pantheon.

Edwards, Richard. 1979. *Contested Terrain: The Transformation of the Workplace in the Twentieth Century.* New York: Basic Books, Inc.

Ehrenberg, Ronald G., and Robert S. Smith. 1987. "Comparable Worth Wage Adjustments and Female Employment in the State and Local Sector." *Journal of Labor Economics* 5 (April): 43–62.

Ehrenreich, Barbara, and John Ehrenreich. 1979. "The Professional-Managerial Class." In *Between Labor and Capital*, edited by Pat Walker, 5–45. Boston: South End Press.

Eisinger, Peter K., and William Gormley. 1988. "The Midwest Response to New Federalism." In *The Midwest Response to New Federalism*, edited by Peter K. Eisinger and William Gormley, 3–17. Madison: University of Wisconsin Press.

Eisenstein, Zillah. 1981. *The Radical Future of Liberal Feminism.* New York: Longman.

———. 1984. *Feminism and Sexual Equality.* New York: Monthly Review Press.

Engberg, Elizabeth. 1993. "Union Responses to the Contingent Workforce." In *Women and Unions*, edited by Dorothy Sue Cobble, 163–75. Ithaca, N.Y.: ILR Press.

England, Paula. 1982. "The Failure of Human Capital Theory to Explain Occupational Sex Segregation." *The Journal of Human Resources* 17 (3): 358–70.

———. 1984. "Wage Appreciation and Depreciation: A Test of Neoclassical Economic Explanations of Occupational Sex Segregation." *Social Forces* 62 (3): 726–49.

———. 1992. *Comparable Worth: Theories and Evidence.* New York: Aldine de Gruyter.

Equality for Women at Work: A Survey of 10 OECD Countries. 1985. Canberra: Australia Government Publishing Service.

Equal Remuneration: General Survey by the Committee of Experts on the Application of Conventions and Recommendations. 1986. Geneva: International Labour Office.

Evans, Sara, and Barbara Nelson. 1989a. "The Impact of Pay Equity on Public Employees: State of Minnesota Employees' Attitudes toward Wage Policy Innovation." In *Pay Equity: Empirical Inquiries*, edited by Robert T. Michel, Heidi I. Hartmann, and Brigid O'Farrell, 200–221. Washington, D.C.: National Academy Press.

———. 1989b. *Wage Justice: Comparable Worth and the Paradox of Technocratic Reform*. Chicago: University of Chicago Press.

———. 1991. "Translating Wage Gains into Social Change: International Lessons from Implementing Pay Equity in Minnesota." In *Just Wages: A Feminist Assessment of Pay Equity*, edited by Judy Fudge and Patricia McDermott, 227–46. Toronto: University of Toronto Press.

———. 1993. "Comparable Worth." In *Gender and Public Policy: Cases and Comments*, edited by Kenneth Winston and Mary Jo Bane, 199–207. Boulder: Westview Press.

Feldberg, Roslyn L. 1984. "Comparable Worth: Toward Theory and Practice in the United States." *Signs* 10 (2): 311–28.

———. 1987. "Comparable Worth: The Relationship of Method and Politics." In *Ingredients for Women's Employment Policy*, edited by Christine Bose and Glenna Spitze, 245–50. Albany: State University of New York Press.

Figart, Deborah M. 1989. "Collective Bargaining and Career Development for Women in the Public Sector." *Journal of Collective Negotiations in the Public Sector* 81(4): 301–13.

———. 1995. "Evaluating Pay Equity in Michigan: A Strategic Choice Perspective." *Industrial Relations* 34 (2, April): 263–81.

Figart, Deborah M., and June Lapidus. 1995. "A Gender Analysis of Labor Market Policies for the Working Poor in the U.S." *Feminist Economics* 1 (3, fall): 60–81.

Filer, Randall K. 1989. "Occupational Segregation, Compensating Differentials, and Comparable Worth." In *Pay Equity: Empirical Inquiries*, edited by Robert T. Michel, Heidi I. Hartmann, and Brigid O'Farrell, 153–70. Washington, D.C.: National Academy Press.

Flammang, Janet. 1986. "Effective Implementation: The Case of Comparable Worth in San Jose." *Policy Studies Review* 5 (4): 815–37.

Franzway, Suzanne, Dianne Court, and Robert W. Connell. 1989. *Staking a Claim: Feminism, Bureaucracy and the State*. Oxford, U.K.: Polity Press.

Freeman, Jo. 1975. *The Politics of Women's Liberation*. New York: McKay.

Freeman, Richard B., and James L. Medoff. 1984. *What Do Unions Do?* New York: Basic Books.

Fudge, Judy. 1993. "The Gendered Dimension of Labour Law: Why Women Need Inclusive Unionism and Broader-Based Bargaining." In *Women Challenging Unions*, edited by P. McDermott and L. Bresleen, 231–48. Toronto: University of Toronto Press.

Fudge, Judy, and Patricia McDermott, eds. 1991. *Just Wages: A Feminist Assessment of Pay Equity*. Toronto: University of Toronto Press.

Gabin, Nancy F. 1989. "The Issue of the Eighties: Comparable Worth and the Labor Movement." *Indiana Academy of the Social Sciences Proceedings 1988* 23 (February): 51–58.

———. 1990. *Feminism in the Labor Movement: Women and the United Auto Workers, 1935–1975*. Ithaca, N.Y.: Cornell University Press.

Gelb, Joyce. 1987. "Social Movement Success: A Comparative Analysis of Feminism in the United States and the United Kingdom." In *The Women's Movements of the United States and Western Europe: Consciousness, Political Opportunity, and Public Policy*, edited by Mary Fainsod Katzenstein and Carol McClurg Mueller, 267–89. Philadelphia: Temple University Press.

————. 1989. *Feminism and Politics: A Comparative Perspective*. Berkeley: University of California Press.

George, Emily. 1982. *Martha W. Griffiths*. Washington, D.C.: University Press of America.

Glickman, Lawrence. 1993. "Inventing the American Standard of Living: Gender, Race and Working Class Identity, 1880–1925." *Labor History* 34 (spring–summer): 221–35.

Gold, Michael Evan. 1983. *A Dialogue on Comparable Worth*. Ithaca, N.Y.: ILR Press.

Golden, Miriam, and Jonas Pontusson, eds. 1992. *Bargaining for Change: Union Politics in North America and Europe*. Ithaca, N.Y.: Cornell University Press.

Goodman, John B., and Gary W. Lovement. 1991. "Does Privatization Serve the Public Interest?" *Harvard Business Review* (November–December): 26–38.

Gordon, David M., Richard Edwards, and Michael Reich. 1982. *Segmented Work, Divided Workers: The Historical Transformation of Labor in the United States*. Cambridge: Cambridge University Press.

Gormley, William T., Jr. 1991. "The Privatization Controversy." In *Privatization and Its Alternatives*, edited by William T. Gormley, Jr., 3–16. Madison: University of Wisconsin Press.

Grant, Judith, and Peta Tancred. 1992. "A Feminist Perspective on State Bureaucracy." In *Gendering Organizational Analysis*, edited by Albert J. Mills and Peta Tancred, 112–28. Newbury Park, Calif.: Sage Publishers.

Green, James, and Chris Tilly. 1987. "Service Unionism: Directions for Organizing." In *Proceedings of the 1987 Spring Meeting, April 1–May 1, Boston, Massachusetts*, edited by Barbara D. Dennis, 486–95. Madison: Industrial Relations Research Association.

Greenberg, Stanley. 1985. *Report on Democratic Defection*. Washington, D.C.: Greenberg Research, Inc., April.

Grune, Joy Ann, ed. 1980. *Manual on Pay Equity: Raising Wages for Women's Work*. Washington, D.C.: Conference on Alternative State and Local Policies.

Gunderson, Morley. 1994. *Comparable Worth and Gender Discrimination: An International Perspective*. Geneva: International Labour Office.

Gunderson, Morley, and W. Craig Riddell. 1992. "Comparable Worth: Canada's Experience." *Contemporary Policy Issues* 10 (July): 85–94.

Hagen, Elisabeth, and Jane Jenson. 1988. "Paradoxes and Promises: Work and Politics in the Postwar Years." In *Feminization of the Labor Force*, edited by Jane Jenson, Elisabeth Hagen, and Ceallaigh Reddy, 3–16. New York: Oxford University Press.

Haignere, Lois. 1991. "Pay Equity Implementation: Experimentation, Negotiation, Mediation, Litigation, and Aggravation." In *Just Wages: A Feminist Assessment of Pay Equity*, edited by Judy Fudge and Patricia McDermott, 160–71. Toronto: University of Toronto Press.

Harrison, Bennett, and Barry Bluestone. 1988. *The Great U-Turn: Corporate Restructuring and the Polarization of America*. New York: Basic Books.

Harrison, Cynthia. 1988. *On Account of Sex: The Politics of Women's Issues 1945–1968*. Berkeley: University of California Press.

Hartmann, Heidi. 1976. "Capitalism, Patriarchy, and Job Segregation by Sex." *Signs* 1 (3): 137–69.

———. 1979. "The Unhappy Marriage of Marxism and Feminism: Towards a More Progressive Union." *Capital and Class* 8 (summer): 1–33.

———. 1993. "Roundtable on Pay Equity and Affirmative Action." In *Women and Unions: Forging a Partnership*, edited by Dorothy Sue Cobble, 43–49. Ithaca, N.Y.: ILR Press.

Hartmann, Heidi, and Stephanie Aaronson. 1994. "Pay Equity and Women's Wage Increases: Success in the States, A Model for the Nation." *Duke Journal of Gender Law and Policy* (1): 69–87.

Hartsock, Nancy C. M. 1985. *Money, Sex, and Power: Toward a Feminist Historical Materialism*. Boston: Northeastern University Press.

Hastings, Sue. 1992. "Equal Value in the Local Authorities Sector in Great Britain." In *Equal Value/Comparable Worth in the UK and USA*, edited by Peggy Kahn and Elizabeth Meehan, 215–29. New York: St. Martin's Press.

Heclo, Hugh. 1986. "Reaganism and the Search for a Public Philosophy." In *Perspectives on the Reagan Years*, edited by John Palmer, 31–63. Washington, D.C.: The Urban Institute.

Heen, Mary. 1984. "A Review of Federal Court Decisions under Title VII of the Civil Rights Act of 1964." In *Comparable Worth and Wage Discrimination*, edited by Helen Remick, 197–218. Philadelphia: Temple University Press.

Heidenheimer, Arnold, Hugh Heclo, and Carolyn Teich Adams. 1990. *Comparative Public Policy: The Politics of Social Choice in America, Europe and Japan*. New York: St. Martin's.

Henig, Jeffery R. 1989–90. "Privatization in the United States: Theory and Practice." *Political Science Quarterly* 104 (4): 649–70.

Hill, M. Anne, and Mark R. Killingsworth. 1989. *Comparable Worth: Analyses and Evidence*. Ithaca, N.Y.: ILR Press.

Horowitz, Morris A. 1994. *Collective Bargaining in the Public Sector*. New York: Lexington Books.

Horrell, Sara, Jill Rubery, and Brendan Burchell. 1989. "Unequal Jobs or Unequal Pay?" *Industrial Relations Journal* 20 (3, autumn): 176–91.

Hurd, Richard W. 1993. "Organizing and Representing Clerical Workers: The Harvard Model." In *Women and Unions: Forging a New Partnership*, edited by Dorothy Sue Cobble, 316–36. Ithaca, N.Y.: ILR Press.

Hyman, Richard, and Anthony Ferner, eds. 1994. *New Frontiers in European Industrial Relations*. Oxford: Basil Blackwell.

Institute for Women's Policy Research. 1993. *Pay Equity in State Governments*. Washington, D.C.

———. 1994. "What Do Unions Do for Women?" Research-in-Brief. Washington, D.C.

Jancey, Marilyn. 1994. Statement of Marilyn Jancey, retired, Everett, Massachusetts, School District. *Joint Hearing on the Fair Pay Act of 1994*. Joint Hearing Before the Subcommittee on Select Education and Civil Rights of the Committee on Education and Labor and the Subcommittee on Compensation and Employee Benefits of the Committee on Post Office and Civil Service. House of Representatives, 103d Congress, July 21. Washington, D.C.: U.S. Government Printing Office.

Jarman, Jennifer. 1994. "Which Way Forward? Assessing the Current Proposals to Amend the Equal Pay Act." *Work, Employment, and Society* 8 (2, June): 243–54.

Jenson, Jane, Elisabeth Hagen, and Ceallaigh Reddy, eds. 1988. *Feminization of the Labor Force: Paradoxes and Promises*. New York: Oxford University Press.

Johansen, Elaine. 1984. *Comparable Worth: The Myth and the Movement*. Boulder: Westview Press.

Johnston, Paul. 1994. *Success While Others Fail: Social Movement Unionism and the Public Workplace*. Ithaca, N.Y.: ILR Press.

Jones, Bryan D., and Lynn W. Bachelor with Carter Wilson. 1986. *The Sustaining Hand: Community Leadership and Corporate Power*. Lawrence: University of Kansas Press.

Kahn, Peggy, and Elizabeth Meehan, eds. 1992. *Equal Value/Comparable Worth in the UK and USA*. New York: St. Martin's Press.

Kahn, Shulamit. 1992. "Economic Implications of Public-Sector Comparable Worth: The Case of San Jose, California." *Industrial Relations* 31 (2, spring): 270–91.

Kaplan, Marshall, and Sue O'Brien. 1991. *The Governors and the New Federalism*. Boulder: Westview Press.

Kates, Carol A. 1989. "Working Class Feminism and Feminist Unions: Title VII, UAW and NOW." *Labor Studies Journal* 14 (summer): 28–45.

———. 1994a. "Pay Equity and Wage Justice." *Review of Radical Political Economics* 26 (2): 1–23.

———. 1994b. "Pay Equity in Local Government: A Case Study." *Labor Studies Journal* 19 (2): 48–66.

Katz, Lawrence F., and Alan B. Krueger. 1991. "Changes in the Structure of Wages in the Public and Private Sectors." In *Research in Labor Economics* 12, edited by Ronald Ehrenberg, 137–72. Greenwich, Conn.: JAI Press.

Kautzer, Kathleen. 1992. " 'We Can't Eat Prestige': The Yale University Workers' Campaign for Comparable Worth." In *Equal Value/Comparable Worth in the UK and USA*, edited by Peggy Kahn and Elizabeth Meehan, 137–64. New York: St. Martin's Press.

Kaza, Greg. 1991. "Lansing with Wolves: Can Michigan's Engler Pull off His Taxpayer's Revolution?" *Policy Review* 57 (summer): 74–77.

Kelly, Rita Mae, and Jane Baynes, eds. 1988. *Comparable Worth, Pay Equity, and Public Policy*. Westport, Conn.: Greenwood Press.

Kessler-Harris, Alice. 1990. *A Woman's Wage: Historical Meanings and Social Consequences*. Lexington, Ky.: University Press of Kentucky.

———. 1994. "Feminism and Affirmative Action." In *Debating Affirmative Action: Race, Gender, Ethnicity and the Politics of Inclusion*, edited by Nicolaus Mills, 68–79. New York: Bantam Doubleday Dell.

Killingsworth, Mark R. 1985. "The Economics of Comparable Worth: Analytical, Empirical, and Policy Questions." In *Comparable Worth: New Directions for Research*, edited by Heidi I. Hartmann, 86–115. Washington, D.C.: National Academy Press.

———. 1987. "Heterogeneous Preferences, Compensating Wage Differentials, and Comparable Worth." *Quarterly Journal of Economics* 102 (November): 727–41.

———. 1990. *The Economics of Comparable Worth*. Kalamazoo, Mich.: W.E. Upjohn Institute.

Kim, Marlene. 1989. "Gender Bias in Compensation Structures: A Case Study of Its Historical Basis and Persistence." *Journal of Social Issues* 45 (4): 39–50.

Kochan, Thomas A. 1995. "Using the Dunlop Report to Achieve Mutual Gains." *Industrial Relations* 34 (3, July): 350–66.

Kramer, Leo. 1962. *Labor's Paradox: The American Federation of State, County, and Municipal Employees, AFL-CIO*. New York: John Wiley and Sons.

Kuhn, Sarah, and Barry Bluestone. 1987. "Economic Restructuring and the Female Labor Market: The Impact of Industrial Change on Women." In *Women, Households, and the Economy*, edited by Lourdes Beneria and Catharine R. Stimpson, 3–32. New Brunswick: Rutgers University Press.

Kuttner, Robert. 1988. "Reaganism, Liberalism and the Democrats." In *The Reagan Legacy*, edited by Sidney Blumenthal and Thomas Byrne Edsall, 99–134. New York: Pantheon.

Labour Research Department (U.K.). 1993. *Redundancy and Transfer Rights*. London: LRD, May.

Ladd-Taylor, Molly. 1985. "Women Workers and the Yale Strike." *Feminist Studies* 11 (fall): 465–89.

Lamp, Virginia B. 1985. "Statement on Comparable Worth . . . for the Chamber of Commerce of the United States." In U.S. Congress, House Committee on Post Office and Civil Service, Subcommittee on Compensation and Employee Benefits, *Options for Conducting a Pay Equity Study of Federal Pay and Classifications Systems*, 99th Cong., May 2, 311–53.

Lapidus, June, and Deborah M. Figart. 1994. "Comparable Worth as an Anti-Poverty Strategy: Evidence from the March 1992 CPS." *Review of Radical Political Economics* 26 (3, September): 1–10.

Larsen, Lex K. 1995. *Employment Discrimination*, 2nd ed. New York: Matthew Bender/Times Mirror Books.

Lewin, Tamar. 1989. "Pay Equity for Women's Jobs Finds Success Outside Courts." *New York Times*, October 7: 1, 7.

Lindblom, Charles. 1977. *Politics and Markets*. New York: Basic Books.

———. 1988. *Democracy and Market System*. Oslo: Norwegian University Press.

Lorber, Lawrence Z. 1985. "Statement . . . on Behalf of the American Society for Personnel Administration." In U.S. Congress, House Committee on Post Office and Civil Service, Subcommittee on Compensation and Employee Benefits, *Options for Conducting a Pay Equity Study of Federal Pay and Classifications Systems*, 99th Cong., April 4, 257–72.

Malveaux, Julianne. 1985. "Comparable Worth and Its Impact on Black Women." *Review of Black Political Economy* 14 (2–3, fall/winter): 47–60.

Marglin, Stephen. 1974. "What Do Bosses Do? The Origins and Function of Hierarchy in Capitalist Production." *Review of Radical Political Economics* 6 (2, summer).

McCann, Michael W. 1994. *Rights at Work: Pay Equity Reform and the Politics of Legal Mobilization.* Chicago: University of Chicago Press.

McColgan, Aileen. 1993. "Legislating Equal Pay? Lessons from Canada." *Industrial Law Journal* 22 (4, December): 269–86.

McCormick, Ernest J. 1981. "Minority Report." In *Women, Work, and Wages: Equal Pay for Jobs of Equal Value,* edited by Donald J. Treiman and Heidi I. Hartmann, 115–30. Washington, D.C.: National Academy Press.

McLaughlin, Doris B. 1970. *Michigan Labor: A Brief History from 1818 to the Present.* Ann Arbor: Institute of Labor and Industrial Relations.

Mellor, Earl F. 1987. "Workers at the Minimum Wage or Less: Who They Are and the Jobs They Hold." *Monthly Labor Review* (July): 34–38.

Michael, Robert, and Heidi Hartmann, eds. 1989. *Pay Equity: Empirical Inquiries.* Washington, D.C.: National Academy Press.

Milkman, Ruth. 1983. "Female Factory Labor and Industrial Structure: Control and Conflict over 'Woman's Place' in Auto and Electrical Manufacturing." *Politics and Society* 12 (2): 159–203.

———. 1985. "Women Workers, Feminism, and the Labor Movement Since the 1960s." In *Women, Work and Protest: A Century of U.S. Women's Labor History,* edited by Ruth Milkman, 300–322. New York: Routledge and Kegan Paul.

Miller, Nancy. 1993. "The Scales of Injustice." *CA Magazine* 126 (4, April): 28–32.

Mitchell, Daniel J. B. 1988. "Collective Bargaining and Compensation in the Public Sector." In *Public Sector Bargaining,* 2d ed., edited by Benjamin Aaron, Joyce M. Najita, and James L. Stern, 124–59. Washington, D.C.: BNA Books.

Moody, Kim. 1988. *An Injury to All: The Decline of American Unionism.* New York: Verso Press.

Murphy, Marjorie. 1990. *Blackboard Unions: The AFT and the NEA, 1900–1980.* Ithaca, N.Y.: Cornell University Press.

Nash, June. 1983. "The Impact of the Changing International Division of Labor on Different Sectors of the Labor Force." In *Women, Men, and the International Division of Labor,* edited by June Nash and Maria Patricia Fernandez-Kelly, 3–38. Albany: State University of New York Press.

National Commission for Employment Policy. 1987. *Privatization and Public Employees: The Impact of City and County Contracting out on Government Workers.* Washington, D.C.: NCEP, May.

National Committee on Pay Equity. 1984–96. *Newsnotes.* Washington, D.C.: NCPE.

———. 1985. "Summary of Pay Equity Activity." *Newsnotes* (May): A–D.

———. 1987. *Job Evaluation: A Tool for Pay Equity.* Washington, D.C.: NCPE.

———. 1989. *Pay Equity in the Public Sector, 1979–1989.* Washington, D.C.: NCPE.

———. n.d. [1990]. *Bargaining for Pay Equity: A Strategy Manual.* Washington, D.C.: NCPE.

———. 1993. *Erase the Bias: A Pay Equity Guide to Eliminating Race and Sex Bias from Wage Setting Systems.* Washington, D.C.: NCPE.

Neathey, Fiona. 1992. "Job Assessment, Job Evaluation and Equal Value." In *Equal Value/Comparable Worth in the UK and USA,* edited by Peggy Kahn and Elizabeth Meehan, 65–81. New York: St. Martin's Press.

Needleman, Ruth. 1994. "The Devaluation and Privatization of Public Service: Race and Gender Implications." Paper delivered at the Fourth Annual Women's Policy Research Conference, Innovations in Government and Public Policy: New Directions for Women. Washington, D.C., June 4.

Newman, Katherine S. 1988. *Falling from Grace: The Experience of Downward Mobility in the American Middle Class.* New York: Random House.

———. 1994. "Troubled Times: The Cultural Dimensions of Economic Decline." In *Understanding American Economic Decline,* edited by Michael A. Bernstein and David E. Adler, 330–57. New York: Cambridge University Press.

Newman, Winn. 1976. "Policy Issues." *Signs: Journal of Women in Culture and Society* 1: 265–72.

Newman, Winn, and Jeanne M. Vonhoff. 1981. "Separate but Equal: Job Segregation and Pay Equity in the Wake of Gunther." *University of Illinois Law Review* 2: 269–331.

New York State Comparable Worth Study. 1985. Albany: Center for Women in Government, October 1.

Offe, Claus. 1984. *Contradictions of the Welfare State.* Cambridge: MIT Press.

O'Neill, June. 1984. "An Argument against Comparable Worth." In *Comparable Worth: Issue for the 80's,* 177–86. Washington, D.C.: U.S. Civil Rights Commission.

———. 1990. "Women and Wages." *American Enterprise* 1 (6) November/December.

Orazem, Peter F., and J. Peter Mattila. 1990. "The Implementation Process of Comparable Worth: Winners and Losers." *Journal of Political Economy* 98 (1): 134–52.

Osborne, David, and Ted Gaebler. 1992. *Re-inventing Government: How the Entrepreneurial Spirit Is Transforming the Public Sector.* Reading, Mass: Addison-Wesley Publishing Company.

Parker, Robert E. 1994. "Race, Sex, Class: The Contingent Work Force in the United States." *Race, Sex & Class* 2 (1, fall): 145–59.

Patten, Thomas H., Jr. 1988. *Fair Pay: The Managerial Challenge of Comparable Worth and Job Evaluation.* San Francisco: Jossey-Bass Publishers.

Paul, Ellen Frankel. 1989. *Equity and Gender: The Comparable Worth Debate.* New Brunswick: Transaction Publishers.

Peterson, Janice. 1990. "The Challenge of Comparable Worth: An Institutionalist View." *Journal of Economic Issues* 24 (2, June): 605–12.

Polacheck, Solomon William. 1984. "Women in the Economy: Perspectives on Gender Inequality." In *Comparable Worth: Issue for the 80's,* 34–53. Washington, D.C.: U.S. Civil Rights Commission.

Power, Marilyn. 1994. "Achieving Pay Equity for Child Care Workers." Paper presented at the International Association for Feminist Economics Summer Conference. Milwaukee, Wis.: July 29.

Power, Marilyn, and Sam Rosenberg. 1993. "Black Female Clerical Workers: Movement toward Equality with White Women?" *Industrial Relations* 32 (2, April): 223–37.

———. 1995. "Race, Class, and Occupational Mobility: Black and White Women in Service Work in the United States." *Feminist Economics* 1 (3, fall): 40–59.

Press, Charles, and Kenneth Verburg. 1985. "Gubernatorial Transition in Michigan, 1982–83." In *Gubernatorial Transitions: The 1982 Election,* edited by Thad Beyle, 221–23. Durham, N.C.: Duke University Press.

Rabkin, Jeremy. 1984. "Comparable Worth as a Civil Rights Policy: Potentials for Disaster." In *Comparable Worth: Issue for the 80's,* 187–95. Washington, D.C.: U.S. Civil Rights Commission.

Reich, Michael, David M. Gordon, and Richard Edwards. 1973. "A Theory of Labor Market Segmentation." *American Economic Review* 63 (2, May): 359–65.

Remick, Helen. 1984. "Major Issues in A Priori Applications." In *Comparable Worth and Wage Discrimination: Technical Possibilities and Political Realities,* edited by Helen Remick, 99–117. Philadelphia: Temple University Press.

———. 1986. "The Case of Comparable Worth in Washington State." *Policy Studies Review* 5: 838–48.

Report of Wisconsin's Task Force on Comparable Worth. 1985. Madison.

Reskin, Barbara F. ed. 1984. *Sex Segregation in the Workplace: Trends, Explanations, Remedies.* Washington, D.C.: National Academy Press.

Reskin, Barbara F., and Heidi I. Hartmann, eds. 1986. *Women's Work, Men's Work: Sex Segregation on the Job.* Washington, D.C.: National Academy Press.

Reskin, Barbara F., and Irene Padavic. 1994. *Women and Men at Work.* Thousand Oaks, Ca.: Pine Forge Press.

Reskin, Barbara F., and Patricia A. Roos. 1987. "Status Hierarchies and Sex Segregation." In *Ingredients for Women's Employment Policy,* edited by Christina Bose and Glenna Spitz, 3–22. Albany: State University of New York Press.

———. 1990. *Job Queues, Gender Queues: Explaining Women's Inroads into Male Occupations.* Philadelphia: Temple University Press.

Reverby, Susan. 1987. *Ordered to Care: The Dilemma of American Nursing, 1850–1945.* Cambridge: Cambridge University Press.

Rhoads, Steven E. 1993. *Incomparable Worth: Pay Equity Meets the Market.* New York: Cambridge University Press.

Riccucci, Norma M. 1990. *Women, Minorities, and Unions in the Public Sector.* New York: Greenwood Press.

Rogers, Joel. 1995. "A Strategy for Labor." *Industrial Relations* 34 (3, July): 367–81.

Rom, Mark. 1988. "The Political Economy of the Midwest." In *The Midwest Response to New Federalism,* edited by Peter K. Eisinger and William Gormley, 18–54. Madison: University of Wisconsin Press.

Roos, Patricia A., and Barbara F. Reskin. 1984. "Institutional Factors Contributing to Sex Segregation in the Workplace." In *Sex Segregation in the Workplace: Trends, Explanations, Remedies*, edited by Barbara F. Reskin, 235–60. Washington, D.C.: National Academy Press.

Rosenberg, Sam. 1991. "From Segmentation to Flexibility: A Selective Survery." *Review of Radical Political Economics* 23 (1 & 2, spring & summer): 71–79.

Ross, Jean. 1993. "Roundtable on Pay Equity and Affirmative Action." In *Women and Unions: Forging a Partnership*, edited by Dorothy Sue Cobble, 49–56. Ithaca, N.Y.: ILR Press.

Rubery, Jill. 1978. "Structured Labor Markets, Worker Organization, and Low Pay." *Cambridge Journal of Economics* 2 (1, March): 17–36.

Rubery, Jill, and Roger Tarling. 1982. "Women in the Recession." In *Socialist Economic Review 1982*, edited by David Currie and Malcolm Sawyer, 47–75. London: Merlin Press.

Sacks, Karen Brodkin. 1988. *Caring by the Hour: Women, Work, and Organizing at Duke Medical Center*. Urbana: University of Illinois Press.

Salaman, Graeme. 1981. *Class and the Corporation*. London: Fontana.

Sawhill, Isabel V. 1986. "Reaganomics in Retrospect." In *Perspectives on the Reagan Years*, edited by John Palmer, 91–120. Washington, D.C.: The Urban Institute.

Scales-Trent, Judy. 1984. "Comparable Worth: Is This a Theory for Black Workers?" *Women's Rights Law Reporter* 8: 51–58.

Schneider, Krista. 1993. *The Human Costs of Contracting Out: A Survival Guide for Public Employees*. Washington, D.C.: Public Employees Department, AFL-CIO.

Service Employees International Union (SEIU). n.d. *Privatization Overview*. Washington, D.C.: Research Department, Winter Commission Report.

Shafran, Lynn Hecht. 1982. "Women: Reversing a Decade of Progress." In *What Reagan Is Doing to Us*, edited by Alan Gartner, Colin Greer, and Frank Reissen, 162–89. New York: Harper and Row.

Shattuck, Cathie A. 1985. "Statement of the American Retail Federation." In U.S. Congress, House Committee on Post Office and Civil Service, Subcommittee on Compensation and Employee Benefits, *Options for Conducting a Pay Equity Study of Federal Pay and Classifications Systems*, 99th Cong., June 18, 672–81.

Shostak, Arthur B. 1991. *Robust Unionism: Innovations in the Labor Movement*. Ithaca, N.Y.: ILR Press.

Smith, James P., and Michael Ward. 1989. "Women in the Labor Market and in the Family." *Journal of Economic Perspectives* 3 (winter): 9–23.

Snyder, Carl Dean. 1973. *White-Collar Workers and the UAW*. Urbana: University of Illinois Press.

Sokoloff, Natalie J. 1987. "What's Happening to Women's Employment: Issues for Women's Labor Struggles in the 1980s–1990s." In *Hidden Aspects of Women's Work*, edited by Christine Bose, Roslyn Feldberg, Natalie Sokoloff, and the Women and Work Research Group, 14–45. New York: Praeger.

———. 1988. "Contributions of Marxism and Feminism to the Sociology of

Women and Work." In *Women Working*, 2d ed., edited by Ann Helton Stromberg and Shirley Harkess, 116–31. Mountain View, Ca.: Mayfield Publishing Company.

Sorensen, Elaine. 1989. "The Wage Effects of Occupational Sex Composition: A Review and New Findings." In *Comparable Worth: Analyses and Evidence*, edited by M. Anne Hill and Mark R. Killingsworth, 57–79. Ithaca, N.Y.: ILR Press.

———. 1991. *Exploring the Reasons behind the Narrowing Gender Gap in Earnings*. Washington, D.C.: Urban Institute Press. Report 91-2.

———. 1994. *Comparable Worth: Is It a Worthy Policy?* Princeton: Princeton University Press.

Spalter-Roth, Roberta, and Ronnee Schreiber. 1995. "Outsider Issues and Insider Tactics: Strategic Tensions in the Women's Policy Network during the 1980s." In *Feminist Organizations: Harvest of the New Women's Movement*, edited by Myra Marx Ferree and Patricia Yancey Martin, 105–27. Philadelphia: Temple University Press.

Spalter-Roth, Roberta, Heidi Hartmann, and Nancy Collins. 1994. "What Do Unions Do for Women?" In *Restoring the Promise of American Labor Law*, edited by Sheldon Friedman, Richard W. Hurd, Rudolph O. Oswald, and Ronald L. Seeber, 193–206. Ithaca, N.Y.: ILR Press.

Spenner, Kenneth I. 1990. "Skill: Meanings, Methods, and Measures." *Work and Occupations* 17 (4, November): 399–421.

Spigelmyer, Sharon. 1985. Testimony of Sharon Spigelmyer, Director, Human Resources and Equal Opportunity, National Association of Manufacturers on Comparable Worth. In U.S. Congress, House Committee on Post Office and Civil Service, Subcommittee on Compensation and Employee Benefits, *Options for Conducting a Pay Equity Study of Federal Pay and Classifications Systems*, 99th Cong., May 2, 375–96.

Standing, Guy. 1989. "Global Feminization through Flexible Labor." *World Development* 17 (7): 1077–95.

Starr, Paul. 1987. "The Case for Skepticism." In *Privatization and Its Alternatives*, edited by William T. Gormley, Jr., 25–36. Madison: University of Wisconsin Press.

State of Maryland Comparable Worth Study. 1986. Annapolis, Md.: Commission on Compensation and Personnel Policies, February 26.

State of Oregon. n.d. Executive Department. Personnel and Labor Relations Division. "Historical Summary—Comparable Worth." Typescript.

Staudohar, Paul D. 1983. "Subcontracting in State and Local Government Employment." In *Collective Bargaining by Government Workers: The Public Employee*, edited by Harry Kershen, 184–90. Farmingdale, N.Y.: Baywood Publishing Company.

Steinberg, Ronnie. 1988. "The Unsubtle Revolution: Women, the State, and Equal Employment." In *Feminization of the Labor Force: Paradoxes and Promises*, edited by Jane Jenson, Elisabeth Hagen, and Ceallaigh Reddy, 189–213. New York: Oxford University Press.

———. 1989. *Mainstreaming Comparable Worth: Reforming Wage Discrimination to Palatable Pay Equity*. Unpublished manuscript.

————. 1990. "Social Construction of Skill: Gender, Power, and Comparable Worth." *Work and Occupations* (17): 449–82.

————. 1991. "Job Evaluation and Managerial Control: The Politics of Technique and the Techniques of Politics." In *Just Wages: A Feminist Assessment of Pay Equity*, edited by Judy Fudge and Patricia McDermott, 193–218. Toronto: University of Toronto Press.

————. 1992. "Gendered Instructions: Cultural Lag and Gender Bias in the Hay System of Job Evaluation." *Work and Occupations* 19: 387–432.

Steinberg, Ronnie, and Lois Haignere. 1987. "Equitable Compensation: Methodological Criteria for Comparable Worth." In *Ingredients for Women's Employment Policy*, edited by Christine Bose and Glenna Spitze, 157–82. Albany: State University of New York Press.

————. 1991. "Separate but Equivalent: Equal Pay for Work of Comparable Worth." In *Beyond Methodology: Feminist Scholarship as Lived Research*, edited by Mary Margaret Fonow and Judith A. Cook, 154–70. Bloomington: Indiana University Press.

Stern, James L. 1988. "Unionism in the Public Sector." In *Public Sector Bargaining*, 2d ed., edited by Benjamin Aaron, Joyce M. Najita, and James L. Stern. 52–89. Washington, D.C.: BNA Books.

Strauss, George. 1995. "Is the New Deal System Collapsing? With What Might It Be Replaced?" *Industrial Relations* 34 (3, July): 329–49.

Strober, Myra H., Suzanne Gerlach-Downie, and Kenneth E. Yeager. 1995. "Child Care Centers as Workplaces." *Feminist Economics* 1 (1, spring): 93–120.

Studenmund, A. H. 1992. *Using Econometrics: A Practical Guide*. New York: Harper Collins.

Sutton, Kathy. 1992. "Fighting for Equal Value: Health Workers in Northern Ireland." In *Equal Value/Comparable Worth in the UK and USA*, edited by Peggy Kahn and Elizabeth Meehan, 165–80. New York: St. Martin's Press.

Teitelbaum, Phyllis. 1989. "Feminist Theory and Standardized Testing." In *Gender/Body/Knowledge: Feminist Reconstructions of Being and Knowing*, edited by Alison M. Jaggar and Susan R. Bordo, 324–35. New Brunswick, N.J.: Rutgers University Press.

Tomaskovic-Devey, Donald. 1993. *Gender and Racial Inequality at Work: The Sources and Consequences of Job Segregation*. Ithaca, N.Y.: ILR Press.

Trade Union Research Unit. 1984. *A Guide to the Hay Job Evaluation Package*. Technical Note No. 94. Oxford, U.K.: TURU.

Treiman, Donald J. 1979. *Job Evaluation: An Analytic Review*. Washington, D.C.: National Academy of Sciences.

————. 1984. "Effect of Choice of Factors and Factor Weights in Job Evaluation." In *Comparable Worth and Wage Discrimination: Technical Possibilities and Political Realities*, edited by Helen Remick, 79–89. Philadelphia: Temple University Press.

Treiman, Donald J., and Heidi I. Hartmann, eds. 1981. *Women, Work, and Wages: Equal Pay for Jobs of Equal Value*. Washington, D.C.: National Academy Press.

Treiman, Donald J., Heidi I. Hartmann, and Patricia A. Roos. 1984. "Assessing

Pay Discrimination Using National Data." In *Comparable Worth and Wage Discrimination*, edited by Helen Remick, 137–54. Philadelphia: Temple University Press.

Troyer, Steve. 1987. "Labour Relations in the Public Service in the United States." In *Public Service Labour Relations*, edited by Tiziano Treu et al., 243–87. Geneva: International Labour Office.

United States General Accounting Office. 1985. *Options for Conducting a Pay Equity Study of Federal Pay and Classification Systems.* Washington, D.C.: GAO/GGD-85-37. March 1.

———. 1986. *Pay Equity: Status of State Activities.* Washington, D.C.: GAO/GGD 86–141, September 19.

Vallette, Robert G., and Richard B. Freeman. 1988. "Appendix B: The NBER Public Sector Collective Bargaining Law Data Set." In *When Public Sector Workers Unionize*, edited by Richard B. Freeman and Casey Ichniowski, 399–419. Chicago: University of Chicago Press.

Vogel, David. 1989. *Fluctuating Fortunes: The Political Power of Business in America.* New York: Basic Books.

Wachter, Michael L. 1995. "Labor Law Reform: One Step Forward and Two Steps Back." *Industrial Relations* 34 (3, July): 382–401.

Wagman, Barnet, and Nancy Folbre. 1988. "The Feminization of Inequality: Some New Patterns." *Challenge* (November–December): 56–59.

Wajcman, Judy. 1991. "Patriarchy, Technology, and Conceptions of Skill." *Work and Occupations* 18 (1, February): 29–45.

Walby, Sylvia. 1986. *Patriarchy at Work.* Cambridge: Polity Press.

———. 1990. *Theorising Patriarchy.* Oxford: Basil Blackwell.

Ward, Kathryn, ed. 1990. *Women Workers and Global Restructuring.* Ithaca, N.Y.: ILR Press.

White, John Patrick, and Thomas S. Crabb. 1988. "An Overview of Public Sector Employment Law in Michigan." *Labor Law Journal* (May): 286–98.

Wial, Howard. 1994. "New Bargaining Structures for New Forms of Business Organization." In *Restoring the Promise of American Labor Law*, edited by Sheldon Friedman, Richard W. Hurd, Rudolph O. Oswald, and Ronald L. Seeber, 303–13. Ithaca, N.Y.: ILR Press.

Willborn, Steven L. 1989. *A Secretary and a Cook: Challenging Women's Wages in the Courts of the United States and Great Britain.* Ithaca, N.Y.: ILR Press.

Williams, Robert E., and Lorence L. Kessler. 1984. *A Closer Look at Comparable Worth: A Study of the Basic Questions to Be Addressed in Approaching Pay Equity.* Washington, D.C.: National Foundation for the Study of Equal Employment Policy.

Winebrenner, Hugh. 1986. "The Implementation of Comparable Worth in Iowa." *Policy Studies Review* 5 (4): 863–70.

Wisscha, Glennis Ter. 1984. Statement of Glennis Ter Wisscha. In *Federal Pay Equity Act of 1984*, Part I. Hearings before the Subcommittee on Compensation and Employee Benefits of the Committee on Post Office and Civil Service, House of Representatives, 98th Cong., April 3 and 4. Washington, D.C.: U.S. Government Printing Office.

Withers, Claudia, and Judith A. Winston. 1989. "Equal Employment Opportunity." In *One Nation Divided*. Washington, D.C.: Citizen's Commission for Civil Rights.

Witt, Mary, and Patricia K. Naherny. 1975. *Women's Work—Up from 878: Report on the DOT Research Project*. Madison: Women's Education Resources, University of Wisconsin-Extension.

Witz, Anne, and Mike Savage. 1992. "The Gender of Organizations." In *Gender and Bureaucracy*, edited by Mike Savage and Anne Witz, 3–64. Cambridge: Blackwell.

"Women Face Barriers in Top Management." 1991–92. *Women in Public Service* (2, winter). Albany: Center for Women in Government.

Wright, Eric Olin. 1978. *Class, Crisis, and the State*. London: New Left Books.

Zavella, Patricia. 1987. *Women's Work and Chicano Families: Cannery Workers of the Santa Clara Valley*. Ithaca, N.Y.: Cornell University Press.

Zieger, Robert H. 1986. *American Workers, American Unions, 1920–1985*. Baltimore: The Johns Hopkins University Press.

Michigan Documentary Materials and Interviews

Advisory Committee for Group One [Classification Redesign Advisory Committee]. 1986–90. Committee meeting minutes; summaries of discussion and action. Lansing: Department of Civil Service.

AFSCME Council 25, Institutional Unit. 1983–86. *Contract Between State of Michigan and Michigan Council 25 AFSCME, AFL-CIO*.

———. 1986–89. *Contract between State of Michigan and Michigan Council 25 AFSCME, AFL-CIO*.

———. 1989–92. *Contract between State of Michigan and Michigan Council 25 AFSCME, AFL-CIO*.

AFSCME Local 567. 1993. Outline for Conference with Judge Stewart Newblatt, Federal District Court. November 10.

Ann Arbor News. Ann Arbor, Mich. Various issues.

Arthur Young and Company. 1981. *A Comparable Worth Study of the State of Michigan Job Classifications*. Detroit: Arthur Young and Company.

Audie-Figueroa, Alice. 1987. Statement on Behalf of the Labor Caucus of the Classification Review Project Advisory Committee to the Civil Service Commission. August 26.

Barker, Melissa A. 1990. Technical consultant's comments. *Summary of Testing of the Equitable Classification Plan for Group One Classes*, 4–8. Lansing: July.

———. 1994. Technical consultant, Department of Civil Service; assistant professor, State University of New York-Potsdam. Telephone interviews, May 18, August 31; interview, Detroit, Mich., May 31.

Bass, E. J. 1990. "Civil Service Report on Top Level Positions." *WIRE* 12 (5, May): 1, 4, 6.

Beal, Cynthia. 1992. Labor relations specialist, Michigan Corrections Organization, Local 526-M, SEIU. Interview, Lansing, Mich., March 6.

Bibbs, Martha. 1982. Memorandum to John Hueni regarding classification progress. August 23.

———. 1992. State personnel director, Department of Civil Service. Interview, Lansing, Mich., September 8.

Blanchard, James J. 1984. Governor of the state of Michigan. "State of the State." Speech. January.

———. 1985. Letter to Mr. Walter Greene, chair, Civil Service Commission. August 2.

———. 1987. "State of the State." Speech. January.

Black, Karon, and MSEA. 1981. *Charge of Discrimination.* Filed with Michigan Civil Rights Commission and U.S. Equal Employment Opportunity Commission. August 3.

Brown, Mary. 1993. State representative, Michigan House. Interview, Lansing, Mich., June 2.

Cain, Michael. 1979. AFSCME Council 25 Civil Service Department. Testimony to the Citizens Advisory Task Force on Civil Service Reform. March 21.

Campbell, Lawrence G., and Robert P. Young. 1985. "Comparable Worth." *The Detroiter* (April): 38–42.

Carter, Joan. 1985. Director of Government Affairs, the Employers Association of Detroit. Remarks to the Comparable Worth Task Force. April 26.

Chamber of Commerce [Michigan]. n.d. "Moving Michigan Forward: 1987–8 Legislative Priorities." Lansing.

———. n.d. "Proposed Legislative Priorities for 1985–6." Lansing.

———. 1984. "Official Policy Relating to Comparable Worth." Lansing: Board of Directors, April 17.

Citizens Advisory Task Force on Civil Service Reform (CATF). 1979. *Toward Improvement of Service to the Public.* Lansing: July.

Civil Service Commission. 1964. "State Employee Relations Policy." Lansing: December 1.

———. 1983–91. Minutes of Civil Service Commission Meetings.

———. 1989. *Rules.* Lansing: September.

Civil Service Commission, Employee Relations Board. 1985. *Impasse Panel Proposed Decision IP 85-02.*

———. 1988. *Impasse Panel Proposed Decision IP 88-08.*

———. 1991. *Impasse Panel Proposed Decision IP 91-01.*

Coalition of Labor Union Women [Michigan]. 1985a. Comments before the Comparable Worth Task Force. May 17.

———. 1985b. Memo to Sam Fishman, president, Michigan AFL-CIO. July 12.

———. 1985c. Letter to Prospective Conference Participants. July 19.

———. 1985d. Memo to Alvarado, Brown, Glazer, Jeffrey, Mason, Massaron. July 24.

Cohn, Joseph. 1992. Labor relations consultant, United Technical Employees Association. Interview, West Bloomfield, Mich., January 24.

Collette, Catherine. 1985. Testimony of AFSCME before the Comparable Worth Task Force of the Civil Service Commission. April 26.

Comparable Worth Task Force [grassroots]. 1982. Minutes of Meetings.

Comparable Worth Task Force [CWTF]. 1983–85. Minutes of Meetings.

———. 1985. *The Report of the Comparable Worth Task Force to the Michigan Civil Service Commission.* Lansing. June.

Constitution of the State of Michigan of 1963 (as amended).

Cooke, Margaret. 1993. Executive director, Michigan Women's Commission, 1977–84. Interview, Lansing, Mich., July 21.

Cooper, Janet. 1993. Director, Legal Affairs Bureau, Michigan Department of Civil Rights. Interview, Detroit, Mich., August 25.

Crain's Detroit Business. 1994. *1994 Book of Lists.* Detroit: Crain's.

Crittenden, Richard. 1994. Project director, Classification Redesign Project, Group Three. Telephone interviews: August 25, 1994; April 29, 1996.

Curran, Hilda Patricia [Pat]. 1991. Former firector, Office of Women and Work, Michigan Department of Labor. Interviews, Lansing, Mich., February 19, February 28, March 28, May 14.

Department of Civil Rights. 1982. "Michigan Civil Rights Commission and Michigan Department of Civil Rights." July 29. Typescript.

Department of Civil Rights and Department of Civil Service. 1971. *Employment Practices Review.* Lansing.

Department of Civil Service. n.d. *Michigan Benchmark System Factor Guides.* Lansing.

———. 1938. *First Annual Report of the Civil Service Department.* Lansing.

———. 1941. *Another Chapter in Civil Service.* Lansing.

———. 1964. "Employee Relations Policy." Lansing: December 14.

———. 1976. "Employee Relations Policy." Lansing: August 20.

———. 1980. "Employee Relations Policy." Lansing: April 25.

———. 1992. Summary Findings—Preliminary Testing of the Group Two Factoring System. Lansing: November 5.

Department of Civil Service, Management Services Division. 1980–95. *Annual Work Force Report.* Lansing: July.

Department of Civil Service, Merit Systems Planning and Development Bureau. 1990a. *ECP Group One: Technical, Office, Paraprofessional and Service Occupations* [Job Specifications and Implementation Package]. Lansing: April.

———. 1990b. Dear Employee . . . April 1.

———. 1990c. *Summary of Testing of the Equitable Classification Plan for Group One Classes.* Lansing: July.

———. 1993. *ECP Group Two: Business, Human Services, Scientific and Engineering Professional Occupations* [Job Specifications and Implementation Package]. Lansing: July.

Department of Civil Service, Merit System Review Project. n.d. *Job Content Survey.*

Department of Commerce [Michigan]. 1987. *Automotive Employment in Michigan.* Lansing.

———. 1991. *The Michigan Economy, 1979–1990.* Lansing.

Department of Labor. 1984. *General Departmental Order GDO-16.* Subject: Office of Women and Work. Lansing: August 1.

Detroit News. Detroit, Mich. Various issues.

Doyen, Joyce. 1992. President, UAW Local 6000. Interview, Lansing, Mich., February 19.

Duley, Margot. 1994. Former president (as Margot Duley-Morrow), Michigan National Organization for Women. Personal written communication, August 24.

Earle, Henry. n.d. [1985]. Representative, Michigan Manufacturers' Association. Statement to Comparable Worth Task Force.

Engler, John. 1991. Governor of the state of Michigan. "State of the State." Speech, January.

———. 1992. *Toward Public Trust in Public Service: Change in the State Classified Service.* Lansing: February 6.

Furlong, Nadine. 1985. Executive director, Michigan Nurses' Association. Statement to Comparable Worth Task Force.

Giese, Elizabeth. 1993. Board member, Michigan National Organization for Women. Interview, Hartland, Mich., June 7.

Granberry, Paulette. 1991. Labor relations specialist, Office of the State Employer. Interview, Lansing, Mich., May 14.

Grattan, Crary E. 1985. General counsel, Michigan State Chamber of Commerce. Testimony to the Civil Service Task Force on Comparable Worth. April 26.

Griggs, Henry. 1986. "MSEA Chartered as AFSCME Local 5." *Michigan AFSCME News* 8 (May–June): 3.

Haener, Dorothy. n.d. [1985]. Chair, Michigan Civil Rights Commission. Statement before the Michigan Civil Service Task Force on Comparable Worth.

———. 1993. Former chair, Michigan Civil Rights Commission. Telephone interview, Ann Arbor, Mich., August 3.

Hall, Millie, and Olga Madar. 1992. Letter to Lewis Dodak. October 2.

Hall, Thomas N. 1991. Labor relations specialist, Office of the State Employer. Interview, Lansing, Mich., May 14.

———. 1994a. Telephone interview, May 20.

———. 1994b. Personal written communication, May 26.

———. 1994c. Personal written communication, August 25.

Helms, Philip W. 1992. Public Affairs director, AFSCME Council 25. Interview, Lansing, Mich., February 19.

Hueni, John. 1983. "Comparable Worth Project." Memorandum to Michigan Civil Service Commission. March 9.

Keeley, Judith. 1994. Michigan Department of Labor. Personal communication, August 1.

Kelley, Frank J. 1978. Attorney General. Letter/opinion for Representative Alfred Sheridan. March 1.

Komer, Odessa. 1985. Vice-president, UAW. Statement before the Civil Service Task Force on Comparable Worth. April 26.

Koucky, Patricia. 1985. Representative, League of Women Voters of Michigan. Testimony on Comparable Worth Task Force Draft Report. April 24.

Landers, Frank M. 1988. *A Bureaucratic View of the Michigan State Government, 1935–1960.* Marshall, Mich.: The Marshall Press.

Legislative Program Effectiveness Unit (LPER), House Fiscal Agency. 1976. *The Michigan Civil Service System: Issues and Analysis.* November.

Madar, Olga. 1992. Consultant, Michigan Pay Equity Network; president emerita, Coalition of Labor Union Women. Interview, Detroit, Mich., July 30.

Massaron, Paul. 1992. International representative, United Auto Workers. Interview, Madison Heights, Mich., September 24.

Maynard, Libby. 1993. Chair, Michigan Democratic Party, 1979–83. Interview, Flint, Mich., July 12.

McCracken, Marian. 1993. Former president, Michigan National Organization for Women. Interview, Hartland, Mich., June 7.

Michigan AFL-CIO. 1981–82. Legislative Programs.

———. 1989–90. Legislative Programs.

Michigan AFL-CIO News. 1979–92. Lansing. Various issues.

Michigan AFSCME News. 1979–92. Lansing. Various issues.

Michigan Citizens Review Committee on Civil Service. 1988. *Report of the Citizens Review Committee.* Lansing.

Michigan Corrections Organization. 1985–87. *Security Unit Agreement between Michigan Corrections Organization, SEIU Local 526-M, AFL-CIO and State of Michigan.*

———. 1987–90. *Security Unit Agreement between Michigan Corrections Organization, SEIU Local 526-M, AFL-CIO and State of Michigan.* December 18, 1987–December 31, 1990.

———. 1990–91. *Security Unit Agreement between Michigan Corrections Organization, SEIU Local 526-M, AFL-CIO and State of Michigan.*

Michigan Democratic Party. 1949–88. State Central Committee Records, boxes 120, 125, 128, 129. Lansing: Michigan Historical Collections.

Michigan Employment Security Commission. 1992. *Employment Report* (November): 4.

———. 1995. "Michigan Women and Teens Have Largest Job Increases in 1994." Lansing: MESC, February 21.

Michigan House of Representatives. 1990. Committee on Labor. Hearings on House Bills 4150 and 4151. March 14; November 12, 14, 28. Lansing.

Michigan Manufacturers Association (MMA). 1986. *Project Northstar: A Look Forward for Michigan Manufacturers and Employers.* Lansing: MMA.

Michigan Professional Employees Society. 1991–93. *Agreement between Michigan Professional Employees Society and the State of Michigan.*

Michigan Public-Private Partnership Commission. 1992. *Final Report. PERM: Privatize, Eliminate, Retain, or Modify.* Recommendations to the Governor on Improving Service Delivery and Increasing Efficiency in State Government. Lansing. December.

Michigan Report. 1971–91. Lansing: Gongwer News Service.

Michigan State Employees Association (MSEA). 1985. Statement of MSEA on the Report of the Comparable Worth Task Force. June 28.

Michigan State Employees Association, AFSCME Council 5. 1989–91. *Agreement between the State of Michigan and the Michigan State Employees Association.*

Michigan Women's Commission. 1982. *Michigan Women* 6 (1): 1–4.

Milliken, William G. 1971. Governor of Michigan. Executive Directive 1971-8. "Equal Employment Opportunity in State Government." September 21.

Mowitz, Carol. 1991. Project director, Classification Redesign Project, Groups One and Two. Interview, Lansing, Mich., March 28.

"MSEA Joins AFSCME!" 1986. *Michigan AFSCME News.* 8 (January): 1.

Office of the State Employer. 1988. *State Employer: The Year in Review.* Lansing.

———. 1991. Employer's Position Statement, Impasse Panel 91–01. Lansing: October.

Office of Women and Work. 1980. "What's Wrong with MBES? A Critique of the Michigan Benchmark Evaluation System." August.

———. 1981. "Impact of State of Michigan Compensation Policy on Salaries for Sex-Type Jobs." August.

Parish, Cheryl. 1985. "A Cost Analysis of the Draft Report of the Comparable Worth Task Force to the Michigan Civil Service Commission." Econostats. April.

Pay Equity Network (PEN). 1985–91. Minutes, newsletters, drafts of legislation. Lansing.

———. 1985. Press Release. October.

———. 1986a. Letter to affiliates. January 27.

———. 1986b. Letter to Governor James J. Blanchard. December 19.

———. 1986c. Letter to Civil Service Commission. December 19.

———. 1987. Letter to affiliates. July 7.

Pollack, Lana. 1993. State senator. Interview, Ann Arbor, Mich., May 24.

Pollock, Mary. 1992. Coordinator, State Affirmative Action/EEO, Department of Civil Service. Interview, Lansing, Mich., April 20.

———. 1994. Telephone interview, July 18.

Revo-Cohen, Lynne. 1994. Partner, Hubbard and Revo-Cohen. Telephone interview, May 25.

Ross, Richard. 1981. Memo to Civil Service Commission. December 17.

Sarri, Rosemary et. al. 1987. *Women in Michigan . . . A Statistical Portrait.* Lansing and Ann Arbor: Michigan Women's Commission, Michigan Equal Employment and Business Opportunity Council, Institute for Social Research. September.

Service Employees International Union [SEIU] Local 31-M. 1991. *Appeal of Decision by Planning and Development Regarding Human Services Support Bargaining Unit Job Specifications.* January 18.

Service Employees International Union [SEIU] Local 31-M. 1989–91. *Collective Bargaining Agreement between Local 31-M, Service Employees International Union and State of Michigan.*

Shattuck, Cathy. 1985. Testimony on behalf of the Michigan Merchants' Council to the Comparable Worth Task Force. April 26.

Slivensky, Joseph. 1990. Director, Merit Systems, Planning and Development Bureau, Department of Civil Service. "Implementation Procedures for Review of Classification Issues and Individual Positions Resulting from the Classification Redesign Project." March 19. Memorandum.

———. 1992. Interview, Ann Arbor, Mich., June 15.

———. 1994. Personal written communication. August 19.

Staff Task Force on Public Employee Relations (STAFER). 1975. *Report.* Lansing: August 5.

The State Journal. 1937–1940. Lansing. Various issues.

Strunk, Sheila. 1992. Trustee and legislative chair, UAW Local 6000. Interview, Lansing, Mich., May 27.

Swanger, Toni. 1994. "Twenty-Five Years of NOW in Michigan: Activists Look Back over Change and Progress." *MetroTimes* (Detroit) (August 24–30): 16.

Technical Subcommittee to the Classification Redesign Project [for Group One]. 1988–90. Committee meeting minutes; summaries of discussion and action. Lansing: Department of Civil Service.

Trombley, Mary. 1994. Telephone interview, July 11.

United Automobile, Aerospace, and Agricultural Implement Workers of America, UAW v. State of Michigan. 1985. Civil Action No. 85CV75483DT.

UAW v. State of Michigan. 1987. 673 F. Supp 893 (ED Mich 1987).

UAW Local 6000. 1986–87. *Agreement between UAW Local 6000 (Administrative Support Unit and Human Services Unit) and the State of Michigan.*

———. 1988. "Position Statement of International Union, UAW and Its Local 6000." Impasse Panel IP 88-08. Lansing.

———. 1988–90. *Agreement between UAW Local 6000 (Administrative Support Unit and Human Services Unit) and the State of Michigan.*

———. 1991. "Brief of International Union, UAW and Its Local 6000." Impasse Panel IP 91-01. Lansing: December 6.

———. 1992a. "Privatization in Michigan: Recommendations to the Governor. A Response to the Interim Report." Lansing: October.

———. 1992b. *Privatization: The Michigan Experience.* Lansing: December.

———. 1991–93. *Agreement between UAW Local 6000 (Administrative Support Unit and Human Services Unit) and the State of Michigan.* January 1, 1991–December 31, 1993.

UAW Local 6000, Pay Inequity Committee. 1987. *Report of Pay Inequity Committee.* Lansing: March 28.

United Technical Employees Association (UTEA). 1991–93. *Agreement between the State of Michigan and United Technical Employees Association.*

Whitbeck, William C. 1991a. Memorandum to Mr. Leonard J. Paula, UAW. Lansing. April 17.

———. 1991b. Memorandum to Mr. Leonard J. Paula, UAW. Lansing. October 28.

Williams, Althea. 1984. President, MSEA. Failure of EEOC, Michigan CRC to act. Statement. August 31.

———. 1985. "The Michigan State Employees Association's Statement of Position before the Comparable Worth Task Force." April 26.

Women in State Government [WSG]. 1980–90. *WIRE* (newsletter).

———. 1984. Statement of Women in State Government before the Comparable Worth Task Force. February 3.

The Women's Assembly. 1985. "Comparable Worth Task Force Presents Half a Loaf." April 26.

Woods, Gloria. 1993. President, Michigan National Organization for Women. Telephone interview, June 21.

Zurvalec, David S. 1995. Vice-president of Industrial Relations, Michigan Manufacturers Association. Interview, Ann Arbor, Mich., May 31.

Index